10/20

Margaret

Great to
& Alberto as a
part of the Darley
Family.

I hope we have
a chance to work
together u your
Role @ Impr.

Let me know if
I can ever help.

Paul Darley

Sold!

The Art of Relationship Sales

Using Emotional Intelligence and Authentic Leadership to Sell More,

Work Your Way up the Corporate Ladder, and What to Do Once You Get There

Paul C. Darley

SOLD! The Art of Relationship Sales

COPYRIGHT © 2017 Paul C. Darley

Published by:

Smart Business Network

835 Sharon Drive, Suite 200

Westlake, OH 44145

Printed in the United States of America

Editors: Dustin S. Klein; Mark J. Baker

ISBN: 978-1-945389-84-9

Library of Congress Control Number: 2017957174

Table of Contents

Introduction from the Author

I've been working on *Sold!* on and off for the past 10 years. While I always felt an inner calling to write a book, I am somewhat surprised that I've completed it. My family and close friends are sick of hearing about it, and my youngest daughter, Sophie, even called me, "The boy who cried book."

I had a goal to complete this book by the time I turned 50. I missed that by a few years, but I feel a great sense of accomplishment to check off this box. It's been a labor of love. I've been working on it mostly on weekends and evenings, while on planes and vacations. I'm kind of worried about what I will do during these times now that I have finished *Sold!*

The essence of this book is about relationships; how a salesperson can increase sales and make the transition to a business leader by using emotional intelligence and authentic leadership as a springboard. While it's a business book, most of the principles can be applied to enriching any relationship.

This book is dedicated to my family and friends. Most importantly, it's a testament to my father, William J. "Bill" Darley, from whom most of these ideas came. As he approaches the end of his incredible life, I felt a need to document Bill's stories, and mine, for future generations of Darleys who I know will be good stewards for our fourth-generation family business. It is a toolbox or playbook of sorts, for them and future generations of Darley employees and family members.

I don't expect *Sold!* to be a best seller, but I signed a contract with *Smart Business* in November 2012 to publish it. My plan was to publish it within a year for distribution to my family, friends, employees and business associates. Thanks for bearing with me as I share stories and the lessons I've learned from them. I've highlighted the key business take-aways for the reader who is under time constraints, looking for just the "meat and potatoes."

In August of 2013, when I thought I was about done, something happened that made me decide to expand the scope of my book.

An interesting story: My wife, Heidi, and I were at a black-tie party with a business associate, Jeff Hupke, and his wife, Molly, who were our guests. The party had a carnival theme, with clowns and guys on stilts. In the corner was a fortune teller, with a long line of people waiting to have their futures read. None of us had ever been to one before, so we grabbed a drink and got in line.

The gypsy was spot-on in describing my guests and my wife. I was next, and shuffled the tarot cards before randomly pulling out four cards. She turned over the first card and asked what trains had to do with my life. I explained that I just finished my civic duty serving on the board of Metra, the commuter rail that serves Chicago. It was fraught with Illinois politics, and I had just resigned that week amidst another front-page news scandal.

She turned over the second card and asked about China. I explained I was headed there the following week. It was our largest export market and consumed 25 percent of my time. With the third card, the fortune teller asked if a family member had recently asked for a loan. Sure enough, that had just happened, too.

When she turned over the last card, she asked if I was writing a book, to which we all gasped. She said it would be life-changing for me. I'm not so sure about all this stuff, but as Bill Murray said in my favorite movie *Caddy Shack*, "At least I got that going for me, which is nice."

In rewriting this book, I was primarily looking for data to support my thesis that companies run by CEOs with a sales background are more profitable than companies run by CEOs who did not come up through sales. I wanted to include additional research to make it more professional and support my theories outlined in the book. The more I researched, the more I learned. While I was cognizant of my own potential confirmation bias, the research supported my theory.

If you are reading the electronic version of this book, it includes links to over 100 articles and videos that I discovered during my research. If you're reading the print version, you can Google the name shown and quickly find a link. All links are available on my website www.soldbypauldarley.com, where you can get to any link quickly. The website also has a library of tools and a blog where you can leave your mark by adding your own tips and thoughts on emotional intelligence, authentic leadership and best sales practices. We would love to hear your stories and ideas that can help others.

I credit my close friend Bill Ryan, CEO of William Ryan Homes, with the name *Sold!*. This book could have easily been named "Souled!", as recommended by my younger sister, Annie Darley, a school teacher who pushed me to use this "homophone" because of the emotional intelligence and relationship aspects of the book.

Thanks also to Annie and Mark Baker, general manager of our Pump Division, and other friends and family who, along with *Smart Business,* helped me edit this book.

Life is a journey. Everyone is different. I'm excited to be able to share my thoughts on selling, emotional intelligence and authentic leadership, as well as document my life's journey. Like some of you, I experienced a great deal of death of family and close friends at an early age — from my brother, mother, and best friend, Vinnie Kerr, before I was 25 years old — and more recently my sister, Krina, and dear friend, Kris Kosich, who both died way too early. I learned from each experience and came to realize that life is too short. I learned early on to seize the day, work hard and hopefully leave my mark. Carpe Diem!

I am positive that within these pages you will find a nugget or two of wisdom that will make you happier person and a more successful sales representative or leader. If you're already a business leader, I hope that you find an idea or two to pass along to your people to help your organization improve and grow. If you find the book helpful, please recommend it to a friend as I'll be donating the profits from this edition to charity. Thanks for reading it!

Good Selling,

Paul C. Darley
October 2017

SECTION I
THE FOUNDATION

Chapter 1

We're all salesmen!

"A good salesman can sell himself before he sells his product."
Anwar Aleitani, GE Energy

I'm proud to be a salesman, but 25 years ago my image as a sales professional took a small, personal hit. I needed my attorney to review some legal documents. It was after hours, and he lived near my home, so I offered to drop them off at his house. His wife answered the door and snarled, "What do you want?"

I was really taken aback and replied, "I'm Paul Darley. I'm here to drop off these papers for your husband."

"Oh, my gosh, Mr. Darley," she said. "I'm sorry! I thought you were a salesman."

There it was — the unintentional dig. And yet, she was sharing a very common misconception: salesmen are beneath contempt, untrustworthy, slime.

I couldn't let that comment stand.

"I am a salesman!" I proclaimed.

While that incident is long behind me, the emotion and feeling attached to salesmen[1] lingers on. Salesmen get a bad rap. Just think of the bile attached to the term "snake oil salesman," or the cliché of the "used-car salesman." Sure, bad salespeople exist everywhere, and there are far too many who shamefully deserve the dark thoughts that floated through the mind of my attorney's wife as I approached her door. But that goes for every profession. There are bad attorneys, bad teachers, bad bartenders, and the list goes on for every profession.

Part of the reason for the negative connotations is that no one likes to be "sold." We all like to believe that we can make our own decisions without the influence of others. We are suspicious of being ripped off, or paying too high of a price for a product or service. It's rooted in our culture. Most of us are familiar with the stereotypical salesman, Willy Loman, in the play, *The Death of a Salesman*. Interestingly, even Gideon Bibles were distributed to hotel rooms to "eliminate gambling, drinking, dirty jokes, Sunday trading and other forms of temptation peculiar to traveling (sales) men." [2]

Here's the irony: We're all salesmen, really. We sell ourselves to future employers when we are job hunting, to our future spouses

---

1   Throughout this book I refer to salespeople as salesmen. The term "salesmen" is not intended to be gender specific. In fact, some of the best salespeople I ever met were saleswomen. For clarity purposes, I generally use masculine pronouns like "he" and "him" at the suggestion of my editor.

2   Source: Journal of Selling and Major Account Management. The Certified Sales Professional: Has the Time Finally Arrived? Neil Rackham, 2007

when we're dating — and yes, goods and services if that's your chosen profession. What's more, the sales channel is one of the most effective ways to get to the top of any business. Roughly 50 percent of college graduates will work in sales at some point in their careers, and a rising number of CEOs have sales experience. It's not always easy, and it might not come naturally to you. But if you are looking to advance your career, you better know how to sell.

Years ago, it was typical for CEOs to come up the corporate ladder more quickly through the operations, finance or engineering departments. With no disrespect, these academic disciplines aren't typically known for people with high emotional intelligence. According to a 2005 article published in the *Harvard Business Review* (HBR), "Heartless Bosses," researchers measured the emotional intelligence levels in half a million senior executives (including 1,000 CEOs) across multiple lines of business on six continents. CEOs scored the lowest on emotional intelligence than any other management level. If you don't believe me, check the article below:

HBR: Heartless Bosses, 2005

Things have changed over the last 12 years, partially because of the focus on emotional intelligence, which we will discuss in Chapter Two. Today, more C-Level executives come up through the sales and marketing channels than ever before. Many executives assume roles in operations after having worked in sales, which makes them better prepared for the top seat. My research, outlined in this book, supports my hypothesis that companies run by CEOs with a sales background outperform peer companies with CEOs who came up through other disciplines.

Why? Because they get it! They know how to connect better with people — their customers, employees, stockholders and vendors — to get things done and deliver results.

In 2011, *Forbes* published an article titled, "The Path to Becoming a *Fortune 500* CEO," which included the following passage:

Forbes: The Path to Becoming a *Fortune 500 CEO, 2011*

"While we all know stories of legendary CEOs who seem born to the role, most CEOs are not born, they are made. People who aspire to the role have to seize the opportunity and set a path: to manage their career choices and craft their experience to make them a likely CEO candidate. What does that path look like? To find out, the CEO and Board Practice at Heidrick & Struggles analyzed the careers of all current Fortune 500 CEOs. *Here's some of what the study discovered:*

"About 30% of Fortune 500 CEOs spent the first few years of their careers developing a strong foundation in finance. This is by far the most common early experience of today's CEOs. As the second-largest constituent, CEOs who started out in sales and marketing roles account for only about 20% of the current big company CEO population.

"A foundation in finance is an important building block for a career. However, only about 5% of these CEOs were promoted directly from the role of CFO – more than half were appointed from the role of COO or President. Though the prevalence of Fortune 500 CEOs with strong financial backgrounds underlines the importance of developing financial acumen, above all, companies value a strong operator.

"For example, while Oshkosh's Charles Szews spent the majority of his career in a variety of finance roles, prior to his appointment as CEO in 2011, he spent four years as COO."

Charlie Szews is my friend and was a highly effective CEO who created tremendous economic value for Oshkosh Corporation's shareholders during his tenure. Before retiring, he landed a major defense order to build the Joint Light Tactical Vehicle (JLTV), valued at $30 billion for the Army. He was replaced by Wilson Jones on January 1, 2016.

Wilson is a beloved, humble leader who came up through the sales channel and then moved on to operational duties, like many CEOs. He possesses high emotional intelligence and knows how to motivate teams through authentic leadership. In his first year at the helm, the price of Oshkosh stock more than doubled. Wilson is quick to give credit to others and praises his teams — a common trait among authentic leaders. Wilson gets it.

This is only one example that hits close to home. Since 2011, the number of CEOs coming up through the sales channel has continued to increase, and the results they produce are similar. [3]

Chapter 3 of this book is about authentic leadership. If you would like to get an early glimpse of what it looks like live relative to employee engagement and motivating a team, check out Wilson Jones in this "Ed Talk" video:

You Tube: The New North, Wilson Jones Ed Talk

The Apple Doesn't Fall Far from the Tree

I've been a salesman all my life. Selling is in my blood and is the foundation of our fourth-generation family business, W.S. Darley

---

3   Oshkosh Stock price on Jan. 1, 2016 was $30.33 per share and rose to over $66 per share on Dec. 30, 2016.

& Co. or "Darley," as we are best known. Darley was founded in 1908 by my grandfather in Chicago. We are a diverse company that manufactures and sells firefighting pumps, fire trucks, and equipment around the world. Over the last 10 years, we've reinvented our company and now over half of our roughly $200 million in annual sales comes from supplying equipment to the U.S. Department of Defense. At the pleasure of my family, I serve as chairman, CEO and president. Typically, when asked by others, "What do you do?" I'm quick to respond proudly, "I'm a salesman. I sell firefighting and defense equipment."

My father, Bill Darley, was the consummate salesman, despite being an engineer by education. The primary purpose of this book is to document what I learned from him and others with the hope of helping you, my reader, grow as a person, a salesperson, and a business leader in your organization. If you *really* want it, the C-suite is waiting for you.[4]

Bill Darley in 1995 at age 67

---

4   The C-Suite typically refers to those who's titles begin with a "C" such as the CEO (Chief Executive Officer), CFO (Chief Financial Officer), COO (Chief Operating Officer), CSO (Chief Sales Officer), and CRO (Chief Revenue Officer).

Like most companies, Darley has had its share of ups and downs. Through it all, our sales team has been the lifeline to the outside world, and it's a role I learned early on. I grew up the seventh of eight children in River Forest, IL, a suburb of Chicago. Our family was frugal, a trait passed down by my grandmother, Mary J. Darley, who came to America in the early 1900s at the age of six with her nine-year-old sister. She began working as a secretary for my grandfather and they fell in love despite a 30-year age difference.

She instilled important values in her grandchildren with a firm, but loving stick. She applied the same skills to overseeing our company for over 40 years after my grandfather's sudden death in 1937 following a heart attack at his summer home in Lake Geneva, WI. That home remains in our family today and we recently celebrated our family meeting there in July 2017. As youngsters, each of her 16 grandchildren spent time with Grandma Darley every summer at the lake. Every day started off with four hours of demanding labor. If you worked hard, there was a chance you would get the afternoon off. It's a modest home, but priceless to those of us privileged to have the childhood memories.

Our hometown of River Forest was an upper-middle class, close-knit community. We lived in a large home that my grandfather had built in 1920, where my brother, Peter, still lives today. Growing up, I was convinced we were the poorest family in town. My parents made me work for everything, and the majority of my clothes were hand-me-downs from my five older brothers.

I learned to sell while in kindergarten. In some respects, it was a necessity to get what I wanted. As a kid, I was always hustling, looking for a sale. You name it, I did it: selling my parents to get their attention, lemonade in front of our home in the summer, hot chocolate in the winter in front of our local grocery store, hot pads that I knitted, paper routes and, later, lawn cutting and snow shoveling jobs that I farmed out to friends. I received my first actual paycheck working at the Lake movie theatre when I was 14. Michael Connelly, the cool kid in town, landed me the job. I don't think the owners ever asked our age when we applied.

Selling was fun, exciting and rewarding. I was even able to sell my parents on allowing me to ride my bicycle 90 miles to Lake Geneva, WI, with Pat Maloney when I was 12 years old. We left at 2 a.m. to "reduce the wind drag." I still can't believe my parents allowed this. It was a different time, and, heck, I was one of eight children.

Outside of our time at Lake Geneva, we did not get too many vacations. But when I was seven years old, we drove to Pensacola,

FL, and my parents left me at a Stuckey's gas station in Tennessee. The "story" is that they were back within an hour, but it seemed a lot longer.

My older brothers naturally picked on me when I was a kid. They would, however, humor me every so often, as I would spend my modest $1-per-week allowance to buy penny candy and then throw it to them from the top of our stairs after shouting, "Who's the king?" Once the candy was gone, I had to be able to jump the banister and quickly lock myself in the bathroom before they could re-establish the pecking order with a weekly "wedgie." I realized that getting to be "the king" for even a few fleeting moments was the best use of my hard-earned money. It somehow satisfied a pain of mine. Today, my brothers and I are best friends who work together and go out to lunch each day when we're not out on the road selling.

I started working in the family business when I was nine years old. On most Saturday mornings, I headed to the office with my father, where I checked the weekly envelopes to make sure no checks or paperwork were missed, or I emptied trash cans. Later, I spent my summers—and practically every winter and spring vacation—doing everything from sweeping the shop floor to cleaning the in-ground water tanks that we used to test fire engines. When you had to clean the test tank, you knew you were at the bottom of the totem pole. In high school and college, I moved to the office, making collection calls, driving the company truck, working trade shows, and taking orders from our equipment catalogs that were known as the "Bible" of the fire industry.

By the time I was 15 years old, I had saved more than $2,000 and had my eyes set on a 1967 candy apple red Ford Mustang convertible that had been in a used car lot for about three months. I knew it would soon be gone. As my 16th birthday approached, I was $500 short of the asking price and I begged my father to help me buy it, promising I would pay him the difference within six months.

On my birthday night, I sat in front of my house waiting for him to come driving down the street in my new car, oak trees arching in his honor. Instead, he came home with a rubber tree plant that he picked up on his way home from work. I was in shock. I had failed at the largest "sale" of my life. I later save up and bought that car, and it helped me land Heidi Jensen, who has been the love of my life for more than 40 years. My biggest sale ever, as my cousin, Ginny Kerr Sofen, likes to say!

When our daughters were younger, each pleaded for an electronic Barbie car for Christmas. As you can imagine, I never gave in. As I had learned from my father, if you get everything you want in life without working for it, you lose the drive. I've preached this to my kids their entire lives: never lose that drive or the "eye of the tiger."

I formally joined the Darley company full-time after graduating from Marquette University in 1985 with a BS degree in Business Administration, with an emphasis in marketing and finance. (Today we require the fourth generation of family members to work outside the company in meaningful employment for three to five years before joining the family business.) It was my responsibility to build a new fire pump division for our company. I was starting at ground zero. I didn't have a customer base to work with. I didn't have a product that the market was screaming for. And, to make it even more challenging, the target market for our pumps was other fire apparatus builders,[5] who viewed us as a competitor. Because we built our own fire trucks, none of these Original Equipment Manufacturers (OEMs) wanted to buy our pumps. Talk about channel conflicts!

On top of that, and unbeknown to us at the time, our two pump competitors had illegal agreements with most of the OEMs, forbidding them from using our product, even if they wanted to do so. In 1996, the Federal Trade Commission investigated this activity and issued a consent order that stopped this restraint of trade. We weren't the ones who blew the whistle, and it's not exciting reading, but if you are interested in learning more, you can read about it here:

<u>Hale and Waterous FTC 1996 Investigation and Ruling</u>

Although this barrier was formally eliminated, the strong relationships between the other pump suppliers and their OEM customers made breaking into these markets extremely difficult. Moreover, these two competitors made good products, offered good service and competitive pricing, and had strong brands. At the time, most fire departments were highly loyal to brands when it came to pumps on their fire trucks. They saw switching costs as being high because of perceived training and service concerns. Many fire departments also kept large inventories of pump parts in their warehouses.

Ten years earlier, I recall telling my father I wanted to call on the largest fire truck manufacturer in the industry. I was only two months on the job, and my father told me I was wasting my time. The company simply wouldn't buy from us. At the time, I thought I did a hell of a job presenting my case and I was sure we were going to

---

5   Throughout this book, I use the term "fire apparatus OEMs." While there are technical differences, for purposes of this book these are manufacturers of what most people call fire engines, pumpers and fire trucks. In 2016, there were roughly 50 fire apparatus OEMs in the U.S., compared to more than 100 in 1995.

land them as a customer. My calls, however, never got returned. My dad was right, but, more importantly, he knew how to motivate me — he'd been doing it since I was a little kid. I stayed on that account aggressively, and today Pierce Manufacturing is our largest domestic OEM customer account, and it remains the largest fire apparatus manufacturer in the country and, arguably, the world.

Blue Oceans

I learned early on that I had to head toward blue oceans, not red ones. A red ocean is bloody because that is where the sharks swim and everyone chases the same customers. A blue ocean holds numerous opportunities because there is less competition, a lack of strong, preexisting relationships, and no channel conflicts. Blue oceans also mean higher profitability.

The U.S. fire apparatus OEM market was a red ocean, so we grew our export and defense businesses while planting seeds domestically. My grandfather, William Stewart Darley, was a world traveler in the early 1900s. From his start, he was exporting all over the world, including selling complete fire trucks to Turkey in 1939. He and my father, Bill, laid the groundwork for our export business today.

Company founder William S. Darley on an overseas voyage in 1928

My father first traveled to China in 1981. By 2010, we had become the market leader of fire pumps imported into China, and export sales accounted for over 60 percent of our pump sales. As fate would have it, our family name "Darley" in Chinese is pronounced "Da Li," which translates as "powerful." Under the leadership of our partner, Liu Long, Darley is now one of the strongest brands in the China fire market.

Bill Darley's first trip to China in 1981 with an NFPA delegation. Darley employees Ron Voisard and Jim Weigle still work at Darley

Bill traveled to well over 125 countries building our brand. My generation followed in his footsteps. I have had a chance to visit more than 80 countries. When I was young, I found it exhilarating to see the world and felt good about bringing our firefighting products to these developing countries. Our equipment was being used to save lives, and customers wanted to work with us because of our high-tech, high-quality products and the ease of doing business with us.

We continued to build our brand in other markets where we had an established presence, such as Asia, Southeast Asia, Latin America, New Zealand, and Australia. Many of my family members had the travel bug as well — it was a real team effort and a significant growth area. We did particularly well in countries that wanted U.S. products and were exciting places to visit. We have a family practice of always calling on local fire departments and distribution partners when on family vacations. It goes a long way.

Will Darley and Ryan Darley are both fourth generation (G4) family members who work in international sales at our company. They are carrying the international relationship torch now and are doing an awesome job.

We also began to expand our Department of Defense business. In 1993, we landed a significant contract for a portable firefighting and damage control pump with the U.S. Navy, beating out our largest pump competitor. The Navy had many problems with our competitor's product. For four years, we poured our heart and soul into winning that contract and finally landed that milestone order. In the years since, we've sold around $100 million worth of this product to the U.S. Navy and more than 40 other navies around the world. It became a springboard for other defense business. We later began manufacturing pumps for the U.S. Marine Corps, U.S. Army, U.S. Air Force, and the U.S. Coast Guard.

As a result, we began bursting at the seams with business. None of this work was done alone; we were supported by incredible engineering, production and customer service teams who understood the mission. Everyone was pulling in the same direction.

To address the channel conflict here at home, we limited our distribution of fire trucks in the U.S. and began promoting them internationally, where we would not be competing with our potential domestic OEMs customers and their dealers. We stayed the course in relentless-yet-patient pursuit of their business. One by one, we began to establish relationships, earn their respect, and, eventually, their business.

Selling is a Process

Selling is a process that needs to be learned. There is no "one-size-fits-all" approach. While selling came very naturally to me, I had to learn how to sell, and I am still learning. So does everyone in your organization; it's not only the people with "sales" written on their business cards. Whether you're a C-suite executive or the employee who sweeps the floor at night, we're all salesmen and an integral part of the selling process. Yes, even the custodian is part of the process. He's selling by making sure the plant is clean, and as he makes his way through the office and shop, he has a smile on his face that others see on a regular basis. Smiles are contagious.

A person still answers our phones at all our locations. We refer to our receptionists as the "Directors of First Impressions." They know they must be upbeat, cordial and professional with visitors and customers who phone or visit us. When transferring calls, they always respond, "It's my pleasure to connect you." It's simple wording, but it goes a long way toward making a good first impression and building a brand.

Recently, Clark Cramer, a 30-year union employee at Darley who crates our pumps for shipping, sent me a text stating, "I'm the last line of defense. I always do my best, and a little more whenever possible, to keep a watchful eye for any imperfections that may not meet our customer's quality expectations." He gets it, and he is one of the right people on the bus, as authors Jim Collins and Jon Gordon like to say in their book *Good to Great*. Here are some great tips from their <u>book.</u>

<u>ATIIM: Jim Collins: Good to Great. Summary of take-aways</u>

Visitors come through our plants all the time. Our shop employees are some of our best salespeople. We encourage visitors to approach any employee and ask any question they want. Our guests can see our workers' attitudes as they're walking through our plants and offices. "Hey, that receptionist is really friendly. That machine operator is very conscientious. And that guy assembling pumps is not only a professional who knows what he's doing, but he's happy and enjoying his work." Whether it's a committee of military personnel, a foreign delegation, or engineers from a *Fortune 500* company, the encounters they have with our employees can be the difference between landing or not landing a deal.

Lack of Formal Sales Training

While selling is such an important part of every business, I've come to learn that surprisingly little attention is paid to the selling process in our nation's universities. Some business schools are beginning to embrace the art and science of selling, but most are barely in their infancy. I complained about this lack of sales classes to Northwestern's Kellogg School of Management (Kellogg) in my graduation interview from its Executive MBA program in 2003. In 2004, I was invited to come back to teach a pilot course on sales.

I was asked to create my own materials for the class. In preparation for teaching the course, I did a great deal of research, interviewed top sales producers, and thought long and hard about my own experiences. I began to document the processes and concepts, which became the impetus for *Sold!*. It was an awesome experience, but I'm still licking my wounds as they have never invited me back, despite having a Kellogg professor on our company board.

During the past year, some universities — including Marquette University — have started to recognize the importance of including sales classes in their curriculum. This *Harvard Business Review* article talks to the importance of this classes:

12

HBR Article: April 2016 *More Universities Need to Teach Sales*

While most *Fortune 500* companies have formal sales-training programs, most mid-size and small businesses offer little, if any, training. They cast their salespeople into the marketplace with almost no guidance. Our company is no different. Hopefully, this book can be a tool for those who are new to sales and do not have the benefit of a formal sales training program, and also for those looking to hone their selling skills and move up the corporate ladder. But it's also a book about building relationships in any setting.

Relationship Sales

There are many different types of selling: retail sales, transaction sales, enterprise sales, soft sell, hard sell, solution selling and consultative sales, to name a few. This book, however, is about relationship selling. Developing a relationship with your customers is critical, but it isn't exactly a revolutionary concept. Relationship selling has been the hallmark of many service businesses, such as banking, for hundreds of years.

Relationship selling is a technique centered on the interaction between the buyer and the salesperson, rather than focusing solely on the price or details of the product. Relationship selling requires a process, and I'll walk you through the process that has been successful for us.

Relationship selling can increase customer loyalty and, thus, customer retention. The traditional sales approach focuses on getting the sale; with relationship selling, getting the order is a byproduct of the relationship. To quote sales coach Patricia Fripp, "You don't close a sale, you open a relationship if you want to build a long-term, successful enterprise." Some other good quotes can be found here:

Canadian Professional Sales Organization: CPSA's Top 50 Sales Quotes to Inspire your sales team

Anthony Florek was my best friend at Kellogg and a professional salesman if there ever was one. He puts it this way: "I never looked at sales as a single transaction, but rather a series of transactions that led to a pathway that created a solution. Solutions build relationships, which form partnerships for life."

Relationship sales apply to all relationships, not just buyer-seller relationships. You can strengthen relationships with your co-workers, direct reports, board of directors, your family, and nearly everyone you encounter. One of the keys to improving your relationships is through Emotional Intelligence (EI).

Chapter 2

Emotional Intelligence (EI)

"At best, IQ contributes about 20% to the factors that determine life success, which leaves 80% to other forces: forces grouped as emotional Intelligence."

Daniel Goleman Ph.D., author of the New York Times bestseller *Emotional Intelligence* and *Social Intelligence: The New Science of Human Relationships*, 1995

A college degree — even an MBA — doesn't carry the weight it once did. Today's highest performing companies are looking for recruits who have high emotional intelligence (EI) to complement their academic and business credentials. In 2016, more than 80 percent of Fortune 500 companies tested and hired people based on their emotional intelligence, putting more weight on their emotional quotient (EQ)[6] than on their intelligence quotient (IQ), or even their experience.

These companies are looking for authentic leaders who know themselves, can adapt to different groups of constituents, can size up a situation, make decisions quickly, and can motivate their teams toward a common goal. Bottom line: They want authentic leaders who can execute and increase shareholder value through motivating their teams. We'll talk more about authentic leaders in Chapter 3, but this article speaks to the importance of EI in top CEOs:

Huffpost: The Top 10 Emotionally-Intelligent Fortune 500 CEOs, 2011

I first learned about Emotional Intelligence in the fall of 2009 through the Young Presidents' Organization (YPO).[7] Within YPO, eight to 10 company presidents/CEOs meet monthly in a confidential setting in a group called a forum. Our YPO Forum was hand selected by Jim Liautaud, who had founded our Chicago Windy City YPO chapter some 30 years earlier. Jim mentored us over a five-year period and it was an incredible learning experience.

As a forum, we studied Process-directed Emotional Intelligence (PdEI) under a program at the University of Illinois at Chicago (UIC); the Liautaud Graduate School of Business. We received a two-year graduate certificate, and we were the first graduates of the program, thanks to our forum founder after whom the college was named.

"Big Jim" Liautaud was an amazing man with a presence that struck you immediately upon meeting him — from his silver hair, perpetual tan, bright blue eyes, and engaging smile and disposition that made you feel you were the most important person in the world. Big Jim had experienced it all in life, from bankruptcy to billionaire. He died suddenly from cancer in October 2015 at the young age of 79,

---

6   **Emotional intelligence (EI)** or **emotional quotient (EQ)** are used synonymously. EI is the ability of individuals to recognize their own and other people's emotions, to discriminate between different feelings and label them appropriately, and to use emotional information to guide thinking and behavior.[1] The term gained prominence in the 1995 book by that title, written by the author, psychologist and science journalist Daniel Goleman.

7   YPO is an organization that unites approximately 25,000 company CEOs and presidents in 130 countries around a shared mission: Better Leaders through Education and Idea Exchange ™.

16

but he certainly left his mark on us and this world. Here is a link from the UIC following his death:

UIC: Remembering Jim Liautaud

His sons, Greg and Jimmy John, are both in our YPO chapter. Greg runs a successful Tier 1 automotive company, and Jimmy John is one of the world's most successful food business entrepreneurs with a freaky fast food franchise business that bears his name. The apple doesn't fall far from the tree.

What is Emotional Intelligence?

Emotional Intelligence has four key components:

1) Understanding who you are (Self-Awareness)

2) Being able to control your emotions and impulses (Self-Management)

3) Being able to properly assess the needs of others (Social-Awareness)

4) Using your skills to motivate and get the desired results from others (Relationship Management)

Emotional Intelligence is about a person's capability to understand who he is, understand his social settings, control himself and act properly in different types of settings, read people in terms of their needs, be a good listener, motivate others to action, and, ultimately, build strong, long-lasting relationships. EI applies at all levels and with all relationships, whether with customers, suppliers, employees, stockholders, friends, family, or sometimes even spiritual ones.

EI will help build relationships and is a vital stepping stone to authentic leadership, which will have people wanting to follow you.

Studies show that those people who embrace the concepts of PdEI earned more promotions, were happier, and saw their salary increase 39.32% higher than their peers who did not embrace PdEI.[8]

Frankly, my emotional intelligence level has always had room for significant improvement, and it still does. True behavior modification takes a lot of practice and engagement. Everyone is a work in process, but understanding your shortcomings is the first step toward improvement. Studying PdEI has helped me become a better boss, co-worker, father, husband, friend and salesman.

---

8   Based on data from the Liautaud Institute

Many think those abilities are natural — you're either born with them or you're not. To some extent, that is true. Some are naturally gifted. Some are born with athletic skills, beauty or a high IQ. And some are born with a high EQ.[9]

A high EQ or having high EI is a critical attribute for a salesperson, and it is often the determining factor in the difference between a good salesperson and a great one. High EQ helps you to empathize and walk that proverbial mile in your customers' shoes. So you might ask, "What is the point of talking about EQ if it's something you're born with and can't increase much?"

Well, just as Olympic athletes continue to train, runway models highlight their features with makeup, and those scholars with genius IQs continue to study, anyone can improve his or her emotional intelligence. Studies by the Liautaud Institute suggest that you can improve your EQ by 23 percent. Based on my personal experience, I would argue it can be raised significantly higher if the person is willing to work at it. As you'll learn, it easy to test.

There are a few different models, but most academics will agree that Emotional Intelligence is divided into four parts: Self-Awareness, Self-Management, Social Awareness, and Relationship Management. [10]

		Recognition	Regulation
Personal Competence		**Self-Awareness** ✓ Self-confidence ✓ Awareness of your emotional state ✓ Recognizing how your behavior impacts others ✓ Paying attention to how others influence your emotional state	**Self-Management** ✓ Getting along well with others ✓ Handling conflict effectively ✓ Clearly expressing ideas and information ✓ Using sensitivity to another person's feelings (empathy) to manage interactions successfully
Social Competence		**Social Awareness** ✓ Picking up on the mood in the room ✓ Caring what others are going through ✓ Hearing what the other person is "really" saying	**Relationship Management** ✓ Getting along well with others ✓ Handling conflict effectively ✓ Clearly expressing ideas/information ✓ Using sensitivity to another person's feelings (empathy) to manage interactions successfully

---

9   Based on data from the Liautaud Institute

10   Source of Chart: *Emotional Intelligence: Why do I need it?* Mary Francis Winters, 2013

Self-Awareness: Self-Awareness means having a better understanding of who you are and knowing your strengths and weaknesses. As you examine yourself, you'll discover what motivates you to action — what makes you tick. You'll also be more aware of the impact you have on others.

It's about becoming comfortable "in your own skin," with who you are, and becoming authentic. Self-awareness, through self-evaluation, is the cornerstone of Emotional Intelligence and can lead to self-actualization, allowing you to achieve your full potential.

Self-examination can come from within, but you can also get honest and direct feedback from people you trust and respect. At Darley, we conduct 360-degree reviews where all employees can give honest feedback on managers.

Family and close friends will often provide the most direct and constructive feedback, but business peers can give you direct feedback as well. My forum-mate Joe Popolo, CEO of The Freeman Company, is known for giving others direct feedback for improvement in an appropriate and tactful manner. Friends can help each other like that, and they can be vital in letting you know where to improve. Remember, if you're asking for areas to improve, you need to take a strong humility pill, as hearing what others truly think of you can be difficult to swallow.

Ask others for feedback on what you can be doing better. When the situation is right, be sure to offer feedback to others without them having to ask. Always start with something complimentary.

People naturally look for feedback after making a presentation. If you have something positive to say, let them know. I can assure you that they will remember it.

The higher a person goes up the corporate ladder, the more everybody is watching his actions. You need to understand how your behavior impacts others. Some employees judge what kind of day they're going to have based on how the boss walks into the office that day. Think about that. The difference between a good day for your employees and a bad day might be whether they think you're smiling or scowling when you walk by their desk.

As you become more cognizant of how your actions affect others, you'll find yourself more focused, more in the present, and a better listener.

I know of several companies that actively practice EI by holding confidential meetings called "forums," with outstanding results. The forums have a mix of people from different levels of the organization.

While we preach about EI at Darley constantly, based on our company's culture, we have not established forums.

Self-awareness should be constantly evaluated. My YPO forum mate, Richard Harris, is the most self-aware person I know. He is a "hired gun" CEO who has run huge conglomerates and recently began his own private equity firm after some soul searching at age 50. He and I studied PdEI together, and he came to grips with who he was as a person and decided his entrepreneurial spirit was moving him to change his life. He is happier and more free-spirited than ever before.

When you understand your strengths and weaknesses, you can stay in your lane and excel at the areas where you are strong. Some of your weaknesses simply can't be changed, and it's imperative to surround yourself with people who are strong where you are weak.

Self-Management: Self-Management is how a person controls himself and how he interacts with the world. It's his emotional reaction to different situations. It means understanding and acting in accordance with expected, versus unexpected, behavior in different types of settings. I confess, this is the area I am weakest and the main reason I have embraced EI.

Being self-aware helps with self-management and allows you to focus and be present. It's about active listening, not being disruptive or thinking about what you're going to say next. Remember — it's not about you!

Self-management can help you control your emotions in highly charged situations without threatening your authentic leadership. While I seldom lose my cool, too many times I have shown poor self-management with respect to conversations, controlling my emotions, making immature comments, not listening, and making low level reactions to things. I'm not quite sure where it comes from. My wife, Heidi, has teased me over the past 30 years, saying I lack a filter between my brain and my mouth. While I still have a long way to go, scores show I've improved more than 50 percent in this area. This is contrary to most EI studies from the Liautaud Institute, and contrary to what Heidi might say.

I maintain an open-door policy at work. Today, when employees walk into my office I put everything aside and try to give them my full attention. If it's more than a minute conversation, we meet at a small conference table in my office where we can meet more intimately, without the distractions of talking over my computer monitors. These meetings are like crossing a set of railroad tracks: if you don't listen well, it can be dangerous. Below are some simple steps to be a better listener:

1. **STOP** everything you're doing. It's more about them and not about you.

2. **LOOK** with your eyes and body facing them, and make your facial gestures in sync with their feelings.

3. **LISTEN** with nods and smiles, short, affirmative phrases, shared experiences and high support. Don't let you mind wander…stay present.

The above works well in any setting: customer meetings, trade shows, at dinner parties and at the dinner table with your family. Focus on the person — what they're saying and what they're not saying.

To be a successful leader, you must be yourself — be authentic. Self-management is not about changing the essence of who you are. Rather, it is about being aware of, and improving on, your weaknesses; regulating your emotions while still being authentic. Put another way, you still need to be who you are, but as you read people, watch their body language, the tone of their voice, their colloquialisms, and then adapt to their environments—some call this the "chameleon effect," or "mirroring." The chameleon effect refers to the nonconscious mimicry of the postures, mannerisms and facial expressions during interactions with others in different social environments.

The reality is that you can't have your guard up all the time. There are times when it is fine to just be yourself without a filter— say, with close friends and family. Like you, I want to be who I am naturally in those relaxed, social settings and be accepted. Real friends don't judge you, but they do let you know when to reel it in. The important point is to be mindful of what you say in certain settings, but keep your authenticity.

Improving your self-management skills impacts far more than your business life. It can help with anything from goal setting to family life to your overall happiness level and, of course, to improving your sales and career path.

Social Awareness: Social Awareness deals with a your ability to be aware of your surroundings and the surroundings of others. It focuses on your ability to listen and size up a situation — how to read and work a room. Increasing social awareness means having a better understanding of what's going on around you and how you fit in. It improves your ability to absorb and interact.

In the business environment, social awareness can help you

be in tune with what's going on in your company, your customer's company, and the industry. When embraced, social awareness can help you be an effective change leader in your business and in your industry. Increasing social awareness is vital for anyone looking to move up the corporate ladder.

Social awareness will also help you manage different organizational and social networks. It is a measure of how you interact in a team environment and what role you play on those teams. You're not always going to be in the leader role. Sometimes you will be second fiddle or first mate; other times you will simply be a follower or cheerleader. Social awareness will help you understand when to lead and when to follow.

Empathy is a large part of social awareness. When you're empathetic, you're tuned in to other people's needs and truly listening to what they say. If you can get to where the person you're conversing with says, "Gosh, I can't believe I'm telling you this!", that's a breakthrough. The next time you're in a social setting, go up to someone who seems alone or sad and try engaging them in a conversation. The impact can be life-changing for both of you.

Relationship Management: Relationship Management takes social awareness and puts it into play across your different networks, environments and relationships. It's about managing relationships to make things happen and being able to better handle the interactions you have with others. It answers the question: How well are you able to build bonds with those important to you while dealing with stress that you and others around you may be facing? Can you build long-lasting relationships? Are you sensitive to the needs of others? Can you motivate others to action? Can you play nice?

In my mind, managing relationships is the single most important trait for a relationship salesperson and business leader to possess. No successful person can do anything by himself.

If you're going to lead, you need people who want to follow you. They'll only follow you if they believe you "get it" and can relate to them. Social awareness increases your chances of moving your team in a direction if you take time to listen to their concerns and take their input into consideration as you move forward. Conversely, if you're headed down the wrong path, they will be likely to provide you open and honest feedback.

Whether a business, personal, family or even spiritual relationship, if you can't build lasting relationships, you're not going to live a happy, productive and fulfilling life. This ability to build loving and compassionate relationships with others is the essence of humanity; what makes us different and allowed us to evolve millions of years ago.

An example: When our children were growing up they had the best principal you can imagine. Mrs. Helen Kwasniewski knew and loved every student at Immaculate Conception Grade School. She would greet each child by name, with a hug for those who wanted one. Despite there being almost 500 students in the school, Mrs. "K" somehow knew almost all the parents intimately. She had a very high EI, and everyone confided in her. In her final newsletter before she retired in 2001, she wrote, "When growing your relationships, remember that people will come into your life for a reason, a season or a lifetime." Similarly, my pal, Dave Gast, likes to say, "Even though your paths might be going in different directions, you know which friendships are for a lifetime."

Relationship management is one of the areas where I score the highest in EI, but I do so in an odd way.

Paul Darley's Quantitatively Quirky List Affliction

About 30 years ago, I realized I had a tendency to put everything into silos to manage my life. I generally rated these silos on a scale of 1-10 so that I knew where I needed to be spending my time and effort. I have silos for work-related issues, such as customer relationship management, operations, financial and employee matters. But I also have silos for my life outside of work, where they are segmented for my family, friends, social, and spiritual life. The lists and silos go on and on. In a busy world, compartmentalizing helps me manage relationships and my life. Taking these lists, buckets and silos into consideration, I can quickly say where my life is on a scale of 1 to 10. But more importantly, I can go to the bucket (or relationship) that needs the most attention.

I'm not exactly sure where this comes from, but Ron French, a neighbor of mine who owns Red E, a boutique clothing store in our town of Elmhurst, IL, likes to call it a "numbering affliction."

I've pretty much created these silos all my adult life, and describe myself as "Quantitatively Quirky," a term my wife, Heidi, and I coined many years ago. Not surprisingly, I began to number my top friends ranging from 1-10. I do it because it's kind of fun, perhaps offensive to some, but primarily because it lets me know with whom I need to concentrate my efforts and it ensures I spend my time with those most important to me.

Part of this may be due to losing my best friend, Vinnie Kerr, to cancer in his twenties and feeling I did not pay enough attention to him in his final years. Perhaps, too, some of it is due to insecurities over losing my brother and mother. With an abundance of drama and death in my life at a young age, it was one of my coping mechanisms. As grim as it sounds, in those days I thought a great deal about "Who's going to carry my casket at my funeral?" I guess I still do.

Best friends since first grade at our wedding rehearsal party in 1987. From left to right: Tom Gorski, Tony Pierotti, Gene Leonard, Jim (Vinnie) Kerr, Paul Darley and Peter Harmon

It could also be because when I first started dating Heidi in high school, her brother, Chris Jensen, posted me at the top of his "Got to Go" list that was prominently displayed on their refrigerator door. Chris was a 6'7" jock, which meant I just had to suck it up. Fortunately, we're great friends today. Heidi's other brother, Pete, has always been supportive, but I do remember him playing "Taps" on his trumpet when I lost their father's prized wrench set while in high school.

Every year or two, I throw a Top 10 party that is incredibly fun. I've put numbers on my top 10 friends in this book where I mention them. Each are incredible family men who contribute to society and live happy and productive lives. My 50th birthday was a stag party at the Adventurer's Club for my Top 100 friends. I was roasted by Don Meyers (No. 3), John Kosich (No. 4), Joe O'Neil (No. 6), and my brother, Jimmy, who was my best man at my wedding. Don's first line of his roast was that I had to invite 200 to get 100 friends there. It was true! It was an incredible night with close friends, family, and business associates who are friends. I've managed to include most of them in this book.

24

Top 10 Party in Miami Beach in 2015. Yacht was courtesy of a YPO friend

Brandon Goehl (No. 10) is one of those guys who really appreciates the friend numbering and ranking system. He is on it because he wants to be so badly ... the other guys merely tolerate me. Brandon is involved with numerous businesses, including managing shows for former Rat Pack member Tom Dreesen.

OK, I've come to accept that not everyone appreciates this ranking system. It sounds quirky, and it's considered by most to be unacceptable behavior. But if you compartmentalize different components of your life, you might find you can handle and cope with more events and people, as well as grow your relationships.

To some degree, everyone ranks their friends. But most don't talk about it freely like I do. Think for a moment: who is your best friend? I've also found that most women don't like or appreciate the concept—although a few do—and they have numbers on my "women's favorite list."

I've listened to my daughters talk about weddings where the bride picks her maid of honor and I've come to learn that the order in which bridesmaids walk down the aisle is a huge deal and is based on their "number" with the bride.

In certain situations, numbering in general makes a great deal of sense. If you're in the hospital for an illness, the doctor will ask you to describe your level of pain from 1 to 10. If you go to China and order a steak, you don't tell them medium-rare; you order it on a scale of 1-10, with 10, of course, being well-done.

Emotional Intelligence in the Workplace

For leaders, relationships are about expressing a vision, telling a compelling story, and motivating people. Social awareness means understanding how your actions impact employees, customers and the marketplace. It means constantly scanning your environments. Today, most successful business people have high EI and those who don't are either working on it or on their way out the door.

A two-year study by the Liautaud Institute in Chicago showed that the business people who participated in the study and worked on their emotional intelligence through forums could show measurable improvements over a control group that did not. The study found participants improved in the following ways:

1. **Self-Awareness** (knowing one's emotions, capabilities and preferences). Co-workers viewed participants as becoming more insightful of their own emotional states and capacities.

2. **Self-Management** (controlling one's emotions and impulses; persistence). Evaluators noted an increase in the participants' ability to exercise emotional control and work more effectively in achieving a common goal.

3. **Social Awareness** (accurate perceptions of the feelings and needs of others). Participants are more empathic with what other people are feeling and their concerns.

4. **Relationship Management** (skill in getting desired results from others). Participants are viewed as better able to work through others to get results.

As a result, salaries and promotions improved significantly. The critical period for comparison is relative changes from Year 1 to Year 2. According to the Liautaud Institute research, EI participants received an 11.09% increase in salary compared to 7.96% among the control group. This represents a 39.32% greater salary increase, and was statistically significant with a single sample test on percentages.

Emotional Intelligence at Home

Jim Fannin is a life coach who coaches athletes and CEOs, including my friend Rob Wilson, CEO of his family business, Employco, which has grown to over 15,000 employees under his leadership. Jim's most notorious client was baseball player Alex Rodriguez. Jim talks a great deal about the 90 Second Rule ™. When you get home from work, the first 90 seconds set the tone for z the evening. Chill out before you go in the door. Don't go in the house talking on your cell phone. Take some time to decompress and then come in ready to engage your spouse and family. You'll find that if you concentrate on your family for the 90 seconds, asking about their day and listening and responding with empathy, you'll pretty much be in good graces with them for the rest of the evening. It's a simple action, and it works. Try it.

When at home with my wife and kids, our family dinners are now consumed by high EI conversations that are more meaningful than ever before. Everyone listens, and we don't interrupt each other. We talk about nearly anything from the happiness scale (1-10) to the best or worst thing that happened since we were last together. We also talk about the "big" things, like what's important to our daughters in a future husband, career, or their goals in life.

The most meaningful discussions focus on what we appreciate about each other. We take time to talk positively. These conversations usually start with something like, "I really appreciate that Sophie recently … I'm proud of her." We've been doing it for about seven years, and you'll be surprised how much people open up, even teenage daughters.

I don't use numbers for my three daughters. Audrey, my oldest, works at Darley and is a hardworking professional who is a natural leader and a lot like me. Maggie is a top corporate recruiter for Insight Global, an IT staffing firm, who lights up every room she enters. Sophie has the biggest heart of anyone I've ever met and has recently began a career teaching 4th grade in Indianapolis. I don't have favorites when it comes to them; I'm proud of them all for their success and happiness in life, which is primarily due to their mother, Heidi, who is my No. 1 on all lists.

Our family at the wedding of my cousin Meg Sofen and Dan Opel in 2014.
Back row from left: Heidi, Paul and Sophie. Front row: Audrey and Maggie

Over the years, I've come to notice that generally women — and mothers in particular — have higher EQs than men. It goes back to our hunter-gatherer roots and the fact that women are nurturers. They are focused on the needs of others and they listen.

I grew up a terrible listener. It runs in my family, which was dominated by males. Thirty-five years ago our company slogan was, "After 80 years you can still talk to a Darley." My mother-in-law, Boni Jensen, used to jokingly say, "Yeah, they might not always listen, but you can always talk to one." Boni has always known how to subtly get a point across to me. When my mother died, Boni took me in as one of her own. Today, she's my biggest fan, and she has one of the highest EQs that I've ever seen in a person — she's blessing in my life. It makes life easy when your relationship with your in-laws and other relatives is strong, especially if you're in a family business.

I believe in EI so strongly that I might go a little overboard with it. Heidi has seen the positive change, but sometimes asks me to tone down the EI when we are at home alone. When I start rambling on about EI, she sings the refrain from *Old McDonald*, "E-I-E-I-O." Perhaps I drank a little too much of the Kool-Aid on Emotional Intelligence. I'm not saying everyone needs to embrace EI as much as I do, but, suffice it to say, if you can improve your emotional intelligence, you and those around you will be the better for it. It is a great tool, particularly for business leaders. The evidence is more than anecdotal. Even Heidi is quick to admit that relationships within our family are greatly improved because of EI.

As you have these types of high EI conversations with those closest to you, your relationship with them will flourish, too. You'll come to find that they naturally flow over into deeper conversations with business associates, friends, and other individuals who are important in your life.

Emotional Intelligence with Customers

Over the past several years, I've made a concerted effort to spend more face time with our best customers and partners. To get the most out of our precious time together, I always ask the hard questions — those things you simply can't discuss easily in an email or on the phone. These are the questions that no one is asking. Those questions can bring your relationship to a higher level. Some professionals would call them critical questions. I call them high EI or code-shifting questions. Kellogg Professor Craig Wortmann calls them "Impact Questions."

Craig Wortmann: Impact Questions worth asking every prospect

They are questions that make the other person pause and think.

28

Some examples could be: What keeps you awake at night? Where do you see your business in five years? What does success look like for you relative to this project? Where is your life on a scale of 1–10?

When you listen, and I mean *really* listen, the power of EI in a business relationship can be profound. We'll talk about code-shifting in Chapter 6, but these times create building blocks or "code-shifts" in your relationship with others. Moments when you truly connect with someone become building blocks for a meaningful relationship. Generally, the more code-shifting moments together, the deeper the relationship — they become the basis for life-long meaningful relationships.

Be sure to let people know how much you value their business and your relationship with them. You probably show your appreciation all the time in emails, but it doesn't have the same impact. While emails have changed our lives from a practical and efficiency standpoint, they can be impersonal. In our rush to communicate promptly, we can lose the personal touch. You can't build long-lasting relationships sitting in your office behind your desk! You must be out face-to-face with your customers!

Emotional Intelligence in a Family Business

In a family business, strong family relationships are the single most important factor for a sustainable enterprise. Trust, transparency and harmony are paramount. Lose these attributes, you lose your business. Family businesses can be the best of business or the worst of business. In our case, it's the best. As my friend, Justin Craig, Clinical Professor of Family Enterprise at Kellogg, likes to quote, "Entitlement and wealth become the enemy" (Jim Ethier, Emeritus Chairman at Bush Brothers). Justin adds, "Family members need to be ready, willing and capable of contributing in a meaningful way." Family members hoping to work in the business must possess *all* three.

We follow many family business best practices, which include having a family council, developing a family constitution with strict rules about joining the family business, and holding family meetings. We also clearly define our family core values, which include Gratitude, Faith, Service, Family Unity, Love and Respect, Stewardship, Integrity, and Attitude.

If you would like to see our family constitution, you can view it at our website:

Soldbypauldarley: Family Business Library

My brother, Stephen, has led these initiatives for over 20 years. Steve served as Chairman of our Family Council and was perfect for these due to his humility, love of our history and high EI. Steve recently retired from Darley after 37 years and my sister, Annie, assumed this role. I know she'll do a great job as well. She is the liaison to our G4 and did an awesome job with our latest family meeting.

We also use EI to guide our family business discussions in a professional and caring manner. Most of our family are outdoorsmen, so when we have an issue that everyone knows exists but no one is talking about, we call it a "smelly moose" issue, kind of like the "elephant in the room." It is a metaphor for a 1,200-pound moose standing on the center of the conference table, but no one will acknowledge it. My brother, Tom, heads up our equipment sales. He is known for being both a peacemaker and someone who points out smelly moose issues in a non-offensive manner. Tom is a natural hunter and great leader who works closely with our customers and employees to deliver results and excellent service.

One of the secrets to our success is that we don't let the small things fester. We address issues when they are small, and no one in our family goes to bed mad at anyone else. It's been a family rule for more than a century. We've worked hard at instilling these values in the next generation.

Brooke Vuckovic, another Kellogg professor, writes, "Many family firms benefit from having leaders who have literally grown up in the business, knowing its mission, values, and culture intimately. But these leaders also face the challenge of dealing with conflict among colleagues who are family members ... Increasing social-emotional intelligence yields long-term benefits for the family and the business. Perhaps the best part: savvy family leaders can cultivate this form of intelligence in their children, creating a gift that truly keeps giving across generations."

See this link for more information about this topic:

Kellogg Insight: Family Business Leaders Should Nurture Their "Social–Emotional Intelligence" Brooke Vuckovic

There is a lot written on best family business practice. If you would like to know more, I suggest you check out the below link:

HBR: Leadership Lessons from Great Family Businesses, April 2015

Our family members are real students of learning from other family businesses. We participate in programs in YPO, *Family Business Magazine*, Northwestern University and we're active members of the Loyola University Chicago Family Business Center in Chicago.

My daughter, Audrey, and I have presented to students at Northwestern on a couple of occasions. That brought on other speaking engagements at Dublin (Ireland) University, YPO and even to a couple of industry trade associations. We donated our stipends to charity. You can review the slides from our presentation at our website:

SoldbyPaulDarley: Paul Darley & Audrey Darley Presentation: Family Business Dynamics and Pitfalls

Non-family businesses can learn from family businesses. My longtime YPO friend, Scott Robinson, recently sold his recruiting firm, but he could not sit on the sidelines very long. He writes some incredible blogs on his website and really nailed it with this one:

Robinson Resource Group: Relatively Speaking: 5 Family Business Strategies that All Companies Can Leverage

Emotional Intelligence with Peers

I belong to several business peer forums. When catching up at our meetings or with my friends and family, we often begin our conversations with the question, "Where is your life on a scale of 1-10?" This overall score takes into consideration personal, family and business issues. Our rule: If your answer is below a 7, then you need to talk about it. It's a great, yet simple way to check in with others and be able to discuss the significant things going on with those individuals closest to you.

Things can change quickly; for example, the illness of a loved one or a business crisis can cause the scale to quickly go down. When significant issues arise in someone's life, checking in like this creates a code-shifting opportunity where you can reach out and offer to help in their time of need. It creates the opportunity for others to share important things in their lives, good or bad, if they should choose to do so.

Some respond negatively to other people with continually high scores, thinking that the person might not be opening up on true feelings or issues in their life. Others might see that person as boastful or feel jealous. I can kind of get that, but it's best if you can just be happy for them and maybe some of it will rub off on you. It seems few are truly happy for someone else's success or happiness. I'm not sure where this comes from.

Truly being happy for someone else's success over your own is not easy, but it does happen. Professional hockey player Gordy Howe was truly happy for Wayne Gretzky when Gretzky broke his NHL scoring records in less than half the time Howe had set them. He even attended all the games where his records were broken and cheered Wayne on. When Gordy Howe died in May 2016, Gretzky was selected as a pall bearer and gave a eulogy at his funeral.

One of the highest rated TED talks, "Happiness and its surprises," by Nancy Etcoff, highlights that there is no English word for "being happy about someone else's happiness." Most other languages have a word for this idea, and it's interesting that we don't. It's well worth the watch:

Ted Talk - Nancy Etcoff - Happiness and its surprises

In our YPO forum, we put Emotional Intelligence into practice at our monthly meetings in a confidential, non-judgmental way. Our forum of nine CEOs also led nine new Chicago Windy City YPO forums that embraced EI. Today, many of the business organizations I belong to utilize emotional intelligence to some degree. At YPO meetings, strict protocol is followed to ensure the most benefit to each member. In our forum meetings, we focus on active listening — the key skill at the center of emotional intelligence — through an eight-step process that I'll talk about more in Chapter 12. Other forums can be a bit less structured.

In these meetings, we have a rule that you can't even have a notepad and pen in front of you. We're focused on whomever is presenting, and we listen with our ears, eyes and body language. Of course, all cell phones and other devices are off. In our case, we sit at a round table; we're all peers. There's no bigwig at the table, regardless of the size of company or net worth. Equality is an important part of YPO and EI, along with being supportive and non-judgmental.

Like these meetings, when out to dinner with family and close friends, we have a rule: cell phones go into the middle of the table so that we can stay focused on each other and being present. First one to check his phone must buy a round.

Is Emotional Intelligence Manipulative?

Fred Jevaney (No. 7) is CEO of a highly successful company, Randall Manufacturing. Fred and I look alike, and everyone seems to think he's my younger brother, yet he is almost 10 years older than I am. We were recently on the golf course together discussing EI. After I explained it, he turned to me and said, "So EI is about being nice to people so that you can get what you want?"

We both laughed because, on first blush, EI sounds like that, but it's not manipulative. If it is used only in these terms, people will see right through it. Instead, it must be natural and authentic, and used for the altruistic reasons.

Fred just sold his company to Safe Fleet, which is a private equity firm that is also buying a lot of companies in the fire industry, including several of our major suppliers. John Knox, the Safe Fleet CEO, is a mutual friend from YPO who is armed with a Harvard MBA and someone who gets it. Heidi is in a YPO spousal forum with his wife.

Prior to studying EI, I didn't dole out many compliments or praise, probably due to my upbringing. It seemed like whenever I was complimented as a kid, it was followed by an insult. I can blame those darn brothers of mine, but I found myself doing it as an adult. Now, I've been able to change that habit.

Today, I give out sincere praise on a regular basis. When you praise others, both publicly and privately, for a job well done, it's a powerful thing for you and the person receiving the praise. No one gets enough pats on the back. Watch what happens when you compliment others in a sincere manner. It's so easy and rewarding. I still can't figure out why so many managers seem reluctant to dole it out.

With friends and family, it seems that no one gets enough hugs either. Growing up, if my brothers showed any affection, it was usually in the form of a punch to the arm. It was almost a culture shock to go to Heidi's house and see her family cuddled up on the couch sharing a blanket. It took me a long time to get used to embracing others, but now I hug friends and family all the time. Hugs can be powerful.

How to get more information on Emotional Intelligence

There is a ton of information available on EI. For the past several years, one of the best-selling business books has been *Emotional Intelligence 2.0*, written by Travis Bradberry and Jean Greaves. It's sold over five million copies and has been translated into 28 languages. Travis has over one million followers on LinkedIn, where he posts great thoughts almost daily. I purposely did not read their book until I was about done with *Sold!*, but it's a great quick read:

Emotional Intelligence 2.0

Harvard's Dr. Daniel Goleman, Ph. D, was the one who put EI on the map with his 1995 book *Emotional Intelligence* and in his *Harvard Business Review* book article, "What makes a Leader," published in 2004. The latter is a brief, must-read article for anyone interested in pursuing EI.

Harvard Business Review article, "What Makes a Leader", 2004

Many one-day business seminars and universities are beginning to offer programs as well, such as Talentsmart and The Liautaud Institute, where I was recently added to their board of advisors.

<u>Liautaud Institute – Emotional Intelligence</u>

Joe Balistreri, CEO of the Liautaud Institute, says it was among the first organizations founded to provide EI training. Google currently has thousands of people on its waiting list:

<u>Fast Company: Inside Google Insanely Popular Emotional Intelligence Course, 2015</u>

Testing your Emotional Intelligence Quotient (EQ)

As discussed earlier, most studies suggest that people are only supposed to be able to improve their EI or EQ by 20-25 percent. My experience suggests that dedicated students can exceed that number in certain quadrants. It's been a couple of years since I completed this University of Illinois PdEI program and, like anything, if you don't practice it regularly, you tend to lose it.

You can find many free online surveys where you can test your EQ. You need to answer the questions honestly, there are no right and wrong answers. If you purchase *Emotional Intelligence 2.0*, you will receive a code where you can test your EQ twice on the above Talentsmart website. You should test yourself once at the start of the book and then again after you begin to put the theories into practice.

As you work on your EI, test yourself regularly so that you can improve on those areas that need work. Here is one such free test:

<u>Maetrix Emotional Intelligence Test</u>

Some will argue that individuals don't change, and some will always be clueless when it comes to "getting it." However, most can improve their emotional intelligence if they really want to and if they're willing to invest the time and effort. In doing so, they'll find they will improve their value to their companies while increasing their own happiness.

There's no question in my mind that learning to be more self-aware makes someone a better all-around person. If you want self-improvement, you can change, too. Anyone can do it. You merely need to start and then practice.

Mindfulness is like EI and has been getting reams of attention recently. Mindfulness is the state of active, open attention on the present. It means staying focused while being aware of your surroundings, but not being distracted. When you're mindful,

34

you observe your thoughts and feelings from a distance without judging as them good or bad. Instead of letting your life pass you by, mindfulness means living in the moment and awakening to the experience. Be present!

In business settings, mindfulness has been proven to improve decision making, reduce stress and improve communications across the organization. According to the below *Harvard Business Review* article, research shows that people spend 47 percent of their waking hours thinking about something other than what they are doing, which impairs their creativity, performance and well-being.

You can test for your mindfulness through the below free HBR link:

HBR: Free Assessment: How Mindful are you? March 2017

One other test that is now free is the Myers-Briggs personality test. There is no test that is so universally used and accepted when it comes to understanding how you and your co-workers are wired so that you can communicate and work more effectively with each other.

Online Personality Tests. Org: The Myers and Briggs Personality Test

The book Strengthsfinder 2.0 is also a great read and includes a password that allows you to take its test. We've done this at a management meeting, and it's been very beneficial to understanding ourselves and each other better.

What's Ahead for Emotional Intelligence

The understanding and popularity of Emotional Intelligence is only going to continue to grow as more people become aware of it.

You may have heard about emotional contagion, which is the phenomenon of having one person's emotions and related behaviors directly trigger similar emotions and behaviors in other people. A broader definition of the phenomenon was suggested by Schoenewolf: "a process in which a person or group influences the emotions or behavior of another person or group through the conscious or unconscious induction of emotion states and behavioral attitudes." The behavior has been found in humans, primates and dogs.[11] I'm not quite sure what that means, but probably two things: 1) Smiles are contagious and 2) live by the Golden Rule and treat people how you want to be treated.

---

11   Source: Wikipedia

The TV show 60 Minutes recently ran a story on Emotional Intelligence in robots. Humanity is an obvious differentiator between robots and people, but this video showing how robots can learn emotions is spooky:

<u>60 Minutes: Artificial Emotional Intelligence in Robots</u>

A lot of people are talking about conversational intelligence and the importance of being able to connect with others. Conversational intelligence helps you to better navigate your social interactions. It's not about how smart you are, but how receptive you are to learn from the small cues in interactions that build trust, partnership and mutual success. Top salespeople typically use conversational intelligence to build strong connections and lasting relationships. This video is dry, but the overall message is strong.

<u>You Tube: Judith Glasser - Conversational Intelligence: How Great Leaders Build Trust and Get Extraordinary Results</u>

At the beginning of this chapter, I mentioned that college degrees and MBAs don't carry the weight they once did. Don't get me wrong; education is critical for advancement. But I'm not entirely sure a strong correlation exists between one's formal education level and their EI. Some of the highest EQ people I've met only had a high school education. They might not have been CEOs, but they were solid citizens who "got it," had deep relationships with family and friends, and lived happy and productive lives.

When you embrace EI, one of the greatest benefits is that you can bring all your relationships to a higher level. It's incredibly rewarding, thought-provoking and personally fulfilling. This doesn't mean you need to be the life of the party, but you'll become more engaged with others and be able to motivate them to make things happen.

If you want to be a great salesman, a better parent, a more indispensable employee or an authentic leader, start practicing your EI. You'll be surprised what doors it opens.

Chapter 3

Authentic Leadership

"Before you are a leader, success is all about growing yourself. When you become a leader, success is all about growing others."

Jack Welch, former CEO, GE

Google the word "leadership," and you'll come up with over 800 million hits. There are that many opinions on what makes a great leader. I don't profess to be an expert on leadership, but over the years I've read reams on leadership. And, more importantly, I've observed many leaders very closely.

I've had an opportunity to be personally exposed to some of world's greatest business, civic, military and religious leaders. Each time I am given this opportunity, I concentrate on their leadership style. What can I learn? What traits do I aspire to? Which am I not impressed with? I cherish these moments and always seem to come away with something valuable.

Before moving on, please take a moment to think of a leader whom you've come to admire. What are the traits of that person that you would like to emulate?

Ready?

Through studying EI, I've come to learn about authentic leadership. While still in its infancy, much has been written on authentic leadership over the past few years. In short, authentic leaders are those who can lead others in a passionate and respectful way through being themselves. People naturally want to follow them.

The authentic leaders I aspire to be more like have certain traits. These people:

- Know who they are, are comfortable with themselves, and are genuine and self-aware

- Have high integrity, are honest and do the right thing, even when it's not popular or easy

- Lead with their heart

- Are forthright, don't play games, get along well with others, and don't throw sand when they're in the sandbox

- Are confident, yet humble, and never boastful

- Embrace and live by the organization's and their own core values, which are almost always aligned

- Build trust and loyalty by doing what they say they are going to do, and then doing more

- Respect everyone and, in return, earn their respect

- Realize they need improvement and work on their weaknesses. They are open to respectful criticism and suggestions for improvements personally and in the company

- Set priorities, take action, and get things done by motivating others
- Are servant leaders — they help others
- Embrace and drive change
- Develop high-performing teams through a "people first" culture
- Are self-starters, mission and goal driven
- Listen. They *really* listen!
- Communicate openly and often, and know how to tell stories to get their point across
- Are example-setters who lead from the front
- Accept others' ideas
- Admit when they don't know things and acknowledge when they're wrong
- Are hardworking and serve as pacesetters for the organization
- Inspire others and are great cheerleaders and good followers when called to be
- Listen to all sides, build consensus, and then move quickly and decisively
- Seek help from others
- Know that nobody does it alone. They don't take all the credit; they deflect praise and take blame when things go wrong
- Are positive, but realistic
- Look for the good in people
- Stay calm in difficult and crisis situations
- Focus on the long-term
- Are transparent
- Are courageous, yet carefully weigh and mitigate risks
- Give back
- Are family oriented

- Are passionate and enjoy what they're doing

- Are empathetic and compassionate

- Are grateful for the things they have; they give thanks to others and to God

- Have balance in their lives

- They get it!

I hate to throw out a Wikipedia definition for authentic leadership, but, it's the simplest and most straightforward definition that I have found:

> *Authentic leadership is an approach to leadership that emphasizes building the leader's legitimacy through honest relationships with followers who value their input and are built on an ethical foundation. Generally, authentic leaders are positive people with truthful self-concepts who promote openness. By building trust and generating enthusiastic support from their subordinates, authentic leaders are able to improve individual and team performance. This approach has been fully embraced by many leaders and leadership coaches who view authentic leadership as an alternative to leaders who emphasize profit and share price over people and ethics…Because the concept itself is not yet fully mature in a theoretical sense, there are many different definitions of authentic leadership, each with its own nuances. However, consensus appears to be growing that authentic leadership includes these distinct qualities:*

> - *Self-Awareness: An ongoing process of reflection and re-examination by the leader of his or her own strength, weaknesses, and values*

> - *Relational Transparency: Open sharing by the leader of his or her own thoughts and beliefs, balanced by a minimization of inappropriate emotions*

> - *Balanced Processing: Solicitation by the leader of opposing viewpoints and fair-minded consideration of those viewpoints*

> - *Internalized Moral Perspective: A positive ethical foundation adhered to by the leader in his or her relationships and decisions that is resistant to outside pressures*

> *"There is empirical research that supports a superordinate construct of authentic leadership that includes these four components."*

I'm sure that you can see the correlations with Emotional Intelligence: Self-Awareness, Self-Management, Social Awareness and Relationship Management — they are all right there!

Authentic Leaders' Effect on Organizations They Lead

Like EI, aspects of authentic leadership are both innate and learned. Any salesperson who wants to move beyond that role and improve himself must possess ambition, drive and a willingness to work hard. What's more, I would argue that these leadership traits are very similar to the traits that define a successful salesperson. And these traits are the essence of why great salespeople can make great CEOs.

Most successful salespeople have similar qualities, and most of the traits of a successful salesperson translate well into running a business, but not all. Those salespeople making the transition won't be strong in all disciplines, such as finance, legal and engineering, so they need to surround themselves with people who are. People who are generally educated in these disciplines seldom migrate naturally to the sales channel, but those who do have a strong competitive advantage due to their special skill set.

Many people who head up organizations — whether a civic committee, a small business or a *Fortune 500* company — don't handle the transition well. With the title comes a great deal of responsibility. Having a "chief" title doesn't necessarily make that person a leader. Leaders bring people together; they build teams. This assembly is critical because no individual does anything on his own, and to succeed as a leader, one must be able to motivate people to act. This HBR article talks to this:

HBR: How the Most Emotionally Intelligent CEOs Handle Their Power, December 2016

The handoff from a predecessor can affect the outcome of the succession process. Many refer to the "Halo Effect" when looking at past CEOs while pointing to their previous success. This McKinsey article addresses this issue head on:

McKinsey: The Halo Effect and similar Management Illusions, 2007

CEOs must groom and support their successors from the time they take the wheel. As my father wrote, "The final test of a leader is that he leaves behind him, in other men and women, the conviction, knowledge and will to carry on." I was fortunate to have him as a mentor for years after taking over the role of president.

As a leader, on occasion it's okay to show your emotional and vulnerable side. We all have emotions and generally nothing hits home closer than family. It happened to me at a recent quarterly company address, when our long-time employee Ron Voisard asked about my father. Ron's been a great mentor to our new international

41

sales team. I also got choked up at our holiday party last December when speaking about how grateful we were to our Defense Advisory Board for its help.

To some extent, everyone needs to multitask. It's a prerequisite for living in a tech-saturated world. Creating networks with manageable silos can help handle the myriad issues coming at you and allow you to deal with the influx of people looking to you for answers. If you're headed to the C-Suite, you had better learn to be present and in the zone, especially on important things. The ability to be extremely focused and to concentrate are critical to be a leader. Everyone is watching you and they can tell easily when you're drifting or thinking about something else. Be present.

Push Decisions Making Down in the Organization

As you move up the corporate ladder, more and more people will come to you for advice and assistance. Many new leaders find themselves overwhelmed because they think it's their role as "Superman" to take on those problems and resolve them. That's a huge mistake.

As discussed, it's important to give your undivided attention to those individuals looking for your advice, but the key is to push thinking and decision-making down in the organization. There is nothing wrong with asking the employee, "What do you think we should do?" One of my all-time favorite HBR articles is, "Who's got the Monkey?" A subordinate comes to you with a problem (a monkey) and tries to take it off his back and give it to you. The key is not to take the monkey!

HBR: Time Management – Who's got the Monkey? 1999

We'll talk more about this in the third section of Sold!.

Find the Right Business Model

Today, most business gurus are preaching that organizations need to excel in **one** of three disciplines:

    a)   Be the low-cost producer like Wal-Mart

    b)   Be the most innovative like Apple

    c)   Be the most customer-intimate like Nordstrom

Yes, the books say you can only pick one area to excel in, and then don't focus on the others. Candidly, I don't buy it. While organizations should clearly play to their strengths, especially if their competitors are weak in that area, I believe a business must be adept

42

in all three areas to contend in today's competitive markets. This is the ante just to get into the game.

If forced to pick **one** for Darley, however, it would be customer-intimacy, because it comes so naturally to us. This fact is probably due to the sense of family that permeates our business—and extends far beyond our walls. We know we can't lose the personal touch, as it's been a guiding principle of our company for more than a century.

Why do some Organizations fail while others Succeed?

How is it that some companies in the same market, with similar products, seem to excel while others flounder? The same question can apply to any organization. For example, when looking at fire departments, why do some have high morale and strong recruiting, while others can't seem to get enough volunteers?

The quick answer, I'm convinced, is leadership. To be fair, it is rarely only one thing that makes a company flounder, but you can usually start at the top when looking for the answer. Leadership books typically focus on the same resounding themes: integrity, knowledge, vision, ability to build a strong team, commitment, and a host of other qualities.

Ten years ago, I came across a study from the University of Chicago that focused on why established companies either hit a growth plateau or took off and reached the next level. You can read about it here:

Overcoming the Growth Plateau, University of Chicago 2006

After researching companies, the study's authors determined the key traits needed to bring an established company to the next level are:

1. Be customer centric

2. Develop a culture where pertinent information is shared with employees

3. Reach and implement decisions without perfect information

That's basic stuff, but I was excited about this study because it's aligned with authentic leadership approaches and affirms much of what we try to do at Darley. This approach was started by my grandfather and then perpetuated by my father and our generation. In short, we always try to treat people fairly, be honest and err on the side of the customer. We also share information openly with our employees and stakeholders, and we make decisions quickly, perhaps too quickly in some cases.

1) *Customer Centric / Relentless Customer Focus*

If you get nothing else from this book, remember this: focusing on the customer is key to success. Everything else flows from that simple concept. It starts at the top of the organization and needs to permeate the business. To become a successful salesman or a successful executive requires a relentless focus on your customer's pain. Resolve his pain and he'll keep coming back.

At Darley, we're obsessed with maintaining and building strong customer relationships. We don't want to merely satisfy our customer's need; we want to delight them! With few exceptions, I firmly believe successful organizations must have a customer-centric structure, which includes everything from the initial customer contact to meeting your commitments. It's astonishing how many companies talk about focusing on the customer, but how few do. At Darley, we do what we say we're going to do. No company is perfect, but we strive to exceed customer expectations. Employees need to feel appreciated and engaged to make this happen at all levels.

Our company has been around since 1908. With more than a century of experience, we've developed a sense of self, and a set of values that we share with our employees and customers. Our No. 1 core value is integrity, and our second is relentless customer focus. If we didn't live up to the values we profess, we wouldn't be able to get away with it.

The second key to success is taking care of your hard-working employees. All our employees can recite our company core values, and they are shared with our customers — on our website and our newsletters, and more importantly, in our actions.

2) *Culture that Shares Information*

I know many CEOs who conduct monthly, or even weekly, company-wide meetings. In large companies, several of them are now broadcasting their message via phone messages or video addresses. In addition to regular email communications, I conduct quarterly addresses at all our locations. One of my 50 business goals each year is to motivate our team through these company addresses. This task isn't always easy because part of being an authentic leader is "telling it like it is." I always speak from the heart, and if things are great, I will relate that fact. If we are not hitting budgets or have significant issues we are dealing with, I let them know. But more importantly, we let them know what we are doing about it and we don't panic.

How much information to share is a tricky question. Over the years, I've had numerous discussions with other CEOs of privately held companies about how much information should be shared with employees. Among these companies, I've seen a trend where when things are bad, CEOs tell them everything; but when things are good, they don't tell them anything. For me, I can't remember what I said yesterday, so I have to be honest and forthright — whether it's motivating or not. Most of our employees appreciate the candor, but I am working on putting a more positive and inspirational tone to ensure that I am encouraging our employees, even during tough times, while still be authentic.

We are constantly sharing information with our employees, stockholders, and other stakeholders, and then monitoring to make sure the communications are not too much or too little. In both cases, our surveys show that 95 percent of our respondents say that the amount of information they receive is "about right." If employees don't know what's going on, they'll usually imagine that things are worse than they are. These situations can get fueled by rumors and speculation and spiral out of control.

At Darley, we also blast out a monthly email video, "Inside Darley," to all our employees, as well as a mailing list of about 25,000 opt-in customers. The three-minute videos are not just about Darley products. In fact, we focus primarily on industry news, leadership tips, sales tools, and other information that our subscribers can use to improve themselves and their organizations. We film these videos in-house. They are very cost-effective and an easy way to get our brand message across, while sharing information that our customers can use. We get a great deal of mileage out of these videos with an open rate of over 20 percent, which means over 5,000 people view it monthly. The cost per touch point is substantially lower than any other media platform we use. If you're interested in registering for our monthly Inside Darley newsletter, please take a moment to do so here:

www.darley.com: Sign up for "Inside Darley" Video

3) *Making Decisions with Imperfect Information*

Too many CEOs like to have every scrap of information possible before making decisions. While one should make all efforts to understand a business situation from multiple viewpoints, CEOs who delay the decision-making process make matters worse. Particularly in timely matters, you should decide based on the best information available.

At Darley, we follow numerous metrics and use that data to make decisions. But sometimes we respond to anecdotal information or what we feel in our "gut" based on our instincts or experience. We do our best to balance those approaches. The more we grow, the higher the stakes. My cousin, James Long, is our data guru at Darley and loves the saying, "If you can't measure it, you can't manage it."

Collecting and analyzing data is good, but those businesspeople who spend too much time mulling over the data are in danger of "analysis paralysis." It's a frustrating situation for everyone in the organization when issues are turned over and over without action. Decide, go down that path, and stick with it. If it proves to have been the wrong choice, recognize it quickly, and change direction, or cut bait. Don't stay in a business because of your sunk costs, as it usually gets worse. As explained in the below article, sunk costs are exactly that—sunk!

Lifehack: The Sunk Cost Fallacy makes you Act Stupid, July 2017

Darley's history and experience gives us a competitive advantage, but we also gain a significant competitive advantage by being able to make decisions and move ahead swiftly. Many of our larger competitors don't have this luxury by nature of their larger bureaucratic structures. Companies can survive small mistakes; they can't survive indecision.

Take new products, for example. Less than five percent of new products brought to market these days are successful. You've got to continue to throw stuff at the wall and see what sticks, but some due diligence, market research and understanding of customer demand must take place before investing too much time and money in new products.

Top executives are human and make mistakes—they are risk takers by their nature—but they recognize that mistakes are opportunities to learn and improve. Indecision prevents you from moving forward, from refining, from making the right decision. To quote UCLA basketball coach John Wooden, who won 10 national championships, "If you're not making mistakes, then you're not doing anything."

Be decisive, but not rash. Plan things out, move quickly, and make sure the financial information being reviewed is accurate. That said, there is nothing wrong with "sleeping on it." Recent sleep studies have proved that your brain processes data and helps the decision-making process while you sleep. This rest results in better decision-making, as this Northwestern University study shows:

Northwestern University Sleep Study: 2012

Authentic Leadership comes in many forms.

I love to learn from our country's military leaders. U.S. Navy Admiral Joe McGuire serves on our board of directors. His best friend is Admiral Bill McRaven, who in 2014 gave the most watched commencement speech of all time at The University of Texas. His message detailed life lessons he learned as a Navy SEAL. His authentic leadership is clearly visible in this YouTube video. I've watched it numerous times, the last time with our family over the Christmas holidays. Everyone was moved.

YouTube: Admiral William H. McRaven, University of Texas Commencement

Sports is one area where you can easily see a plethora of authentic leadership, partially because it shows up so quickly in the win/loss column. While I've always migrated to sports that I'm actively participating in, such as fishing, hunting, golfing and skiing, some great examples are found in the leadership of sports teams.

Prior to 2016, the last time the Chicago Cubs won a World Series was 1908, the same year our company was founded. It's tough not to love the authentic leadership style of the Cub's manager, Joe Maddon. He knows how to motivate his young players and build a team. He is known for his peculiar quotes, including, "I've never been a bulletin-board guy to create my motivation. Your motivation has to come from within." And "Don't ever permit the pressure to exceed the pleasure." During the 2016 playoffs, his motto of "Try not to suck" sold thousands of tee shirts and hats. Good stuff!

Joe Maddon reminds me a bit of Kevin O'Sullivan, who is our sales rep based in New Zealand. Kevin spent most of his life as a leader in the New Zealand Fire Service. He is an authentic leader who does an awesome job with our customers. After the Cubs won the World Series in 2016, he joked to me that New Zealand invites other countries when they have *world* competitions.

As any great athlete knows, there is no substitute for hard work. While I'm not a huge Notre Dame fan, football coach Lou Holtz said it best: "Winners embrace hard work. They love the discipline of it, the trade-off they're making to win. Losers, on the other hand, see it as punishment. And that's the difference."

Find your own Style

In the early 1990s, when I first became president of Darley, I would stand up during our quarterly company addresses (at a time when our employee morale wasn't as high as it is today) and say, "If you're not happy here, you should leave!" I remember some challenging discussions with my father during that time. He would tell me to stop the rhetoric about asking unhappy employees to leave. "You're going to lose a lot of good people," he would say. I did not challenge him on much over the years, but on this I did because in my heart I felt it was the right thing to do, and a part of becoming an authentic leader. Ten years later, Jim Collins validated this concept in his book, *Good to Great*, as he talked about getting the right people on the bus as a critical first step in taking a company to the next level.

If the business has people who don't want to be on the bus or who are not a part of the program, everyone is better off when that person is not with the company. This attitude should start at the top and permeate the culture. Our Team Darley employees understand this important premise, and it makes for an incredibly strong team across the entire organization.

Not all of Jim's companies in *Good to Great* or the ones highlighted in his second book, *Built to Last*, are doing that great, but it's a concept that few can argue with today. In our case, we lost the losers and kept the good people. Everyone was glad the unhappy people left. Who wants to be around that negativity?

It was what I truly believed, and it was part of my authenticity. If you know who you really are and passionately believe what you're saying is right, people will naturally trust you and want to follow you. Everyone should find their own style, whether it's your selling style or leadership style. It's an ongoing process of self-awareness and self-improvement. Hone your style through social awareness and self-management, based on feedback you get from others.

Ultimately, I did tone down the "get the hell out of here" message, particularly after several people I didn't necessarily want around left. I may mention it when reviewing our annual employee survey, but today, my message is more one of letting our employees know where we are headed and thanking them for their dedication and hard work that helps to create a winning environment, and I always stress the importance of serving our selfless customers at all expense—something we call "The Darley Way!"

Chapter 4

The Darley Way

"At Darley, we will continue to live with integrity, accountability, hard work & commitment."

Bill Darley, 1998

If you're not in the defense or fire industry, I won't be disappointed if you breeze through our company history in the first half of this chapter. But please take time to read the second half, which talks to our company's rich culture and our approach to business.

Proud History

Like most established, successful companies, Darley has a proud history. In our case, it spans more than a century. My grandfather, William S. Darley, was born in Chicago in 1877, not long after the Great Chicago Fire of 1871. At the age of 31, he founded our company in 1908 after successfully selling two other companies in which he was a partner.

William S. Darley in 1908 the year our company was founded

William S. Darley modeled our company after Sears Roebuck by offering a complete line of municipal supplies, including fire and police equipment, sold through catalogs mailed across the U.S. In 1926, following a historic meeting with Henry Ford at his home in Florida, William began manufacturing fire engines and offered them through his catalog.

At that time, most of the other fire truck manufacturers made their own cab and chassis and offered their trucks at a price of $4,000 to $5,000. My grandfather introduced a complete fire engine for $690. It was a true paradigm shift more than 90 years ago, and it completely upset the market. When Rich Karlgaard, publisher of *Forbes* learned of this story, he commented, "People talk about disruptive technologies as if they are a new thing." If you're interested in watching the 15-minute interview, below is a link:

Forbes Insights: Paul Darley and Rich Karlgaard, 2013

In the early 1930s, the other fire truck builders put pressure on fire pump suppliers not to sell us pumps. With a full order book in our Chicago factories, my grandfather was forced to make a decision: either get out of the fire truck business or build his own pumps. He chose the latter.

He hired Pete Yates, the Chief Engineer of our primarily pump supplier, America Steam Pump Company of Battle Creek, MI, with the understanding that Pete could return to his hometown of Chippewa Falls, WI, to build the pumps there. The lumber industry had recently moved west from Northern Wisconsin, and a surplus of German craftsmen lived in the area. Chippewa Falls is 350 miles from our headquarters in Chicago, and in those days it took several days to travel there. My grandfather's love of hunting and fishing in the north must have influenced his decision.

Our primary manufacturing plant remains in Chippewa Falls today, and it's one of the most state-of-the-art facilities in our industry. All our products are still 100 percent manufactured here in the U.S. by incredible employees with sound Midwest values and work ethic. No parts are outsourced overseas, which is a significant competitive advantage. While it may make our products a bit more expensive, it's offset by the higher quality, resulting in lower warranty rates (less than 0.5% of sales). Since we control the entire manufacturing process, we can also offer customized products and quicker deliveries.

My grandfather died in 1937. He had instructed my grandmother to either sell the company or have young manager and relative, Joe O'Reilly, run it. My grandmother was an active president, but she entrusted Joe. Joe was one tough businessman, which was fitting for the day, and he was a trustworthy and hard pounding steward until my father came of age almost 30 years later.

During World War II, our company shipped thousands of pumps and hundreds of fire trucks to the U.S. Army and Navy. Our company received the Army/Navy Award for Excellence in War Time Production three times during the 1940s. One of those original awards hangs on my office wall today.

After the war, Darley fire trucks were left around the world and became a catalyst for our international business, which today accounts for roughly half of our firefighting business. My father, Bill, grew our international and domestic fire truck business over the next 40 years.

From left: Bill Darley, Pat Long and Reg Darley at our board of directors meeting in 1999.

54

Succession Planning in a Family Business

In 1990, Bill established an executive team consisting of my brother, Peter Darley, who led our Fire Truck Division; my cousin, Jeff Darley, who managed our plants in Chippewa Falls; and me, who led sales and marketing.

As part of his succession plan, Bill watched and worked closely with us, and he asked that we submit business plans on what we would do if he named us president when he planned to step down from this role in 1996. I wrote an incredibly lengthy and detailed plan that was more than 400 pages (which included starting a new defense division) and he realized at that point that I, as his youngest son, felt very strongly about taking this role. In 1997, he advised us that he could not pick a successor. He was not going to pick one of us and then have that person not be supported by the family after he was gone.

Bill asked us to work it out together and decide. He said he would accept our recommendation regardless of what it was—it could be co-presidents, rotating presidents, or hire a new president from the outside ... it did not matter to him; he would support it. Ultimately, both my cousin and my brother threw their support behind me, based on my communication and organizational skills. In fact, we spent so much time working through this process over two years that we took our eye off the ball with respect to company operations — it was the only year we lost money in our 110 years in business.

From left: The executive team of Peter Darley, Paul Darley and Jeff Darley in 1997 after they recommended Paul for president of Darley

In 1998, Bill stepped down as president, following this unique succession plan that has been featured in *Family Business Magazine* and is taught at several family business programs at universities.

Bill Darley on a Canada fishing trip after stepping down full-time in 1997.

Perhaps some thought it was taking the easy route, but it was ingenious. In his words, "I'm not going to rule from the grave."

If you're interested in reading more about this, please check out the below articles:

Family Business Magazine Planning a Smooth Succession Bill Darley

New York Times, Family Businesses Learn to Adapt to Keep Thriving – Darley

At the time, we could have easily become another family business failed succession statistic. We even looked at selling the company. Research shows that approximately 30 percent of all family-owned businesses survive into the second generation, and only 12 percent survive into the third generation. Surprisingly, only 3 percent of all family businesses operate at the fourth generation, as we are today.

Of those companies that don't make it long term, 70 percent fail to transition successfully. Of these, 60 percent fail due to problems with communication and trust, 25 percent fail due to a lack of preparation from the next generation, and 15 percent fail from other issues (e.g., poor tax or financial planning, legal advice). Therefore, roughly 85 percent of family business transitions fail due to a lack of communication, trust, or next-generation competency.[12]

In our case, the transition process made us much stronger as a team. It has helped us to work closely together today in what most

---

12   Source: Williams and Preisser, 2003

family business books call a "Cousin Consortium." These are quite popular in G3 or older family businesses. If you would like to learn more, the below website has a very clear definition:

SMEToolkit.org: The Cousin Consortium

Don't get me wrong: it takes work, and we still have our share of conflict, but it's always with the company's best interests at heart. It's never self-serving.

In 2008, we added a fourth member to our executive team, my cousin, James Long. We have three family branches that own the business, and now all three are represented on the executive team. We felt it was important that all branches of the family be recognized, and it helps with family harmony when the management mirrors the ownership. In our case, my father's family had two representatives based, in part, on his proportioned ownership.

We follow the book with respect to adhering to family business best practices. Darley today is owned primarily by 15 members of the third generation (G3) — all bloodline descendants of my grandfather. Of the 15, nine family members currently work in the business. The stock is pretty much evenly distributed among the G3. In addition, 31 family members from the next generation own stock (G4), six of whom currently work here. We've never hired in-laws, and while we don't have a steadfast rule against it, we feel we have enough bloodline family members and resulting dynamics without adding in-laws to the mix. That said, our family communicates openly and is truly one the primary reasons for our success.

The fact that we're a family business permeates our walls and gives us a strategic competitive advantage. For us, being a family business does not apply only to decedents of our founder, as roughly 25 percent of our employees have a relative who worked for us in the past or currently works at Darley. Whether their last name is Normand, Whitlaw, Monpas, Anderson, Beighley, Bond, Deutsch, Hayes, Hughes, Nicolai, Potaczek, Praxmarer, Schimmel or Gasper, they are significant stewards and contribute greatly to our rich culture and sense of family.

Our customers love our application sales engineer, Lairy Normand. Lairy is 25-year employee, and, like many of our employees, a lot of his family works at Darley. His brother, Gene, is our production manager and serves on our management team. Lairy's daughter, Amanda, is an engineer who drives our Lean initiatives. His cousin, Dan, is a pump assembly mechanic. In total, these four family members have a combined 100-plus years of experience at Darley. Lairy reflects: "I always wanted to work for a company where everyone knows your name. We get that not only at Darley, but with our awesome customers. The personal relationship is so important, and they know we care."

It's critical in family businesses that room is made for other non-family at the top of the organization. In our case, we purposely have more non-family than family members on our 15-member management team. We always have a G4 family member as a guest at all management meetings.

Darley Growth after the Succession Plan

From 1998 to 2017, we went on to grow our business more than 1,000 percent by expanding our core pump business, purchasing four businesses (Odin Foam in 1997, Ohler Pump in 2007, Self-Testing Systems in 2014, Fireboy-Xintex in 2017) and expanding into new markets such as defense distribution. We also diversified into several lateral growth markets and began manufacturing water purification equipment, residential firefighting systems, and even drones.

In the early 2000s, our business began to grow significantly. We realized if G4 family members came onboard at the same rate as our generation, our company would not be large enough to support the next generation. This thought has been the key driver for our growth over the past 15 years. We didn't know much about the defense distribution business when we went into it, so we had to surround ourselves with good people who did. It worked, though not without fits and starts. We established a defense advisory board, brought top level military onto our board, and hired veterans who know the market. We listened and learned from them and constantly modified our strategies.

In 2001, we partnered with a key supplier, Propoly, and started a new company called Polybilt. Propoly is a family business run by Tim Dean, who is a trustworthy partner with whom we are culturally and strategically aligned. Polybilt provides patented plastic fire truck bodies, as well as bodies to the tow truck industry and other markets. Today, we have Polybilt licensing operations in several overseas markets including Asia, Africa, Europe and Australia.

In 2007, we bid on a large government pump contract. We lost the award to a company called Ohler Pump, headquartered near Waterloo, IA. This family business was established in 1947. We purchased it within four months of Ohler winning that pump award. It is still run by family members Rob and Kurt Bond. These guys are incredible operators with solid Midwest work ethic and strong family values that are completely aligned with our family.

58

Darley's Ohler Plant in Janesville, IA

In 2007, we were also awarded two significant Department of Defense contracts to provide equipment to support our warfighters. We started a new Defense Division that same year. These contracts hold an annual value of almost $1 billion, but our actual sales in this division were just over $100 million in 2016. We are growing and gaining market share each year, and this $1 billion in annual revenue from these contracts could become a reality within the next 10 years.

In 2011, Darley was awarded a major fuel transfer pump contract with the U.S. Marine Corps. valued at $85 million, which was primarily performed out of our Ohler plant. We've continued to grow this operation and have invested heavily in our people, new plants, and state-of-the-art-equipment.

In 2014, we purchased Self-Testing Systems, which manufactures patented residential fire sprinkler systems. Jeremy Taylor, the previous owner, stayed on with us, and in 2016 was instrumental in helping us win a multi-million-dollar contract with the Federal Emergency Management Agency (FEMA) to retrofit its mobile housing units with fire sprinkler systems. We supplied hundreds of these systems following Hurricane Harvey in August of 2017.

In 2017, we purchased Fireboy-Xintex (FBX) of Grand Rapids, MI. It is a 30-year-old business that engineers and manufacturers fire suppression and detection systems for the marine market, RV, Department of Defense, and other niche markets. FBX also has manufacturing operations in Poole, England. FBX has roughly 75 percent of the recreational fire suppression marine market with more than one million systems in service. Larry Akins will stay on as CEO and as a 20 percent partner for up to five years. FBX is ISO9001 certified and manufactures extremely high-quality products. It was a great fit for a lot of reasons, but mostly because of the trustworthy and competent leadership team in place, a testament to Larry's ethos and authentic leadership style.

Today, Darley has seven divisions in our company, with roughly half of our business coming from firefighting contracts and half coming from defense contracts. Of our fire equipment business, roughly half of that business is overseas. In fact, over the past five years, we've received Exporter of the Year Awards from both Illinois and Wisconsin, as well as 2015 Ex-Im Bank Exporter of the Year for Sub-Saharan Africa.

I feel funny talking about it, but the following is a testament to our hard-working employees at Darley. In recent years, our trophy case has grown to include awards such as the Illinois Family Business of the Year; Inc. 5000 fastest-growing companies in America for each of the last seven years; one of the fastest growing companies in Chicago twice; and Ernst & Young Entrepreneur of The Year Award Finalist.

In 2017, we were one of 16 companies awarded the Department of Homeland Security FEMA Small Business Excellence Award. The 16 companies were selected by FEMA from a pool of more than 10,500 small businesses. The Defense Logistics Agency (DLA) recognized us as one of its best contractors numerous times. We were also named the Best Midsize ($100-$350 million) Board of Directors by *Private Board Magazine* and received an A+ grade and complaint-free award from the Better Business Bureau.

The recognition is nice, but it's not a key driver for us, and we seldom apply for these awards. They just seem to happen as a byproduct of our passion and our team's hard work and commitment.

Darley's Culture

We have a rich culture, and speaking for our generation, we truly feel honored, privileged and humbled to be caretakers and stewards for Darley. If you have a chance to visit one of our locations, you'll quickly sense it from the old catalog covers, photos, and memorabilia that fill our walls, but more so in our people.

Circa 1901, my grandfather handwrote the following note. It remained on his desk throughout his incredible career.

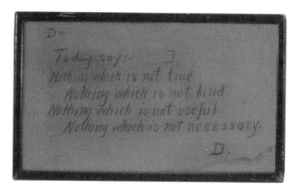

It reads, "Today say: Nothing which is not true. Nothing which is not kind. Nothing which is not useful. Nothing which is not necessary." This message is on display in our corporate headquarters, along with the very first fire truck we ever built in 1926 and a lot of other memorabilia. My brother-in-law, Randy Freedman, has been awesome in helping us locate and document our rich culture and history through Darley antiques and memorabilia he's found online.

Our Team Darley members and our rich culture are the backbone of our success. In our 2017 annual employee engagement survey, we received the highest ratings in our company history, with better than a B+ grade point average. When we asked our employees, among other things, if they felt our company was headed in the right direction, over 95 percent responded that they agree or strongly agree. These results are supported by our employee retention rate of over 97 percent and our ability to attract great new talent — two critical benchmarks for any organization.

61

Part of the reason for these strong results is that we involve our employees in the decision-making process and keep them posted on our progress. We are constantly imbuing our culture into our team, not only in our company-wide quarterly meetings and message boards, but also in our daily actions. We encourage our employees to respectfully challenge management and each other if they see anyone act in ways that are not aligned with our core valves. They are engaged at all levels, and it makes for a trustful and healthy work environment.

Patrick Lencioni, in his best-selling book, *The Advantage*, writes, "The seminal difference between successful organizations and mediocre or unsuccessful ones has little, if anything, to do with what they know or how smart they are; it has everything to do with how healthy they are."

I wholeheartedly agree, but also feel that an organization must have purpose. We asked our employees, "Do you feel our vision and mission statement of service to warfighters and firefighters gives you a deep sense of purpose and inspires you to work with enthusiasm and commitment?" and virtually every employee in our company responded with a resounding, "Yes!"

When you're in the business of supporting firefighters and warfighters, it's easy for our employees to understand and appreciate the higher sense of purpose that we have as a business. This sense of higher purpose in life seems more important to Millennials[13] than other generations.

"We have a proud past, a great team, we know where we are headed, and we are honored & humbled to serve those who protect us all so selflessly."

Paul Darley, March 1, 2015

© W. S. Darley Sensitive and Proprietary Data

---

13   Millennials (also known as the Millennial Generation[1] or Generation Y) are the demographic cohort following Generation X. No precise dates denote when the generation starts and ends; most researchers and commentators use birth years ranging from the early 1980s to the early 2000s.

As I look back at our catalog covers from the past 100 years, it's hard not to be proud. We have a proud past, a great team, we know where we are headed and we are honored and humbled to serve those who protect us all so selflessly.

Our employees understand and respect our rich culture. To quote Chinese billionaire Guangchang Guo, chairman at Fosun Group, "An opportunity sustains an enterprise for a year; good management sustains an enterprise for a decade; good corporate culture sustains an enterprise for a century."

Core Values

At Darley, we talk about our core values, but more importantly, we live by them. Our employees were involved in the process of developing them. All Team Darley members carry small laminated cards that include our core values, mission statement, vision and strategic plan as shown below.

CORE VALUES

INTEGRITY
We shall act in an honest, ethical manner, and we will do what we say we are going to do.

CUSTOMER FOCUS
Everything we do shall be focused on taking care of our customers in a prompt and fair manner, while meeting or exceeding their quality expectations.

RELATIONSHIPS BASED ON RESPECT
We shall strive for relationships built on trust and mutual respect - with our employees, customers and suppliers.

EMPOWERMENT / RECOGNITION
We shall encourage an atmosphere that empowers our employees to make the right decisions for our customers. We shall recognize the efforts of our employees on a job well done and encourage their input for continuous improvement while maintaining a family business environment.

INNOVATION
We shall continue to develop innovative products and embrace technological advancements based on solid engineering and testing.

CELEBRATION
We shall take time to have fun and celebrate our Team Darley victories and special efforts.

YPO NEXT GENERATION

10

© W. S. Darley Sensitive and Proprietary Data

Strategic Planning

In AD 60, the Roman statesman Lucius Seneca stated, "If one does not know to which port his ship is sailing, no wind is favorable." It's a profound strategic metaphor. I'm surprised by the number of large and mid-sized companies that have no formal strategic plan, or if they do, they don't share it with their employees. There is no way to execute a plan unless at least the top managers know where they are headed and can lead their team toward the established goals.

At Darley, we follow the book with respect to strategic planning, which among other things, means going through an annual SWOT (**S**trengths, **W**eaknesses, **O**pportunities, **T**hreats) analysis, reviewing our 4 Ps (**P**rice, **P**roduct, **P**lace and **P**romotion), 4 Cs (**C**ompany, **C**ollaborators, **C**ustomers, and **C**ompetitors), and focusing on our five-year strategic plan and our one-year business plan. We involve all our employees in the strategic process, and we openly share our plan with all employees and key stakeholders[14].

As a result, all our employees know exactly where we are headed. They live by our vision, mission, and strategic direction, and everyone is rowing in the same direction to get us there. Because everyone is a part of the process, they also understand their specific role in helping us to reach our goals and objectives.

We Know Where We Are Headed

VISION STATEMENT
To be a global, family-owned and professionally managed company with a long term perspective for our stakeholders as the first choice of fire, emergency and tactical professionals worldwide.

MISSION STATEMENT
To passionately serve the world's first responder and tactical communities by providing high quality, safe and innovative products with unmatched commitment and service.

STRATEGIC DIRECTION

DEFENSE / GOVERNMENT FOCUS
We shall continue to pursue state and federal government opportunities, and to support our US Military and Homeland Defense markets, to help make our country safer.

EXPORT
We recognize and shall continue to build on our role in the global economy as we service existing markets and pursue new emerging markets.

TECHNOLOGY
We shall continue to invest in new technologies to stay ahead of the competition, scale our business and to bring products to market in a timely and cost effective manner.

CORE MARKET EXPANSION
We shall continue to grow our core markets in the pump industry, while expanding in high growth adjacent markets such as new water markets, EMS & Rescue.

EMPLOYEE GROWTH
We shall continue to foster employee development and create an environment of trust and mutual respect in the workforce where our employees know the expectations, rewards and consequences of their actions. We shall ensure employees have the education and resources to achieve their potential.

PARTNERSHIPS
We shall continue to form partnerships with our customers, suppliers and employees.

BRANDING
We shall continue to position ourselves as a provider of high value goods and services and continue to create demand for our products in the fire, emergency and tactical markets.

During the most recent recession in the late 2000s, our company, like many others, was at a crossroads. We had a choice: Should we continue to expand into new markets or contract and go back to our knitting? We chose to continue with our long-term vision and plan, but we slowed things down a bit so that we could watch our cash closely and not stray too far from our core markets.

Before this recession, never in my life had I been so attuned to learning how other companies were dealing with the economy. I took much solace in learning that what we were doing is what the business gurus were recommending in the top academic periodicals. At the same time, we were also turning to our outside board of directors, peer groups, and industry statistics like never before.

---

14   Stakeholders are anyone who can affect or be affected by the organization's actions, objectives and policies. Some examples of stakeholders are bankers, lawyers, directors, employees, owners (shareholders), etc.

At Darley, we have a detailed annual business plan, a five-year strategic plan and even a 100-year plan—we think in terms of decades, centuries and generations.

Our current five-year strategic plan was kicked off on January 1, 2016. We invited all employees to participate and had more than 50 from all areas of the company involved in the planning process.

As we move through this progression, we take an analytical look at the last five years, but more importantly, we focus on what we want to look like five, 10, and even 100 years from now. During this process, we look at megatrends and ask the critical or high impact questions: Why? Why not? Can we do it better? Who will our next leaders be? How will changes benefit our employees and customers? For us, it's a very emotional process.

We're adding exceptional new talent to Team Darley by onboarding a new generation of family and non-family leaders. It is critical that we get buy-in and have everyone on the same page.

The University of Chicago MBA program teaches the Business Canvas Model, developed by Alex Osterwalder in 2010. We use something similar.

Business Canvas Model developed by Osterwalder in 2010

In all our strategic thinking, we have been guided by Wayne Gretzky's famous quote on breaking Gordy Howe's scoring and point records in the NHL in roughly half the time. When asked how he could do it, Gretzky responded, "I never went to where the puck was; I always went to where the puck was going to be." With that in mind, we strive to have new products (and services) engineered and available before the market realizes that it has a latent need.

We did not achieve all our goals set forth in our last five-year plan, but we did manage to more than double our business since we last went through this process five years earlier. Our growth plans for the next five years are even more aggressive. All this planning and goal-setting is in the hope of building a strong, diverse and sustainable business for future generations—one that can continue to passionately take care of our customers and employees.

The older my generation gets, the more important this legacy becomes. When reflecting on his own succession, my father would often recite one of his favorite quotes, "Son, be wise and make my heart glad" (Proverbs 27:11).

One of Bill Darley's favorite quotes when talking to his children

The Darley Way

While not as formalized as our core values and strategic plan, we also have some basic covenants that all our employees understand. They are the unwritten rules about how business is done here. We live by these guidelines because they are a part of our culture. We call them "The Darley Way."

- We follow our core values

- We create raving customers (Darley Disciples and Darley Demanders) by treating people how we want to be treated

- We're honest, friendly, respectful, engaging and appreciative

- We build close relationships when we become the customer's advocate and err on the side of the customers

- We know speed is a competitive advantage, so we are quick to respond to our customers and changing market conditions

- We are easy to deal with and empower our employees to take care of our customers

- We under-promise/over-deliver

- We don't take ourselves too seriously. We enjoy what we're doing and have fun

We started this chapter talking about relationship selling. Finding and solving customers' pains, aiming to exceed their expectations, and developing raving customers or "disciples" are all ways to develop those relationships. We'll talk more about these approached in the next section.

SECTION II
THE ART OF RELATIONSHIP SELLING

Chapter 5

The 50 Ps of Selling

"Every sale has five basic obstacles: no need, no money, no hurry, no desire, no trust."

Zig Ziglar, Sales Author, Speaker and Coach

I am often asked, "Are salespeople born or made?" While some are born with a natural proclivity for sales, I firmly believe nearly anyone can learn to sell, if they're willing to invest the time and have reasonably high emotional intelligence. Relationship sales is more of an art than a science. No secret formula exists for becoming a great salesperson, but you can do certain things to increase your chance of success.

Sales may not be your focus in your business, but selling impacts virtually every aspect of our lives. It doesn't matter if you are trying to sell your child on studying, asking for a nicer seat in a restaurant, or trying to convince the bank to give you a loan. As discussed in Chapter 1, we are all salesmen!

The best salespeople make it look easy and fun. They are relaxed and have a natural ability to relate to different types of people, and know how to guide a prospect through the sales process. Some might call it "the gift of gab." I call it high EI.

In the chapters ahead, you'll find some of the qualities, approaches and sales tactics implemented by those exceptional sales reps who are in the top 20 percentile — the producers. They won't all apply to you, and you may already be putting some into practice. But hopefully, you'll find more tools to add to your toolbox that will improve your chances of increasing your sales and advancing your career. Ultimately, you should follow a process that best works for you, while embracing the processes, core disciplines and values that your organization extols.

Marcus Lemonis, the CEO and chairman of Camping World, has a hit show on CNBC called "The Profit," where he invests in fledgling companies and turns them around to save jobs and make money. He focuses on three things — people, process and products. It's a good, simple approach that seems to work well for him, as he's invested more than $60 million into these ventures. At Camping World, he grew annual sales from $100 million to $3.3 billion in less than 11 years.

I'm proud to say Marcus is also a Marquette University graduate, about 10 years behind me. Like him, I was also involved in our student government, and we both ran for president of the student body and lost. A good life lesson in public service, humility and perseverance for both of us.

Philip Kotler, a world-renowned marketing professor at Kellogg, is highly regarded as the "Father of Modern Marketing." He popularized the idea of the "Four Ps of the Marketing Mix" framework almost 50 years ago, which includes Product, Price,

Promotion and Place (or distribution). It was later expanded to 7 Ps, adding Physical Evidence, People and Process. Some versions go to 9 Ps, including Partners and Presentation.

Today, his theories are taught in almost every business school around the world using the 14th edition of *Marketing Management*. It's the hallmark of modern day marketing. If you want to learn more about this, click the following link:

Philip Kotler: Marketing Mix

Sales and marketing, while different, tend to get lumped together, which I've done in this section.

As I began to put my thoughts together for Sold!, almost every topic about relationship selling began with the letter "P" or could be described by a word beginning with this letter. It simply worked out that way, so I ran with it.

With respect to this book, I certainly am not trying to "one up" the father of modern day marketing. Instead, I am honoring him by continuing his work. Leveraging off Kotler's 4 Ps above, I developed my own list of Ps relative to relationship selling. I've combined a few to boil them down to 50 Ps, since some are similar or related.

Don't get hung up on the Ps; it's a part of my quirkiness. Have fun with it! This concept is generally reserved for smaller lists, so students and practitioners can remember them. You're not going to be able to remember all 50 Ps, but you'll remember some. The most important takeaway is it's not about you — it's all about your customer! Adopt a "people-first" culture where your employees are empowered to delight your customers.

The 50 traits are divided into five sections. Each is prioritized, and all are appropriate for one sales situation or another. Only one is a stretch on the "P" concept (#11 – Phollow-Up), but it's so important and is missed by too many sales reps who could be great if they were better at it. No sales book could be complete without it.

Moving forward, keep in mind there are only three ways to increase sales:

1. Sell more current products to current customers

2. Sell current products to new customers

3. Sell new products to current and new customers.

Selling new products to new customers is by far the most difficult and costly. But if you're in a stagnant or declining market with new competition, it might be your only choice for growth, or survival.

Selling Products vs Services

My 50 Ps come primarily from a manufacturing and distribution perspective, as that is where I have the most experience. But most these principles apply to the service industry as well. Today in the U.S., the service industry is significantly larger than the manufacturing and distribution industries combined.

Relationship selling in the service industry can be more difficult than in manufacturing or distribution because many buyers have a natural tendency to view services as a commodity with little differentiation.

Those in a service industry (and let's face it, we're all in a service business on some level) must maintain and grow current relationships while building new ones if they want to stay in business. As a rule, the longer the relationship, the stronger it is, and the more difficult it is for the customer to leave. Usually, the switching costs increase with time.

Banks are good about maintaining long-term relationships while drumming up new business. Switching a banking relationship usually has a long selling cycle and seldom happens — unless a significant event occurs.

My daughter, Audrey, was a middle-market banker for MB Financial, a Midwest business bank, until recently when she joined our company. Love her as I do, I still wouldn't break the relationship with my banker to move to her bank. I've got paralysis when it comes to our banking relationships because the switching costs are so high. I have my personal investments and loans with Fifth Third Bank, as well as our company 401k and profit sharing plans. Moreover, our banker, Doug Alwin, and the bank president, Bob Sullivan, do a great job servicing us. For the most part, I feel that they Love My Business (LMB) and deliver VIP treatment.

I get calls from bankers every week hoping to earn our banking business. They have tickets to sporting events or educational forums. I seldom, if ever, take them up on those offers because I don't want to feel beholden to them. However, I am always respectful, because it is important to maintain relationships with other bankers. I meet with them once a year shortly before our line of credit is up for renewal. Smart business people get this practice, as everyone needs a Plan B. Nothing is forever when it comes to business relationships. It's good to have your feelers out and ensure you have relationships with other vendors, whether they be bankers or pump suppliers. You never know when you might need them.

The insurance industry is similar. Our company is one of the oldest customers with Liberty Mutual Insurance Co.; Darley has been insured by them for more than 100 years. Our broker, Arthur J. Gallagher & Co., is a publicly traded company with a market cap of more than $10 billion, yet it is still a family business. We receive outstanding service from Dave "Zeke" Kulhanek, and the company's CEO, Pat Gallagher, still contacts me regularly. Pat has given his personal attention to me on an insurance issue that was extremely significant to our small company, yet almost insignificant in his world. I was amazed by his LMB service. He was our advocate with Liberty Mutual and he truly had our back.

Pat and I enjoy hunting and golfing together, and I am as committed to his family as it is to us. Their company commissioned a book called, *The Gallagher Way*, about their family business and how they've grown to be successful through passionate customer service and taking care of their employees and customers. To get a sense of what they stand for, check out the link below:

The Gallagher Way

The service industry is changing drastically due to automation. When was the last time you went to a bank teller or used a travel agent? Growing up, many of my friends made a great deal of money in a short period trading commodities at the Chicago Board of Trade and Mercantile Exchange. Electronic trading meant the end for most of them, and the open outcry pits went from holding more than 5,000 traders to less than a couple hundred today. My brother-in-law, Jimmy Farmer, and golfing buddy, Greg Pozen, are still standing, but they are looking at their options.

Many lacked transferable skills — and certainly not at salaries that they were enjoying previously. The ones with grit, such as Michael Connelly, Bobby Sanfilippo, Quintin Sullivan and Dave Heinle, made the transition, but it wasn't easy. Dave tried selling life insurance for a couple of years, which is one of the most difficult sales jobs. He studied hard and passed his Certified Financial Planner (CFP) Test and now is a financial investment manager and is nailing it. Steve Skrine started a restaurant. John "Spider" Kenna sells Pierce fire trucks for Global Emergency Vehicles and is one of the best sales reps in the country. JJ Dwyer, a friend since grade school, was one of the conservative ones who invested his money and didn't spend wildly like most others. He retired before the age of 50. There's a good lesson here.

It's said to never go low bid on legal and accounting services because you get what you pay for. Legal services are a changing market, too. With the glut of graduating law school students coupled with online services like LegalZoom and other outsourced legal firms, personal relationships don't have the impact they once did. That said, I grew up down the street from our corporate attorney, Ed Tiesenga. He and his new partner, Mike DeBoer, merged firms after Mike's firm had been representing our company and family for almost 70 years. They both know our business, do a great job, and treat us fairly. While we hire specialist law firms at times, we view ourselves as partners for life.

We have a similar relationship with our accounting firm Shepard, Schwartz & Harris. Partners Gregg Wirtschoreck and Stan Lazar make us feel that we are the most important customer they have. One of their tax accountants, Chris Glowacki, even conducted a tax presentation at our 2017 family meeting. Stan and Greg are kind of opposites, but make a strong team with their yin-yang approach to business. Those teams are often the strongest.

Chapter 6
The Sales Foundation. Build Relationships.
Solve a Pain.
Follow a Process.

"Most people think 'selling' is the same as 'talking.'
But the most effective salespeople know that listening is the most
important part of their job."

Roy Bartell, Sales Trainer and Speaker

1) People (Relationships)

2) Private Conversations/Principled

3) Pacify a Pain

4) Process

5) Prospecting

6) Penetrable/Potential (Qualify the prospect)

7) Preparation/Practice/Pitch/Pre-call Planning

8) Pertinent/Pithy/Precise/Pointed

9) Primary Point of Contact

10) Presentation

This chapter covers the premise of relationship sales — the foundation. By utilizing emotional intelligence and authentic leadership, you'll find you will grow relationships and increase sales as you head up the corporate ladder.

1) *People (Relationships)*

There is *no one way* to build relationships. Relationships are built over a series of positive interactions (code-shifts) that earn each other's trust over time. Once trust builds, so does mutual respect and a natural likability, and your relationships will deepen. By definition, building strong relationships is the basis of relationship selling.

As you build relationships, your business will grow, and so will you. Salespeople with low EI are incapable of building long-standing, strong relationships. They might succeed at some getting orders, but their business is unlikely to grow, and they're likely to lose customers. This deficiency ultimately costs the organization, because lost customers are hard to get back.

Building and maintaining relationships is Business 101 and Life 101. Any first-year business student could tell you, it's far cheaper to keep and build on existing customers than it is to find and develop new ones — most studies suggest it's at least seven times more expensive.

Always remember the lifetime value of customers. You may have a $50,000-a-year customer, but if she's with you 20 years, she should be viewed as a million-dollar customer.

It's said the best salesmen will do 80 percent listening and 20 percent talking. Think of being on your first date with the girl of your dreams. You asked questions, really listened and wanted to know everything about her. You sold yourself by your natural desire to discover more about this person. In high school, I used to make a list of things to talk about when I would call Heidi. I still do that today with important customers.

Trust and Respect

In 2015, Harvard Business School professor Amy Cuddy released a book, *Presence,* in which she noted that people quickly and subliminally answer two questions when they first meet a new person:

1) Can I trust this person?

2) Can I respect this person?

Most people size up others in seconds. Cuddy has been studying this subject for 15 years. Psychologists refer to these two qualities as "warmth" and "competence." She observed that in business settings, trust is more important that competence, which is contrary to what most people believe intuitively. Competence, however, is critical, but it is evaluated only after trust is established. In fact, if you try to come off as too competent too early in a relationship, it often backfires and has a negative impact. Your body language can express a great deal too, as explained in Cuddy's TED Talk.

TED Talk: Amy Cuddy - Your body language shares who you are

You can improve your chances of making a good first impression in many ways, and we'll talk about those later in this chapter.

At Darley, most of our contracts are based on a handshake. While we have formal contracts with our largest customers and suppliers, we seldom refer to these contracts because a mutual trust exists. We both abide by the letter and spirit of the agreement. If you find yourself referring to a contract with a customer or vendor to see if it's been breached, it might be time to re-evaluate your relationship. Chances are it is not as profitable as you think, and it's probably not enjoyable either.

Generations of leaders at Darley have understood that business is about relationships. In 2008, my father, Bill, wrote these words for our company newsletter, *The Darley Times*: "At Darley, we understand the importance of honoring contracts, but we place the trust of personal relationships above all else."

Relationship selling doesn't stop with your customer, well, at least not your traditional customer. You need to build relationships with other "customers" vital to your business and life, whether they are distributors, end-users, suppliers and especially your internal customers — your employees — to make and deliver on the sale. No one does it alone.

2) *Private Conversations/Principled — Relationships Built on Trust & Respect*

Virtually all relationships, not just business relationships, are built on a foundation of trust. Trust is built over time in part by sharing things in confidence with one another in private conversations. It is critical that you keep private conversations private. By its very name, if you want to become someone's *confidant*, you must know how to keep things *confidential*. Become a confidant for others and you'll grow your relationships. Once trust is broken, it's difficult, if not impossible, to rebuild.

One of the most natural ways to build relationships is by keeping your word and doing what you say you are going to. People will begin to trust you when they find you are reliable and have their backs. You earn their trust over time. Trust, respect and integrity are paramount as the foundation of any relationship.

When was the last time you spent meaningful and quality time relationship with a business associate? These times create great code-shifting moments and allow you to deepen your relationship. If you get them, don't squander these opportunities and waste them on small talk. That doesn't deepen relationships. The same applies to time spent with close friends and family.

Mixing Business and Pleasure

Many business relationships are built when you're outside of the business setting. Many of my business associates are also close personal friends. The two go hand in hand. While I don't socialize much with our employees, I do mix business and pleasure with suppliers and customers. When a natural trust and likeability exists, it can be extremely powerful.

Building long-lasting business relationships is very fulfilling, rewarding and gratifying. Tom Gorski, a close friend since first grade, runs Gorski-Osterholt Advertising, a 50-year-old business started by his father. They designed our corporate logo with the flaming "D" in 1974. Tom prides himself on his close personal and business relationships. "When I'm with close customers on the golf course or any social setting, I almost never discuss business. It's more about the bond that we build."

Fellow YPOer and Kellogg classmate, Artie Collins, was able to build his company NPN 360 into a successful printing business based largely on work with friends and family.

It is interesting to note the number of "players" who like to golf, hunt and fish, especially among CEOs. I'm not quite sure why this is, but I suspect it has something to do with being balanced, grounded, in touch with nature and with people who are important to you. It also has something to do with being competitive and natural "hunters" in all that they do.

You can learn a great deal about a person on the golf course, and there's no better time to have deep discussions than while sitting in a duck blind. I've been caught more than once bringing a small notebook with topics to discuss into a duck blind with customers. You have a captive audience for at least several hours. These are great code-shifting opportunities.

Paul Darley & Wilson Jones, CEO of Oshkosh Corp. on a duck hunting trip

Some of my best times with my father were while golfing, hunting and fishing. He always sent family, friends and business associates framed pictures of special times together. Try it. They make for great personal gifts and it's high EI. If you mail it to their office, chances are it will be displayed there.

Code-Shifting

Research conducted by psychiatrist Abigail Brenner, MD, shows seven building blocks for a great relationship: Trust, Commitment, Intimacy, Respect, Communication, Empathy and Equality.

Psychology Today: 7 Building Blocks for a Great Relationship, Abigail Brenner

In every meaningful relationship, building blocks or times shared together create a transitional shift in the relationship. I have coined the term "code-shift". It reflects this building block experience in a relationship where two or more people bond together based on a shared experience. They develop their own "code" or "common language" based on their experience together and it becomes the foundation that shifts or strengthens their relationship.

Deep code-shift moments are generally significant memories that become building blocks in a relationship. The strongest code-shifts are created during times of crisis or jubilation. Think of the bond formed by those who experience life-threatening experiences, such as soldiers or firefighters.

A common "language" is developed through code-shifts. A simple example is a code language such as "Pig Latin" that you spoke when you were a kid. When you did, you built a bond with your buddies. These experiences become stepping stones or building blocks in a relationship. People use references from past experiences together to describe a current situation and build a bond.

You know you've had many code-shift moments with someone when you relate to current situations based on your past relationship together. Your relationship builds as code-shifts develop through an accumulation of past events. Not all the events are necessarily significant. For example, you could be referring to a past situation with inside jokes. I'm teased in our family for misusing words or phrases. In a recent conversation with my mother-in-law, Boni, I suggested that she extend a "fig leaf" to someone with whom she had a disagreement. I obviously meant "olive branch," but it stuck. Silly, but even small code-shifts become building blocks.

You can even have a code-shift with yourself. Have you ever traveled somewhere or experienced something that was life changing for you? In many ways, these are transformational experiences that can mark times when you changed (shifted) as person.

The strongest relationships are when you can look at each other without having to say anything and you both know you're on the same page. These instances require little explanation.

When my sister, Krina, died of cancer in March of 2017 at the young age of 59, it was a watershed moment for my family. Experiencing the love among my family during a crisis was a code-shifting moment for us all, as we bonded more than we had in years.

The power of code-shifts can be seen in many sporting teams. The NFL dynasty of the New England Patriots is a shining example. The relationship between quarterback Tom Brady and wide receiver Julian Edelman is so strong that they are now featured speakers at business seminars. Brady stresses the close bond among players, deeming the earned "trust and love and respect" of his teammates to be "most important." Their code-shift bond is so strong, it seems Brady and Edelman have a sixth sense when it comes to knowing what the other is thinking.

Boston Globe: Tom Brady, Julian Edelman open up on Patriots' sense of accountability at Tony Robbins event, June 2017

As Donna Carroll, president of Dominican University, likes to say, "Moments create momentum." You can see this concept in play in both the Patriots and Dominican University.

Generally, these code-shifts are upward, but they can be downward, too, causing harm to a relationship.

Rumor Mill

People like to spread rumors, which can take a life of their own and spread quicker than they did in 5th grade. Our rule at Darley: we simply don't discuss or spread rumors, good, bad or indifferent.

People who like to spread rumors think that it shows they are in tune with the marketplace. But it generally backfires, and they are perceived as untrustworthy. As a result, the gossipers find it's tough to build true relationships as people will think, "If they are constantly talking about others, what are they saying about me?" It's just easier not to go there.

We don't speak ill of competitors, even if something negative appears in print. We view it as unprofessional and unnecessary. Negative selling never works in relationship sales. If a customer complains about your competitor, it's fine to listen and acknowledge, but don't pile on. My dad was a fisherman and loved to say, "You never saw a fish mounted on a wall that had its mouth closed."

You'll find that most industries are much smaller than they first appear. If you get marked as someone who doesn't tell it like it is, it will tarnish your reputation for life.

We all know that much of what's on the internet is untrue, fake news, or, at best, inaccurate. But if it's in print and may impact our business or that of a customer, we may share it under the right circumstances.

Don't Exaggerate – Don't Puff – Stay within the Lines

Some salespeople get so excited and focused on making the sales that they tend to exaggerate or make promises they can't keep, just to get the sale. This approach almost always fails and is another reason why salespeople get a bad rap.

This practice is considered "puffing," and it can get you into trouble as it can lead to mistrust and loss of confidence. In layman terms, it means exaggerating when selling. Legally, it means "expressing an opinion or judgment that is not made as a representation of fact. Puffing is generally an expression or exaggeration made by a salesperson or found in an advertisement that concerns the quality of goods offered for sale. It presents opinions rather than facts and is usually not considered a legally binding promise. Such statements as 'this car is in good shape' and 'your wife will love this watch' constitute puffing."[15]

It is critical that you always stay within the lines. Grandma Darley would always say, "If you don't want it on the front page of the newspaper, then don't do it!" That stuck with me. You are judged by the company you keep. General Peter Schoomaker would say, "If you wrestle with a pig, you're going to get dirty." He served as Chief of Staff for the U.S. Army. I learned a ton from him when he served on our company board of directors.

It's important to have formal policies and guidelines in place. Poor sales policies almost brought down Wells Fargo in 2016. At Darley, all our employees sign a Code of Conduct that describes our expectations and rules for dealing with customers and suppliers. It clearly outlines what behavior is acceptable and unacceptable, and what measures will be taken if an employee violates the code. Our international sales reps and customers are trained and must agree to act in compliance with the Foreign Corrupt Trade Practices Act (FCPA).

Integrity is our number one core value, and we have a zero-

---

15   West's Encyclopedia of American Law, edition 2. Copyright 2008 The Gale Group, Inc. All rights reserved.

tolerance level when it comes to violating this sacred covenant.

3) *Pacify your Customers Pain*

A large part of relationship selling is finding your customers' pain and helping them solve their problems. Most salespeople are very familiar with their company's products or services and try to sell clients on the merits of those offerings. While it's vital that a salesperson know his products inside and out, the product's features often have little to do with customers' needs. People buy for emotional reasons more than anything else, but they still need to find ways to justify their emotions. This has been proven in numerous studies and is discussed in this McKinsey article:

McKinsey: The "Moment of Truth" in Customer Service 2006

Often customers won't come right out and tell you what their real need is. Sometimes they don't even know. You've got to draw it out. You can find out what they need by getting close to them and asking prodding questions. It takes practice, and it takes place before you talk about your company and the features and benefits of your products.

Getting close to and understanding your customers' pain does take time and energy, but it's critical for relationship selling. Everyone has hot buttons. You need to find them and help your customers and prospects resolve them.

If selling a complex product, companies should send engineers, customer service and other technical support teams with sales reps to new target high-profile customers. Engineers can experience firsthand product application and understand the customer's need. Support staff are also able to put a face to a name and help build relationships with customers. Typically, it's healthier for the company if multiple people have an established relationship with a customer and the organization itself owns the relationship. This idea is especially true if you have high turnover on your sales team.

Sell me on that corner

I use a couple of simple exercises to illustrate the importance of knowing a pain. Whenever I'm interviewing prospective sales reps, as well as other employees who will have customer contact, I point to the corner of the ceiling in my office toward the end of the interview and ask them to "Sell me on that corner." Most (even seasoned sales reps) respond immediately by saying things like, "It a great corner. The drop ceiling is straight. The lighting is nice and soft." I usually stop them in less than a minute. Before reading on, think to yourself for a moment. What would you have said?

Ready?

The answer I am looking for is, "What's important to you in a corner?" I use the corner metaphor because it so strange and people remember it. It also catches people a bit off guard and shows how they might naturally respond under times of sales pressure. About 95 percent of people don't give me the answer I'm looking for. I will also accept, "What is your budget?" which can tell me a great deal about that person.

Sell me on this pen

Similar stories have been told. In the 2013 movie, "*The Wolf of Wall Street*," the main stock broker character (another example of sales reps being stereotyped in a bad light), says at the beginning and end of the movie to his new recruits, "Sell me on this pen."

I first used the "sell me on this pen" exercise with my daughters over 20 years ago. I pulled a ballpoint pen from my pocket and held it before them.

"Sell me this pen," I told them. Their answers were pretty much what you'd expect.

"It writes very smoothly and the ink is a great shade of blue," one replied. "It looks cool, and it's our most popular model," replied the other.

All that might be true, but it doesn't get to the heart of the issue. As you can guess, the answer I was looking for was "What are you looking for in a pen?"

Because they didn't take the time to learn about my concerns, the girls had no idea what their customer — in this case, me — needed in a pen. Ink color and a smooth and consistent flow are good qualities in a pen, but those details are not what was most important to me. Moreover, every pen provides these.

Back then, and still today, I spend considerable time creating hand-written notes to our customers, employees and myself, and my hand quickly fatigues (primarily because I didn't follow the instructions from the nuns at St. Luke Grade School). It quickly begins hurting my fingers and makes my poor handwriting even worse. The Paper Mate Profile has a soft rubber pad where my fingers hold it. As a result, an ergonomic grip eases the fatigue. My pain, literally and figuratively, is solved, or at least eased, with a well-designed inexpensive pen.

I also own a Monte Blanc pen that was a gift from a foreign customer years ago. I seldom use it except for signing special contracts. One reason is because it's too big for my hand, but the main reason is that I tend to lose pens. I don't mind losing a $1 pen, but I would feel terrible losing a $300 pen.

The lesson here is simple: Take time to learn about and consider the needs of others first, truly listen to them and put their needs first. It's not just good selling techniques. It's good manners and it's living by the Golden Rule.

As salespeople, we are all anxious to rush in and extoll all the virtues of our product. Over the years, I've watched way too many fire truck sales reps charge into fire stations anxious to get an order. They immediately begin to talk about their company, the features and benefits of the body construction, the size of the compartments, the paint job, or the great Darley pump. In their haste and pressure to win an order, they forget to slow down and ask the fire chief or committee member, "What's most important to you in your new fire truck?"

One group who gets the concept are commercial and residential realtors. They will quickly ask, "What are you looking for?" and then, "What's your budget?"

I've noticed this ability to size up the customers' needs comes more naturally to women and Millennials. I'm not quite sure why that is, but it's notable. For women, I think they're generally more sensitive to the needs of others than men.

It's good to see this in Millennials because this generation receives flak about being self-absorbed. Here's a 15-minute video that "tells it like it is" with respect to Millennials. Don't let the title mislead you.

You Tube: Simon Sinek –This is Exactly What's Wrong with This Generation

It seems every generation is naturally critical of the generations behind them. I'm sure that Millennials will be critical of Generation Z, also known as Gen Edge — those born in 1995 and after. They are just beginning to enter the workforce and much attention will soon be paid to them. These two generations are clearly different, as pointed out in this article:

The Sound: The generation after Millennials are NOT like Millennials: We call them Generation Edge. Millennials vs Gen Edge, 2014

I have incredible admiration for the "Greatest Generation," especially those men and women who served during World War II.

The Pain is Seldom Obvious

When I was 29 years old, we landed a multi-million-dollar contract with the U.S. Navy. We worked closely with Larry Gallagher, a Department of Defense contract engineer. He was involved with creating specifications for the order, and he had a pain he needed addressed. He worked for a large bureaucratic organization that was hard to navigate. Most of the outside firms who had contact with his organization were difficult to deal with as well. On the other hand, we were very easy to work with and responded quickly and professionally to all his requests.

Today, more than half of our business is with the federal government. We know the rules and clearly stay within the lines. While we won the Navy contract based on the merits of our products and our bid, the relationship with the customer was important.

4) *Process*

Like anything else in your business, sales is a process. While the process is certainly different at every company and may vary from customer to customer, the more organized and process-oriented you are, the more successful you will be. You must have discipline and commitment to the process. You need to modify your sales approach on a regular basis to address changing market conditions.

As previously stated, each year, we begin our sales process with a high level strategic planning session where we conduct a careful review our 4 Ps (**P**rice, **P**roduct, **P**lace and **P**romotion). We also review our 4 Cs (our **C**ompany, our **C**ollaborators, our **C**ustomers, and our **C**ompetitors). These reviews frame the competitive landscape and help the bigger issues come to mind. We then conduct our SWOT Analysis for each division of our company, and the plans are shared openly with all employees. From these analyses, we modify our annual business plan and sales strategy.

If you're looking to enter new markets, you need to be guided by Michael Porter's "Five Forces" analysis. Within his framework, you examine barriers to entry, the threat of substitutes, bargaining power of buyers and suppliers, and industry rivalry. Industries with less rivalry among competitors are typically more profitable, because companies don't make decisions simply to spite their competitors. This video sums it up nicely:

HBR Video: The Explainer: Michael Porters Five Forces Analysis

At Darley, we manufacture a variety of products and distribute more than 100,000 SKUs[16] in catalogs and websites for military personnel and firefighters. Our defense equipment is sold face-to-face by a sales team of recently retired veterans. Our firefighting equipment is sold through a website, catalogs and a team of firefighters who sell equipment on their days off. Our core business is manufacturing firefighting pumps which are sold to different fire truck builders (OEMs). Each product line requires a unique selling approach.

Once you have a strategic sales process that works for your organization, training on the process is critical. If the processes that are in place at your company work, stick with them. But if you are looking to make improvements, take note of the following.

Our basic sales steps are:
1. Prospecting
2. Preparation
3. Preparing a script
4. Practicing
5. Presentation (after carefully listening)
6. Phollow-up (Follow-Up).

We use a few simple tools to help with this process including keeping a journal, customer relationship management (CRM) software, and customer forecasting.

Use a Spiral Three-Section Notebook/Journal

It may not sound like much and it may be old school, but our employees are required to keep a daily journal in a three-section, spiral-bound notebook. They are to document phone conversations, company and customer meetings, daily tasks, goals, follow-ups, and thoughts where the company can improve.

In a typical day, most go through anywhere from two to four pages in their notebook, so the notebooks generally last about a

---

16 Stock Keeping Units are generally assigned to different models of products.

quarter. They put a circle next to each discussion that requires action, and then check it off once completed. Once the notebook is full, notes that require action or follow-up should be transferred to the front section of your new notebook, a Microsoft task list, and onto the customer's CRM account so that you create a permanent record.

The third section of the notebook is for ongoing projects. A three-section notebook is better than a legal pad because the pages stay together and last longer. It might not look as professional as a slick portfolio, but it's more practical.

If a customer calls in 2017 and says, "Hey Paul, we talked about XYZ on Jan. 29, 2015," I refer to my notes. Some might argue that such detail and notetaking is a legal risk. Perhaps. But I'd argue that the benefits outweigh the potential risks. These notebooks should be destroyed after three years (or whatever period is in line with your corporate record-keeping policies).

You probably keep all your appointments in Microsoft Outlook or Google calendar, but try printing out the next six months (in monthly view) and stapling it inside of your notebook. That way you can reference it quicker than you can through a smart phone or computer.

Keep a red file folder for urgent priority items and a yellow medium priority file folder for those unfinished printed documents that can't be easily stored electronically. Go through it daily. You'll be amazed at how quickly you tackle those items.

Customer Order Forecasting/CRM

For every significant Darley pump customer, we establish and get their buy-in on an annual forecast. We do so to properly plan our production requirements and make sure we have the resources to meet their delivery expectations. On a quarterly basis, we share the performance against the forecast with the customer.

You should not need an excuse to reach out to customers on a quarterly basis, but this gives you one. It also allows the sales manager to see which sales reps follow this simple task and which do not. Most our customers like to see a scorecard and take comfort in the fact that we track their performance, as it shows we value and appreciate their business.

Try it. Most other suppliers don't take the time to add their customers to an annual forecast, and you'll set yourself apart if you do. We use this information internally, so we can plan our production requirements, but, equally important, it allows us to quickly "red flag" a customer if behind forecast and commend those customers who are ahead.

90

Most companies use some type of Customer Relationship Management (CRM) tool to manage quotes and sales calls. Commitment to use these systems must come from the top, and all sales staff should be on board. My experience is that you don't need an expensive system. Simple low-cost CRM programs like Sugar, Pipe Drive and others fill most CRM needs.

5) *Prospecting*

In some respects, it's good to cast a wide net when prospecting, but it's critical to qualify your prospect early in the sales process. Not everyone is going to be a potential prospect, even if it appears so at first glance. You must qualify and segment different customers to align with your process.

Cold Call Phone Etiquette

The most difficult way to begin relationship selling is by cold calling, but sometimes it's necessary if you're new to a sales team or entering markets where you don't know *the players*. Today, with caller ID, you'll most often get a person's voicemail. Since roughly 95 percent of these calls will not result in a return call, you'll increase your chances by leaving a clear, succinct and personalized message that is not too long.

Be sure to leave your name and phone number, repeating it twice slowly. State the purpose of the call and the action that you are asking the prospect to take. When you leave a voicemail, let the prospect know you will be following up with an email that can easily be responded to if there is interest.

Caller ID also expedites the conversation when receiving calls. When answering your phone, always address the person by their name with another natural greeting. It's okay, to say "Hello," but it must be followed up with his name. If the person is returning your call, thank them for doing so with your initial greeting. It saves time, it's the polite way to answer and it shows high EI. At Darley, we update our outgoing voice message daily, so that those calling know if you're in the office or not.

Do research on LinkedIn to see if you have mutual people you may know, including others in the industry. It's OK to mention them by name, if you have their permission.

Customer Segmentation

I used to believe market segmentation was hogwash and didn't apply to our niche business, but now I'm a huge believer in it. Market segmentation is simply a marketing strategy that involves dividing all current and prospective customers into subsets of customers who have common needs.

At Darley, we segment our fire customer base by type of customer (OEM, dealer or fire department) and then into five groups. We give them names that are kind of crazy, but easily remembered. It not only helps us to know where to allocate our resources, but when communicating internally, everyone understands where that customer is on our priority lists. Customers can move from one segment to another. Our segments are:

1. **Darley Disciples** — These are key OEMs, distributors and others who are great company advocates or raving fans. They spread the good news and drive most our sales. We enjoy working with each other and have a symbiotic relationship. We spend most of our time, energy and resources ensuring that our "Darley Disciples" are happy through our "Concierge" VIP or LMB service—they feel that Darley "Loves My Business" because we do! Typically, based on sheer volume, they are our most profitable customers. We devote a great deal of face-to-face time with these customers on sales calls and target many communications, such as our company newsletter, the Darley Times, and our monthly Inside Darley video, at this customer segment.

2. **Darley Demanders** —These are fire departments and other end-user customers who specify and "Demand" Darley products in their specifications and think of us first when looking to place an order. We treat them like partners. Word-of-mouth is significant in our industry, and these customers help spread the good news on the internet and in their local communities. We see them at trade shows and reach out through monthly communications.

3. **Darley Don't Knowers** — Even though our company is more than 100 years old, some customers still don't know us, especially in the new markets we serve. We try to build our brand awareness with this market segment, so when they have a need, they will think of us. A lot of our branding with advertising, social media and trade shows can generally reach them.

4. **Darley Don't Carers** — They don't have a need for our products. Either we don't apply to their job or they're simply not in the market. They have no preconceived notions about Darley. Often, they are the customers who come to know us and will work with us when the time is right for them.

5. **Darley Despisers** — Every company has some detractors for one reason or another. We don't waste any time on the "Darley

Despisers." While they might not actually despise us, for one reason or another, we can't get any traction with them.

You can't be all things to all people, and market segmentation really works if you start to breathe it and then infuse it into the culture of your company.

You should design and implement strategies to target each segment based on their needs and your available resources by using sales visits, media channels, blogs, print advertising, and other touch-points that best allow you to reach each customer. You can also create market segments by your product types. We'll talk more about market segmentation in Chapter 10, as it applies to the Pareto Principle.

No Jerks

While you won't find it in any of our formal company policies, we have one other segment at Darley: an implicit "no jerks" policy. We don't want to deal with customers, suppliers, employees and others who are, for lack of a better word, "jerks." (I have heard of other companies that use a stronger word that is inappropriate for a family business like ours, but I trust you get the point.) It's now a code-shift for us and ingrained in our culture.

There are some customers we don't want any longer because they fail to pay their bills on time, are difficult to deal with, or are simply jerks. Life is too short, and with this group of jerks usually comes a lack of profitability and an array of problems.

Sometimes a simple association with these types of people can hurt your brand, as others recognize these difficult customers and associate you with the same behavior.

Hunters and Farmers

In most sales organizations, people play different roles, but almost all models include some type of "hunter" and "farmer" roles. Some salespeople prefer to work from the office helping customers, while others have a tough time being "caged up" there. Both roles are critical to the organization.

The hunters are usually the extroverted relationship and business development people who go find and close new business. They are road warriors who love the thrill of the hunt. They spend time with current customers and maintain those relationships, but they generally migrate to new business opportunities.

The farmers are the ones back in the office who act as inside sales or account managers and who keep clients happy by cultivating and maintaining existing relationships. They generally support both the end-user customer and outside sales reps, and they take care of your existing customers 24/7. Customers often go to farmers first in a time of need because the hunters can be hard to reach and don't have quick access to the information needed.

Hunters will initiate and close the sale, then turn it over to an inside rep. In relationship sales, the handoff from a hunter to a farmer can be a tricky and result in a long process that may harm a relationship. Some customers feel abandoned if the sales rep they thought they would be working with unexpectedly turns them over to someone they don't know. This territory can be dangerous.

The best sales reps are both hunters and farmers. At Darley, all our sales reps are both. It's required because we "hunt as a pack." We all work together to land new customers — "Darley Don't Knowers" and "Darley Don't Carers" — but we also make sure our current customers — "Darley Disciples" and "Darley Demanders" — remain happy. Some of our sales reps are compensated on commission and share in commissions when hunting as a pack. This can get tricky and needs to be clearly defined in compensation agreements. The best plans promote commission sharing when a team approach is used.

Find the Decision Maker

Once inside an organization, you need to find the decision-maker. It often isn't who you might expect, so be careful as you navigate these waters.

When working with large organizations, always try to get an audience with the "top dog." If you can't get an audience with him, keep him posted along the way. Often the CEO won't be involved in the decision-making process, but if you can communicate with him and then reference him in your conversation, it can be helpful. Yes, name drop when the time is right. Some might argue that name dropping is inappropriate. I realize it can be risky and should only be done if what you say regarding your relationship with the CEO or top dog is factual. If it's not, word will get back that you bend and/or stretch the truth.

It's good to ask respectful, prodding questions to see who is involved in the decision-making process. In large organizations, the decisions are often made well before it gets into the hands of the buyer or purchasing agent.

Networking/Connecting

I'm not a huge fan of the cliché, "It's not what you know; it's who you know," but it's true in many respects. I can't stress enough the importance of networking, but the term is so overused that I prefer to call it "connecting."

94

You have many ways to connect with existing and potential customers. Technology has only added to the ways we develop those relationships. LinkedIn, Facebook and other social media channels are good, but be careful with what you post. Many careers have been damaged due to what was a seemingly harmless post.

I belong to many beneficial business and social networks, from the Young Presidents Organization to industry associations. Participation in these groups goes a tremendously long way toward building relationships and providing opportunities you might not find elsewhere.

You need to connect the dots, but you should also be a connector and help to open doors for others.

I've collected roughly 30,000 business cards over the years. It is critical that you find a way to quickly and efficiently save this data. It's easier today than ever before with business card scanner apps that are free or nearly so. Important contacts should always be added to the company mailing lists, CRM programs, and email distributions, with each contact's permission. Further, be sure to share V-Cards with new clients.

When at a trade show or conference, never eat alone. You should always find someone to network with — you might be surprised where some of these chance encounters lead. If you find yourself in a long cab line from the show to airport, share a cab with the person in front of you or behind you.

Conferences/ Trade shows

Trade shows offer great opportunities for prospecting and connecting with a variety of clients, vendors and partners to build your company and personal brand. I'm amazed by the number of attendees and exhibitors who don't know how to work a room or a booth.

Simple things can turn-off potential connections, like sitting in your booth, not greeting people properly, a name tag not clearly displayed, or being lethargic in the booth because you closed the bars the night before with people who were not prospects or important partners. Here are some good tips:

Trade Show Buddy: The Do's and Don'ts or Trade Show Exhibiting

The name tag goes on your right side in most situations, which makes it easier to read your name when shaking hands with others. Most will put them on the left for some reason. I suspect it has something to do with most people being right handed, and it's easier to put on.

Be liberal in sharing your business cards with people and always pack twice as many business cards as you think you might need.

6) *Penetrable/Potential - Qualify the Prospect*

In 1985, we were working the International Association of Fire Chief's trade show in Atlanta. Our team was very young and unseasoned, so my father decided he would show us how to "work the aisles" and sell a specific prospect on Darley. The prospect was wearing an official fire chief show badge as my father fished him out of the aisle and into our booth. We watched as the "master salesman" extolled the virtues of our company, explained the features and benefits of our pumps and other products while walking him around the booth for about five minutes. When he was done, my father asked what the prospect thought, to which the man responded, "Do you want a woman tonight?"

Yes, it was a pimp working the show floor. Remember, you need to qualify the prospect early in the sales process. In this case, the pimp was trying to sell the wrong guy. They each should have qualified their prospect first.

Some of the 3rd and 4th generation Darley family members with the first fire truck we ever produced in 1926

Not everyone is a prospect. You need to determine early on which potential customers are penetrable and which ones are not. You will encounter some customers who are not going to buy from you no matter what you do. I'm not saying you should totally ignore them, but I learned early on not to spend too much time or resources on the long shots. Be cordial with them, even if they let you know that they don't have the time of day for you. Someday, they may.

Some potential customers will have no interest in you or your products. It is quite possible they have no pain as it relates to you or your services. I get several calls a week from private equity firms and investment bankers looking to purchase our company; I respectfully and quickly let them know not to waste their time because we have absolutely no interest in selling our company now. Sometimes you need to know when to move on.

Mike Mikoola, CEO of Global Emergency Products, who is the Pierce fire dealer for Illinois and Indiana likes to say, "Selling is a numbers game." This sentiment is shared by Jeremy Taylor, who joined us when we purchased his company, Self-Testing Systems, in Albuquerque, New Mexico. Jeremy pays close attention to his "kill ratio" which is the number of orders received compared to the number of quotes issued for a particular product.

Channel Conflicts

Channel conflicts come in many forms and can undermine a company's business model while making potential customers less attracted to your products or services. Since most companies sell through several channels simultaneously, channels sometimes find themselves competing to reach the same set of customers. When this happens, channel conflict is virtually guaranteed. In turn, such conflict almost invariably can harm relationships if not managed properly. If you want to learn more, the below site is pretty good for quick business summaries:

Business Jargon: Channel Conflict Management

7) *Preparation/Pre-call Planning/Practice/Pitch*

Salespeople often have difficulty setting up sales appointments. Many of the problems they have are because of the process they go through — or to be more accurate, *fail* to go through.

Make appointments well in advance, and immediately send an email and Outlook meeting invitation, so there is no misunderstanding on where, when and how long the meeting will last. Remember, you need to be careful with time changes in different time zones. Always specify the meeting time in the time zone of the customer.

Ask the customer if they would like to see specific materials in advance (literature, drawings or quotes, for example) and be sure to send the material early enough to give them time to review. Always call or email to reconfirm the meeting 24 to 48 hours before the scheduled time. Once you have an appointment, the real work begins.

Prepare for each call by doing your homework on past sales

history and any recent correspondence in the company file folder or CRM program. Review the customer reports and/or minutes from previous meetings, and share those in advance of the meeting with the customer. Prepare and share an agenda for the meeting in advance, if appropriate, such as follow-up meetings on larger scale projects.

If you conduct customer surveys, be sure to review the customer's responses to your survey to find out what is important to them and how they rate you. Most surveys are never responded to, and many customers never have any action taken. If he gave you low marks or made recommendations, be sure to discuss these points together, but most importantly, let them know what action you have taken. Always bring survey results with you and discuss them in detail. Leave a paper copy if appropriate.

The more you know about your customer and his business, the more effective you can be. Everyone is busy these days, and you show respect for their time when you are well organized in advance. Further, take time to review his company's website, Facebook posts, internet search results, and run a credit report through a firm such as Dun & Bradstreet or Experian.

Following these critical steps lets customers know you care about them and their business, and you are focused on their needs. Because you are prepared to discuss those customer-specific issues, your relationship will grow stronger and you'll be better positioned to ease their pain. Don't be creepy about the amount of information you know from your research, but drop subtle comments on things you know, especially when the information is pertinent to your relationship.

Make sure to let each customer know you are going there just to see them. When you call to set up a meeting with a customer, never say, "I am going to be in the area. Can you meet with me?"Instead, a customer must feel he is the only focus of your visit. He might not say it, but if you tell him you happened to be in the area, he is probably thinking, "Don't waste my time if you are in the area, especially if you're visiting my competition."

While it is smart to book your sales calls within a proximity to one another (time and cost efficiency are good practices), customers don't care about that. Saving your own time and energy solves your pain, not theirs, and usually turns them off.

As a rule, never call on a customer unless you've had meetings set up well in advance. "Just dropping by" can be considered unprofessional and rude.

As part of your preparation, it is imperative that you practice your "pitch" numerous times and in front of different audiences. Video record yourself on your smart phone and watch it. You might be surprised how you look and sound. Conduct a dry run with your co-workers and, ideally, family members; they'll usually give you honest and critical feedback that others won't.

Use a script, so all your salespeople present a clear and consistent message, but use one that is not canned. Well-prepared salespeople find out what's important to their perspective and current customers ahead of time, instead of going in giving a rehearsed robotic-like sales pitch. No one likes to be given a sales pitch, and most see right through them.

The secret to the pitch is that it can't sound like a pitch! Giving a compelling pitch is not easy and it takes time to learn. Practice makes perfect.

Steve Jobs was the master at pitching new Apple products. His presentations always seemed natural and conversational. While it was clearly a pitch, it didn't come across that way. He would literally practice for days and weeks in front of his family and business associates. "How Steve Jobs Made Presentations Look Effortless," is a great *Forbes Magazine* article.

Forbes Magazine March 2015: How Steve Jobs made Presentations Look Effortless

As part of your meeting planning process, you should set specific goals for each sales call. What does a successful meeting look like in your eyes? What will be your ask?

8) *Pertinent/Pithy/Precise/Pointed*

Everyone's time is important, so it's critical that you make the best use of the prospect's time once you get in front of him. "Proper Planning Prevents Poor Performance" — (a bunch more Ps!). Make sure that the information you present is pertinent to him — how is it this good for him? How will it make him more money? How will it save time or money? How will it make his life easier? How will it make him look good to his boss?

Under certain circumstances, pithy presentations can be very effective. While "pithy" may have negative connotations, meaning "terse" or "curt," it also can mean "engaging and concise." When the time is right, everyone appreciates straight talk and it can energize people to action. Don't waste his time with useless information, such as features and benefits that simply doesn't matter to him.

Ask customers what their needs are prior to the meeting and again at the start of the meeting. You won't always get a firm answer, but if you do, you can focus in on what's most important to them and you'll save each other valuable time.

During your communications, always be straight-forward with the customer. Don't play games or B.S. people; most will see right through any attempt at subterfuge, and it's usually a major turnoff. Stay focused and on point, yet be open and ready to go where he leads the meeting.

9) *Primary Point of Contact*

Every business relationship starts with a handshake, an email or a phone call. Since you only get one chance to make a good first impression, and knowing that people size you up quickly, it's important that you get off on the right foot.

The Handshake

With that notion in mind, when the time comes for the in-person meeting, the first interaction is key. Much can be said about handshakes.

Every personal contact should start off strong — offer a firm handshake (not too strong) and make sure to look customers in the eyes and say their name. How you come off right out of the box lays the foundation for how your relationship is going to go in the future.

The term "upper-hand" is an interesting one; figuratively, it means the person who has the power or control over someone else. Literarily, it has the same meaning as well. When shaking hands with someone who is clearly in a state of power, it's important to always let them have their hand on top of yours. When in doubt, shake with your palm open and facing up. Showing respect during a greeting varies greatly around the world. It's interesting to see pictures of world leaders and their practice of this age-old ritual.

The Week: Upper-hand President the Most Powerful Handshake in the World

In May of 2017, French President Emmanuel Macron confirmed that the prolonged and awkward handshake with President Trump had a deeper meaning. "My handshake with [President Trump] was not innocent, not the alpha and the omega of a policy, but a moment of truth," Macron said. An interesting position from the president of a country that has received significant assistance from the U.S. over the years.

Video: President Trump's handshake with Macron

In Asia, for example, it is critical when meeting a person with higher authority that the reverence is shown through a lower bow.

Say their name

There is no sweeter sound then someone saying your name. It's important in both business and in social settings. It's not difficult to offer a firm handshake, look someone in the eyes, and say their name when you meet them, but watch how many don't do follow this custom. That said, don't overuse their name in the conversation; when you do, it sounds unnatural and insincere.

The average person in the U.S. will meet 10,000 people in his or her lifetime. If you're in sales, the number is at least double that. If you meet a great deal of people, it can be tough to remember names, which only gets more difficult the older you get. One way to remember names more easily is using word association. Here is a link to a recent *Forbes Magazine* article:

Forbes Magazine: How to remember names

After my mother died, my father remarried a wonderful woman, Fran Trankina. My dad only had two loves in his life, and both were tremendous women and soulmates to whom he was married for over 25 years each. (He would joke about how he was going to deal with these two relationships once he gets to heaven.) For most of their marriage, Fran traveled domestically and internationally with my dad on business trips. She had an incredible knack for remembering names, but also recalling specific details about the person's personal life. It would not be unusual for her to meet someone once and then reference the discussion, such as a child in school, several years later. She has high EI and was a great "wingman" for my dad.

It's always best to initiate the greeting. As you introduce yourself to people who you've met before, but knowing that they might not remember your name, it's helpful to say your name as you extend your hand for your greeting. Something like, "Hello John, I'm Paul Darley, we met briefly at the FDIC conference last year." Busy people really appreciate this approach and it will get you noticed. Ideally, you should have your full body facing them when you extend your greeting.

As my relationship with people starts to grow, I like to give people nicknames as a way to quickly greet them warmly. This is particularly helpful if their name doesn't naturally roll off your tongue. Many people don't have nicknames, and they often find them endearing. If you do give someone a nickname, you should wait until your relationship builds and ask them if they have one. If they don't, and you want to use one, be sure to get their approval first.

I nicknamed John Kosich about 15 years ago. "Johnny K" was the perfect name, and it's now used by almost everyone who knows him. He is a highly successful commercial real estate developer and has positively impacted the lives of many people through his energetic personality.

I've also given nicknames to my daughter's fiancés –both are great young men who treat our daughters with love and respect. While their nicknames are meant to tease them, Stephen Welch (Lil' Buck) and Chris Teets (Kitty Cat), are good sports about it.

Whenever I meet the child of a friend, I always make them stand up, look me in the eye, give me a firm handshake and say, "Hello, Mr. Darley." I let them know that if they address me like this the next time we meet and I can't call them by their name, I'll give them a $2 bill. It helps me remember their names, but more importantly, it teaches them the importance of properly engaging with the people they meet. It has become my mark. It's important to learn how to engage with other people at an early age so it becomes habit. Not all the children I meet will grow up to be salespeople or comfortable socially, but if this simple skill becomes a habit, then they've gained something far more valuable than the $2.

As eloquently stated by Mary Kay Ash, "Pretend that every single person you meet has a sign around his or her neck that says, 'Make me feel important.' Not only will you succeed in sales, you will succeed in life."

My wife, Heidi's, favorite quote is, "People won't always remember what you said, but they will remember how you made them feel." Make everyone you encounter feel important, because they are!

The Business Card Exchange

Most meetings begin with the exchange of business cards, a courtesy for most Americans. Some people exchange business cards with a sly handoff. Others throw them across conference tables like they're playing poker. Most receive the card, then stick it in their pocket without a glance.

People should show more reverence when exchanging business cards. During my world travels, I noticed that in many places, particularly Asian countries, casually receiving or giving a business card is considered rude. In doing business in parts of Asia, there is an established etiquette to the process. When a businessman hands you his card, he presents it to you with two hands; you're expected accept the card like a gift, receiving it with two hands. You then examine it and then look at the businessperson, maybe ask a question or make a comment about something on their card. Making notes on a business card is common in the U.S., but before you do, ask the person if it's OK. Never do this in Asia.

Your business card should, of course, have all critical contact information on the front. Don't put a fax number on your business card. Who uses a fax machine anymore? I do, however, put both my cell and home phone numbers on my business card. I don't get many calls at home, but it gets across the point that I'm accessible day or night. Also, many people use business card scanners on their cell phones, so make sure that your card is easily scanned for clarity.

The back of your business card is great real estate for pertinent information and oddly few people utilize it. On the back side of my card, we not only list our eight websites, but I also have a simple, strong message: "If you should know of anyone who is not 100% satisfied with our products or services, I will consider it a favor to be notified." I stole this idea from Scott Campbell, who is one of most professional fire apparatus sales reps in our industry. He has sold hundreds of fire apparatus to the New York City Fire Department (FDNY) over the years, and they are one tough customer. We are very proud to have the entire fireboat fleet of FDNY equipped with Darley pumps. Here is an article from a recent Darley newsletter where we featured FDNY.

Darley Times Newsletter: Fall/Winter 2016

Email Correspondence

Every business person needs to shut out the unceasing torrent of information, data and noise that flies in from every direction. Some managers suggest that executives only check their emails two to three times a day. While an admirable goal, I've found that I check it at least hourly when not in meetings or on the road. It can become a real rat race or "email jail" if you don't keep up, and most customers expect replies immediately, especially from our company.

A recent Darley advertisement featuring Paul Darley's home and cell phone numbers. "If you know of anyone who is not 100% satisfied with Darley products or services, I would consider it favor if you let me know."

Everyone in your company should use the same format and font. Your signature should contain all critical information, but at the same time, don't take up "too much" space. Your email signature should be the same size as a business card.

If you have an important conference coming up, it's fine to add a logo for the show with your booth number, inviting people to join you. However, you should not add this information more than 60 days before the show and you should remove it immediately when the show is over.

It's a good practice to put your email signature on all external communications at the beginning of the email discussion, but don't continue to add it to each subsequent email or on internal emails. When people do, it's frustrating to go through all that when reviewing the contents of previous emails. Don't ever include your signature on internal emails.

Many tend to hit "respond all" and do other annoying email responses that cost companies money in lost productivity. If you're on the "CC" line of the email, it is for informational purposes only, and you are not expected to reply. At our company, when sharing information, we'll write NRR, which stands for No Response Requested. This article is one everyone should read:

Business Insider: Email Etiquette Every Professional Needs to Know. Jan. 2016

When out of the office for more than half a day, it's always best to turn on your out-of-office attendant on and include your cell phone for emergencies.

The Toast

At some point in your relationship, you'll may have an opportunity to make a toast. If it's a toast at a first meeting or at a significant event, it's even more important. No matter where in the world you are toasting, it's essential that you look the person you're toasting in the eye. It's overlooked for some reason, and many find it to be disrespectful. Proposing a toast can be a great code-shifting moment, but be sure to practice your toast in advance. This article below gives some great tips.

Science of People: How to give an Awesome Toast

Further, if you go to Asia be sure to read up on how to toast properly there. If someone toasts you, you are expected to toast him back. If the person is in a position of higher authority, make sure that your glass is lower than his when a toast is made. While in Asia, never drink any alcohol without toasting someone at the table.

10) *Presentation*

Okay, it's Show Time! As important as first impressions are, even a good start can easily turn negative. As a rule, work to listen more than you talk. The goal of a first meeting is to find common ground, a mutual link where you and the perspective client can connect with one another and lay the foundation for a long-term relationship.

You should arrive at the destination at least 30 minutes in advance, parking out of view. Review your presentation and all company notes so it's fresh in your mind. Then mentally prepare, relax, and get in the zone. Perhaps you find that comes by listening to your favorite songs or just clearing your mind. Today, the music I listen to is a bit more mellow and quieter than it was 25 years ago.

Ideally, you should always walk in the door five minutes before the scheduled meeting. Let the receptionist know that you are early for the meeting and are happy to wait. It's best to stay standing, but if you sit, be sure get up and approach your customer when he arrives; don't make him walk to you. Greet him with a warm but professional approach — looking him in the eyes, giving a firm handshake, and saying his name.

Most meetings are 30 or 60 minutes and the length is generally established in the Outlook calendar invitation. If the closing time for the meeting has not been confirmed, it's always good to check how much time you have while getting settled in.

Notice if they offer you something to drink. If they don't offer you something, it's a pretty good indication of both the length of meeting and how interested they are in you and your products or services. When hosting others at your office, always offer them something to drink, regardless of your relationship — it's simply being polite.

When you arrive in the meeting room, some small talk is important before making a presentation. Ask questions and find out what is on his mind. Never present without this critical step. Give the person your undivided attention. Listen! Do not interrupt them. As the casual introductory conversation winds down, reach for your laptop or paper materials.

Adjust your tone, breathing and vernacular to match that of the client. If the customer is informal and relaxed, then approach it casually. If you're calling on a larger prospect, the tone is generally more formal. Be guided by the chameleon effect and use code-shifts from prior experiences together to quickly find common ground, if your relationship is established already.

Before you begin with your formal presentation, be sure to take some to clarify the goals and main objectives of the meeting and ask the customer if he has anything specific he would like you to cover. If an agenda has been presented in advance, you should look at the list briefly together to be sure you're on the same page. If there are smelly moose (sensitive issues that no one is discussing due to conflict avoidance) or other critical issues that you are working on together, you should acknowledge and address those head-on at the start of the meeting.

Presentation Style

You need to adopt a presenting form that fits your customer's style and the nature of the meeting. Some like PowerPoint presentations. Others just want to hear what you have to say without a formal presentation. Knowing what kind of presentation clients are comfortable with is important.

For example, if your customer is quiet, ask questions. Some questions can be open-ended, but not all. Ask about his product, his family, or how your company is doing for him. While some salesmen will say it is hokey, when you walk into somebody's office and see a golf trophy or a picture of customer's family, ask about it. On the contrary, asking others about their lives outside of work is a natural part of emotional intelligence and easy pickings for conversation and code-shifting opportunities. If it's up on their wall as a "seeable," it's a good indication it's something he is proud of or passionate about. It's a straightforward way to find common ground to connect, but it must be natural.

The Script

At Darley, we have two basic scripts that we customize based on the sales meeting. One is a simple call report and the other is a formal PowerPoint presentation.

It's important that presentations are interactive — that you are not merely talking to slides, but getting feedback along the way. Get a feel for how your customers want to interact. Some prefer to control most of the meeting and will do most of the talking — then you just listen. Other customers will barely say a word. Either way, you need to find a way to connect with them.

No one presentation is the same for each customer or prospective client, and different approaches should be taken during each phase of the sales cycle. The customization comes from including past purchase history (on the first four or five slides), adding their logo on materials (quickly lifted off their website), highlighting new products that may be of interest to the client, and other customization based on the information that you learned about during your preparation period.

Also offer to give the customer a copy of the presentation and any other documents on paper or on a memory stick. (When working with federal government customers, know that memory sticks are prohibited.)

Listening should be the easy part, but so many salespeople are not good at it. Remember to give the customer time to talk. Listen to them and respond to their needs. Ask them the questions that others are not asking — probing, high EI, impactful and code-shifting questions.

Their responses might surprise you. It's OK to take hand-written notes in your notebook during this part of the meeting, but make sure that it's not a distraction. If action items come up, put a circle next to the note to ensure that you can quickly identify them at the close of the meeting. Customers are impressed that you've been listening if you can quickly identify the next steps from the meeting.

I have witnessed too many sales reps constantly checking their smart phones during meetings. That's bad business and horribly impolite, especially if you're the one who called the meeting. Some salespeople like to keep meeting notes on their cell phone — don't do it because it appears as if you're checking your emails or on the internet, and it is a distraction. It shows disrespect to everyone at the meeting. You've got to stay engaged and in the moment. Turn off your cell phone before you go into the meeting!

Use your notebook to take notes during the meeting, but don't bury your head in your notes — jot down notes somewhat cryptically, so you are looking at your customer most of the time. If you're in a position where you can't write a note, ask the person if it's OK if you make a note on your phone. Ideally, you should keep a small notebook in your pocket for these types of situations.

As you summarize the action items from the meeting, be sure to ask, "Did I understand you correctly … ." You can end this with a variety of clarifying questions, including "The most important thing to you is … ."

Remember: action items are important, but it's what you do with that information that becomes key. Most feedback given to you is actionable.

The Ask

When the meeting starts to come to an end, make sure you ask for something. You should ask for an order, but if it seems way too premature in the sales cycle, then ask for something else — like another meeting in two weeks, an introduction to the engineers, or a reference of anyone they might know who needs your products.

While it might not always seem appropriate, a good time to ask for something from your customers is when you summarize the action items from your notes. If in doubt, ask for the order. You probably won't receive one right there on the spot, but someday you will.

When vendors come to see us, we always like to have an order prepared for their products or a check for them for invoices that aren't even due yet. Few vendors ask for the order, but when they do, you can see their hearts soar if you give them one. Everyone likes to get an order on a sales call. They remember it, and it will be the first thing they mention when they get back to the office.

Our company has been the predominant pump player in the wildfire markets for years. Today, the U.S. Forest Service, Bureau of Land Management, California Department of Forestry, and many other federal and state wildland customers standardize based on Darley pumps because of our reliable performance and compact design. When my brother, Jim Darley, first joined our pump sales team about 20 years ago, one of his first sales calls was to a Darley Demander, the Colorado Forest Service. We had talked about "asking for the order" before he left. When he arrived back from his trip I was anxious to hear if he got an order. He responded, "No, but I got a return." We still laugh about it today, and since then he writes more orders at Darley in our pump division than anyone on our team. Jimmy has high EI, and customers love him.

Chapter 7

Separate Yourself From the Pack; Be Professional, and Enjoy the Ride

"A sale is not something you pursue; it's what happens when you are immersed in serving your customer."

Author unknown

11. Phollow-Up (Follow-Up)

12. Point of Difference (Be different or die)

13. Presence/Personality/Persona (Likeability)

14. Proclivity/Predispositions

15. Professionalism/Polished/Politeness/Proper Manners

16. Promptness/Punctual

17. Personalize/Personal Service/Praise/Propriety/Promises and Pledges

18. Pleasure/Passion/Purpose

19. Positivity (Happiness)

20. Pragmatism/Practicality

The difference between a typical Major League Baseball player who has a .250 batting average and a Hall of Fame player who bats .300 is that the All-Star gets just one more hit in every 20 at bats. Surprisingly, few sales reps take the few extra steps to separate themselves from the pack. As in baseball, the extra steps are easy if you're willing to commit to excellence and put in the hard work and commitment.

So, you've made it in the door and have begun to start new relationships, or you're beginning to grow the ones you already have. This chapter is about those things that absolutely anyone can use to improve his "salesmanship" to become an all-star sales representative. Nearly anyone can apply these best practices to be more productive and happier regardless of your profession, from being a mother to running a company. Some of these ideas are tactical, but most are simply common sense and good manners.

In all cases, you need to prove to others that you are reliable and trustworthy. Earn their respect and eventually you'll earn their support and business.

11) *Phollow Up (Follow Up)*

OK, I realize that this isn't a true "P," but no relationship-selling book could ever be written without stressing the importance of following up. While I'm always amazed by the number of salespeople who don't ask for an order during their sales call, I am even more astonished by the people who don't follow-up properly — if at all — after a meeting or a trade show.

It doesn't matter what business you are in; following up is essential and a common courtesy that produces results.

Asking for the order does not necessarily mean you will get an order, but as anything in life, if you don't ask, you don't receive. If you're selling a sophisticated product, only 2 percent of the sales are made on the first contact, and 80 percent are made on the fifth to 12th contact. Statistically, per the below study, 48 percent of salespeople never follow-up with a prospect, 25 percent send a follow-up and stop, and 12 percent make three contacts and stop.

Trade shows are worse, where 72 percent of all leads are never followed up. There is no excuse for failure to execute. This below article gets the point across big time.

Succeed at Selling: Follow up effectively or fail big time

Ideally that evening, but certainly within the 48 hours following the meeting, send an email to your customer thanking them for the meeting and highlighting the discussions, specific action items, and specific dates for anyone at the meeting. If the action item is theirs to do, be sure it's politely requested.

Once back at the office, make sure to follow up with any outstanding information or materials you promised. It's part of the relationship-building process. It can take years to build a relationship and only a single incident to destroy it. When you promise to get back to a customer with something, make sure you do it … and promptly.

You should copy or blind copy yourself on your follow-up, so you can easily file the latest correspondence for future follow-ups. Be sure to set follow-up dates in your Outlook calendar or CRM system.

If you send them detailed drawings, price quotes, or other attachments, suggest that they start a file folder on your company in Outlook or MS Office. If the material is on your website, use clean-looking hyperlinks via an HTML setting. When it's in an email form, you may find that some will respond and act merely to keep the ball rolling on getting the email out of their inbox.

The Power of Hand Written Notes

It's amazing how a simple thing like a hand written thank you note can separate you from all the other people who walk through his door. Few do it these days … and they're missing a valuable opportunity. Try it.

You might find that when you put pen to paper, you may get more reflective in your thoughts, more so than if you're talking on the phone or writing an email. Most important, you'll stand out as being different.

When you see someone you know mentioned in an industry magazine for something positive, write him a handwritten note of congratulations along with a copy of the article. If you see it on the internet, it's fine to forward it to him electronically, but handwritten notes go a great deal further.

Over the years, my father would send me personal hand-written notes acknowledging an accomplishment of mine, perhaps from an industry publication. He encouraged me to start a scrapbook, which I did. Today that scrapbook is filled mostly with materials that I received from him. My most prized possessions in there are his hand-written notes of encouragement.

My favorite is a copy of my paycheck from 1981 where I was making $3.35/hour. The note attached to it was written in 1998 by my father shortly after I was named president. It says, "You've come a long way from humble beginnings. You've earned where you are today."

One person who follows this practice is Jim Johnson, president of Pierce Manufacturing, our largest domestic commercial customer. Jim, an attorney by education, is an impressive 6'3", yet he is incredibly humble and has very high EI. Jim is probably the busiest guy in our industry; still he takes the time to send hand-written notes to others on everything from a job well done to thanking them for something. Jim is polished, which is reflected in the professional and personal touches he brings to everything he does from the corner office.

12) *Point of Difference (Be Different or Die)*

I was raised with a Jesuit education and taught to question everything. As a result, I've always been a bit of a contrarian. I like to zig when everyone else is zagging. I always ask what will happen if we go against the norm or act differently from whatever everyone else is doing. The most successful wealth managers typically follow this strategy. They avoid the herd mentality that exists in so many things in life. Warren Buffett didn't make his billions by trading like everyone else. Jobs, Wozniak, and Gates all thought differently about computers; that they could be put in the hands of consumers.

In one sense, being different is testing the norms. Before you can challenge those rules, you must know them. The average salesperson follows expectations, and certain well-known standards. Differentiate yourself by going above and beyond what is expected. You'll impress the prospect, and doing so could open new opportunities that would not be explored otherwise.

It's a simple fact that most customers view your products or services as a commodity and believe your products are basically the same as your competitors. Therefore, you must find a way to be different and give them a compelling reason to choose you over your competitors.

Many companies sell similar products. For example, you can get many of the same items at Sears, JCPenney, or Kmart — mostly the same brands and models, with variations in prices and sometimes model numbers to confuse the discriminating buyer. These companies have failed, in large part, due to a lack of differentiation.

Radio Shack was once an electronics powerhouse. Then along came CompUSA, Best Buy and other electronics stores that offered something more, something better. Best Buy quickly became the leader, but by virtue of its real estate platform, will have a hard time competing against the likes of Amazon.com. Amazon is changing the world … if you're in bricks and mortar retail, you better have a sustaining point of difference.

Similarly, in China, Alibaba has put thousands of smaller and mid-sized retailers out of business. Before they closed their doors, many referred to these stores as "Alibaba showrooms," since customers would go to see the products firsthand and then go online and purchase them from Alibaba at a lower price. Like the companies they represent, salespeople must differentiate themselves from other sales reps if they hope to succeed. They need to break away from the pack and not get tied up with industry or company groupthink, which rarely leads to differentiation.

An Exercise to Find your Point of Difference

Nobel Prize winner and economist John Nash discovered that for a "player" to win in any competitive situation, he would need to act according to the actions of the others in the game. For example, if your competitors continue to seek new clients through a cold calling strategy, your smarter move would be to try something different.

Differentiation takes original, creative thinking, and it must come naturally to you and your company to be sustainable. Harder yet, you need to be able to pivot your company and yourself to take advantage of changing market conditions.

When you're thinking strategically and working *on* your business, rather than *in* your business, ask yourself, "Why are customers *truly* buying from us?"

Take a minute to write down your answer to this very important question: *Why do customers really buy from you?*

Ready?

You probably listed one or more of the following:

1. We deliver good value

2. We have high quality products

3. We're the best in town; we're experts in our field

4. Our customers keep coming back due to the personalized service we deliver

5. We're price competitive

6. They like me

Here's a little inside secret: The six responses listed above are most likely being offered by *all* your competitors. It's the ante to get into the game. If you are in business and making money, you've got to be delivering on these just to get your foot in the door and find a seat at the table.

I see the answer quite a bit differently. Simply put, you must do something better than your competitors and it needs to be important to your customer. It needs to satisfy a pain point or a business need. The salesperson who can address that pain in the most concise and efficient manner will usually earn the business.

One of the ways you can beat your competition is by coming up with a different approach to market strategy, particularly when it can't be easily replicated by them. Look at what Ikea did by creating a new space in the retail furniture market. It changed the furniture buying experience by offering low price products assembled by customers in their home, at a fraction of the price of other furniture stores. At the same time, it created a paradigm shift to what is now known as the "Ikea Effect," where customers place a disproportionally high value on products that they partially create.

13) *Presence/Personality/Persona (Likability)*

Have you ever met a person who has a natural presence? It happens occasionally, but most of us, will never possess this ability to naturally capture the audience. I met former President George W. Bush on several occasions, and he had it. First Lady Laura Bush had an especially natural presence.

In our industry, a few people have this strong natural presence. Wilson Jones, Jim Johnson, Dan Peters, Jim Hebe, Eric Schlett and John Witt have it. Each are prolific industry leaders, but their common denominator is that each man has high emotional intelligence. They are great, engaging salesmen, and they make whomever they are

116

with feel special. Despite the leadership positions they hold, they are down-to-earth, likeable, and people naturally gravitate toward them.

Over the past 30 years, John Witt has sold more fire trucks than anyone else in North America. With the build of a NFL lineman, he is an imposing man, yet he always tells it like it is and has an uncanny ability to build relationships. Like the others, John has grit, having made his mark at a young age through a strong work ethic and passion.

As a salesperson, you can improve your presence, make a stronger impression and sell more. That said, presence for our purposes means both having a presence about you and being present when you are with others. These two goals are aligned, and most people achieve them through working on their EI or mindfulness.

When you get the meeting, stay 100 percent focused on the customer with your senses. Listen to what he is saying and not saying. Study his body language. Don't think about what you're going to say next. A typical sales rep only spends about 15-20 percent of his time in front of the customer. Be sure to be present during these times, and you'll begin to see your presence grow.

People buy from people whom they naturally like and want to be around. Having presence has a lot to do with being likeable. Likeability comes from being engaged, consistent, listening and showing more interest in hearing what the other is saying than trying to impress him by talking. Dr. Travis Bradberry conducted a study at UCLA on likeability. This link is a great quick read:

Talent Smart: Travis Bradberry 13 Habits of Exceptionally Likeable People

While it's always a good idea to know what to do to be likable, it's also good to have an idea of those things that make someone unlikeable.

Talent Smart: Travis Bradberry Unmistakable Habits of Unlikeable People

I go fishing in Canada each year with the Leonard family, a close group of lifelong friends who are extremely likable. The seven Leonard brothers, each either a dentist or lawyer, are a great family with an incredible sense of humor. The alpha male, Gene Leonard, has been my best friend since first grade (Yes, he's No. 1). The Leonard clan likes to call me "Tommy Boy" after the 2000 movie where Chris Farley plays a fledgling sales rep trying to save his family business.

In the movie, Tommy Boy uses his personality and natural charm to sway a hard-nosed waitress by being himself. He gains confidence and learns that he must be himself if he's going to succeed in sales. David Spade tells Chris Farley (Tommy Boy), "Selling is about being relaxed, having confidence, having street smarts, and the ability to read people; these people are buying you." It's a great video clip.

YouTube: Tommy Boy - Why I suck at sales

I knew Chris Farley and attended Marquette a year ahead of him. We weren't close, but we had many mutual friends. He had a presence even back then. A tragic story with many touching life lessons. Chris had a big heart and I'm proud to say I knew him, but don't let your presence get the most of you.

One last thought on being present: When I was 15 years old, I couldn't wait to be 18. When I was 21 years old, I wanted to be 30, and so on. Now that I'm in my early 50s, I've come to realize that, in some respects, I was always looking forward to the future and I did not take time to enjoy each phase of my life as much as I should have. Enjoy each phase of your life — each part of the journey. There is no turning back the clock. As Bill Keane wrote, "Yesterday is history, tomorrow is a mystery, today is a gift of God, which is why we call it the present."

Eric Schlett is a good example. He is Executive Vice President of PennWell Fire Group, which owns most of the publications and websites in our industry. PennWell also runs our largest and best trade show, The Fire Department Instructors Conference. Eric is a player who has spent most of his life working hard, often at the expense of family relationships. He has three older sons, was recently remarried, and now has a three-year-old daughter. Because of missing so much of his sons' early years, Eric is totally immersed in his daughter's life and, in some respects, has been given another shot that he's not missing this time around. Now he is more present than ever before when he is with both family and customers.

14) *Proclivity/Predispositions*

A proclivity is a natural inclination or predisposition toward a skill. Some simply aren't cut out for a career in sales and never will be. Some salespeople are "natural born salesmen." They have a natural talent, ability or predisposition for sales. They have high EI, especially in the Social Awareness and Relationship-Management areas.

You can see the EI in their small actions. It comes innately to them, and this proclivity helps them to succeed. They can work a room. The best salespeople are generally extroverts who get energized by spending time with others and add that same energy to the room.

They can relate to a wide variety of topics that allow them to connect with diverse groups of people.

Proclivities applies to all professions. Some are predisposed to be priests, accountants or engineers. The same applies to companies. Typically, individuals and companies that concentrate on capitalizing on their strengths and stick to their knitting generally outperform those who stray from what they are inherently good at.

Selling is about being different and doing those things that you have a natural proclivity for when your competitors don't. You'll find good economic value creation in this space.

15) *Professionalism/Polished/Politeness/Proper Manners*

Like it or not, people will judge you quickly based on your appearance, the way you speak, carry yourself and how you dress. Dressing professionally and improving your professional and polished image is the easy part. The more difficult part is building a professional image through your actions, but it's simple: If you keep your word, stay within the lines, work hard and do what you say you are going to do, you will build your personal brand and earn the respect of others.

Many small things contribute to the branding effort — everything from the clothing you wear at trade shows to the thickness of the paper used on your business cards to the cleanliness of your buildings. It's said you can tell how well a company is run by checking out the restrooms. I can tell you this point certainly applies to restaurants, and I've seen it in companies, too. I insist that our bathrooms at Darley be cleaned daily and several times a day when we have large groups in for training.

Seemingly little things contribute to the perception the industry forms of your company and you. The trivial things add up. They create a composite picture that becomes your company's and your own personal brand.

At Darley we hire heroes, and over the past 10 years we have been hiring many veterans and firefighters. Most of them are very polished and help us to create a strong brand in our defense markets. George McCullough, our Defense Division manager, is a perfect example of someone who is professional and polished. As a West Point graduate, professionalism was instilled in him at an early age. Most of our veterans are great corporate citizens who ultimately end up doing a phenomenal job as sales reps, but they must learn how to sell.

Of course, little things can add up to a negative brand image as well. Not long ago, I took a long-time customer, Ron Heiman, out to dinner. Ron and I have been friends and business associates for more than 30 years and we are always direct with each other. Ron told me one of my salesman called on him wearing wrinkled pants. It might not sound like a big deal, but it was to him, and to me as well. In this case, I gave the employee a clothing allowance and told him it should never happen again.

The same applies to other bad habits. Most people will find the smell of cigarette smoke, bad breath, body odor, chewing tobacco, offensive. Personally, I view every salesman as a reflection of myself. They must be polished and there is really no place for potential offensiveness in the world of professional sales.

If you're in sales, you eat out with large groups. Often, the most fun and memorable dinners are not the fancy white tablecloth places, but rather in the more laidback places. Regardless of where the meal is, you should have proper manners. Whenever making dinner reservations for a party of five more, request a round table; it makes it easier to converse with everyone at the table.

Good habits and manners start at an early age, so it's important that you instill them in your children.

You can learn a great deal from basic etiquette. Emily Post wrote the book on etiquette in the early 1900s, but many of her principals on good manners still apply today at home, in social settings and in business.

Three quick dining tips: First, when out to dinner, remember to wait until everyone has their meal before digging in, unless "there are more than eight, then you don't need to wait." Second, your water is on the right side and bread plate is on the left. If you can't remember which, hold your hands out in front of you and touch your index fingers to your thumb. Your right hand will form a "d" for drink and your left hand will form a "b" for bread. Some will also remember it by the acronym BMW (Bread, Meal, Water). Last, if someone asks for you to pass the salt, you should always pass the salt and pepper together, since they are a pair, and never use them on the way. Here is a good link on basic business etiquette:

Emily Post Institute: 10 Tips on Business Etiquette

In external emails and other communications, it's simply common courtesy to be polite and include words like "please." For our internal company purposes, it is acceptable to adopt a policy where emails that say, "thank you" or "understood" or "you're welcome" are implied in all communications.

It helps to streamline things and reduce the amount of email traffic.

Grammar

People judge others quickly by the way they speak and write. When you have important emails, compose them in a Word file that will at least catch the basic grammar mistakes better than Outlook, and then sit on them for at least a few hours or longer. Ask others to review. You'll be surprised how many errors you'll find when you proofread your own correspondence a second time after letting it rest.

Here's a quick tip on when to use "I" versus "me," which I seem to see the most. It's not, "Me and John are going on a sales call." Two errors with this sentence. The first hint to remember this rule is to always put the other person first because it's polite and proper English. The second rule is to take the other person out of the sentence, so it's "I am going on a sales call." Thus, putting "John" back in, it becomes "John and I are going on a sales call," which is correct. Also, most will say, "Do you want to go with on a sales call with John and I?" because it sounds better, but it's improper English. Remember to take the other person out, so in this case it becomes, "Do you want to go on a sales call with me?" Putting John back in, the sentence becomes "Do you want to go on a sales call with John and me?"

Another that I see too often is the misuse of "to" and "too." "Too" should be used when there are "too many" or "I want to discuss this, too." If you can substitute the word "also," then use "too." Another group that gets mixed up is "there," "their," and "they're."

- There is a memo.

- Their memo is written.

- They're waiting on a memo.

Lastly, use the word "farther" when referring to distance and "further" when expanding on a point. Here are some good basic grammar tips. If you weren't paying attention in high school English classes (like me), it's never too late to learn and to improve your grammar:

"Proper Grammar Tips."

Avoid the Word "Honestly" and Phrase "To Be Honest with You"

When speaking with others, particularly in a sales setting, avoid using the expression, "to be honest with you." Many believe that this phase implies that you are not always honest. Obviously, this is not the case with most people, but enough seasoned business people know this rule that it's worth avoiding. Try using, "To be frank, blunt, or candid" instead.

I frequently used this phrase until about 20 years ago, when a seasoned salesperson brought it my attention. I was taken aback at the time, but it stuck with me and I now correct our salespeople if they use it. Here is an article that spells it out:

<u>Lifehacker: Increase your credibility by Avoiding the Use of the Phrase "To Be Honest"</u>

Bill Lacek (No. 9) is CEO of Lewis Plastics. We've had this conversation about "to be honest" numerous times. This past summer, the police showed up at his house after his neighbor's car had been stolen while parked in front of the house. Bill told them, "To be honest, I have no idea what happened, and I didn't hear anything." While he was clearly not a suspect in the case, he felt nervous and somehow guilty after using this phrase.

It was interesting that Donald Trump used the phase numerous times when on the hot seat during the presidential debates. *Candidly*, I can't even recall what he said next. I would think he would know better, but it was a minor faux pas of his considering all the other things he did and said. Despite his crass approach in so many areas, he still won, and I truly hope that he can "Make America Great Again" with a fresh business approach to government. I've become a supporter since the election, as I've tried to do for every president.

Earn it and Support Those Around you as you Work up the food chain

In large companies, salespeople progress through the ranks the same way — salesperson to regional sales to divisional sales to director of sales to vice president of sales to Chief Sales Officer or Chief Revenue Officer. The titles might differ by company, but the natural progression remains the same. To quote sales guru Harvey Mackay, "To me, job titles don't matter. Everyone is in sales. It's the only way we stay in business." I could not agree more.

In smaller companies, promotions are a reward for a job well done, and in other cases, they seem to come with time. With the new title must come authority, empowerment and accountability. It's important that the title comes with the ability to make decisions and to take care of issues when they arise. If they can't or don't, it can hurt your brand. The person must earn his title. Every day. "What have you done lately?" is frequently heard in sales offices.

As you work your way up the organization, you are held to a higher standard with each new position, and it's important to not step on others on your way up. Don't bully those around you. If you do, you'll find that you will have no support if — and when — you get to the top. You won't be able to command their respect or cooperation if you do make it.

122

While I can't say that I like everything about the leadership approach of former Chicago Bear's coach, Mike Ditka, I can't deny that he is authentic and tells it like it is. He was wise to talk about some of the bad behavior of NFL players in 2015, "When you gain status in life, there comes a thing called responsibility and obligation." The same certainly applies to when you become a leader in any organization.

Expense Reporting

I always keep a close eye on expense reporting of our people, especially early in their career with us because it can tell me a great deal about a salesperson both in terms of how quickly they file their expense report and how honest they are in reporting. It is an easy and quantifiable way to quickly judge someone's integrity, accountability and organizational skills.

Our company policy requires expense reports to be filed electronically within two weeks of incurring an expense. Typically, the offenders who don't file in a timely manner are "too busy taking care of customers." If a sales rep can't do something as simple as filing a timely expense report, it's a pretty good indication that he is disorganized and won't stay on our team long. And unless drastic changes are made, they generally are not cut out for management in the future.

Our basic tenant is to spend company money as if it were your own. In 1994, we were the first pump company to introduce a new firefighting technology called Compressed Air Foam Systems, or CAFS. We built a demo truck and sent our employee, Troy Carothers, across the U.S. conducting demonstrations. Troy is one heck of a salesman who customers like and trust. Troy was always frugal and spent our money as if it were his own. I remember approving one of Troy's expense reports that showed "leftover pizza" in the place for dinner. I've never looked closely at an expense report of his since.

While many relationships are built after hours, we won't approve late-night expenses from inappropriate venues. I'm no prude, but I do feel a bit like Tom Cruise in this video, a spoof from his hit movie, "A Few Good Men." This is funny!

You Tube: A few good salesmen

16) Promptness/Punctual

I've always been a stickler for prompt and punctual behavior. I'm not sure where it comes from, but like many CEOs, it's a real hot button for me. Part of it may stem from my 20 years of YPO experience. YPO forum protocol says if you're late for a meeting, even by one minute, you must pay a $100 fine. It's about respecting others' time and showing deference to the importance of your commitment.

I've imparted that same philosophy at our company, but without the financial penalty. At Darley, all meetings start on time regardless of who's in the room. The habitually late soon get the picture. If not, it's a pretty good gauge of that person's commitment to the organization or, at a minimum, his lack of organizational skills, which must be corrected if he is to stay with us.

It applies even more so to sales calls. If you're going to be late, call and let the customer know in advance. You better have a good reason, and never give more than one reason for being late. Don't lie, or they'll know you are not being truthful. Most look down and to their left when they are lying. Here are some other tips on how to tell.

Resourceful Manager: 10 Absolute Give-aways that Someone is Lying to you, 2014

As part of this practice, with customers and within the company, we never use the phrase "as soon as possible" (ASAP). ASAP has been banned here because it means different things to different people. For some, it is, "whenever I get around to it." To the customer who is anxiously waiting for a response, it could mean one minute. It means he doesn't know when he'll get the information and it can easily strain a relationship unnecessarily. We always state specific dates and times when we will act. If you can't make a commitment, contact the customer in advance with a revised expected date.

When it comes to evaluating prospective suppliers — or recruiting employees — punctuality is high on my list. This trait is due in part because it is so cut and dried when so many other qualities are intangible and subjective. It also quickly tells me a great deal about a person, like expense reporting.

17) *Personalize/Personal Service/Praise/ Propriety/Promises & Pledges*

James Owens (No. 5) runs sales for a $100 billion investment management firm, LSV Asset Management, where he is a partner. He is one of the most successful sales reps I know because he gets it. James is professional, customer centric, and he under- promises and over-delivers. James is a chip off the old block; his father, Jim Owens, was the CEO of Caterpillar for more than 10 years. James takes after his father and he became a success on his own. His rule: pick up the phone and call a customer a day.

We adopted the same policy years ago. It doesn't sound like much, but too many salespeople are solely reactionary. They don't work on building relationships through outgoing unsolicited personal

124

contact and personalized service. They miss the critical opportunities, like a simple phone call to build relationships, which can create code-shifts or building blocks in your relationships.

Pick up the phone and talk with your customers. Ask how they are doing, how your company is doing for them, discuss their performance against forecast, ask if they have any opportunities where you can assist them. Your communication with customers cannot be all electronic; it's difficult to build long-term relationships through emails and social media because you lose that personal touch — the personal connection to the customer. You're not disrespecting their space or time if you call with a purpose and add value. Many sales reps are uncomfortable or afraid of this straightforward approach. If this describes you, learn to get over it or look at a new career.

I realize that how people interact with each other is changing, and I worry about it. I watch toddlers with their heads in an iPad, playing games, and I think about the potential negative impact that this early use of technology will have on their social skills later in life. No matter how technology advances, verbal communication will never go away when it comes to building true relationships.

Blending Old School Methods with New Technology

I'm not immune to changes in technology. I have three daughters. Like most teenagers, as they went through high school they had a natural tendency to disconnect with their parents as they engaged in activities and social relationships. To keep the connection, I began communicating with my kids through text messages. They all had phones in high school, but they rarely use them to make calls. They're texting, Instagramming and Facebooking. If I wanted to know what was going on in my daughters' lives, I had to learn to use their preferred method of communication.

Use the new tools that are out there to build and connect with your network, but don't forget the personal contact of a handshake and a phone call. Leverage electronic platforms, but don't rely solely on them. Things can be misconstrued in emails. Tones can be missed and nuances can be misunderstood in electronic communication, even with an emoji. Never underestimate the power of the personal verbal communication.

Facebook, LinkedIn, WhatsApp, Twitter and Instagram will only grow in importance. Some next-generation business people seem content to conduct most of their personal social communication through these avenues. They're quite adept at using LinkedIn on the business side. Some social media influencers on Instagram can make upwards of $5 million through product placement.

In the "old days," we used a Rolodex. Younger employees are much more diligent about populating their contacts in Outlook and other apps. Whatever tools are used, executives need to make sure employees build their networks in an organized fashion that is shared with their counterparts with the company. Team players don't hoard information.

Use the method that your customer prefers, but don't be afraid to deviate at times. Many of our international customers prefer to communicate via Skype and WhatsApp, which we use.

It's a pretty good bet that today's technologies will soon be replaced by a new generation of tech tools that Gen Z and future generations will embrace. Today's young executives and sales reps will soon have to adopt new ideas and technologies. Whether executives use old school tools or modern ones, they are just that — tools to enable communication. How those tools get used, while keeping verbal communications, is key to their success.

Propriety/ Pledges (Exceed Expectations)

Trustworthiness is at the root of every successful salesperson, which is earned by doing what you say you are going to do. And then doing more. Effective people know and live by this trait.

Over time, you are going to lose some customers. But if you lose them because you broke promises or commitments, it's simply unacceptable. Never make a promise you know you can't keep.

Propriety is the ability and willingness to meet the customer's *external* expectation of business customs and behavior. Everyone has minimum expectations and you need to act with propriety in all your customer dealings. If your customer's expectations are too high or you simply can't meet them, it's best to address that head on. Don't set yourself up for failure.

Ideal customers are those who set reasonable expectations and allow your team to meet and exceed those by under-promising and over-delivering. Everyone uses the phrase "exceed expectations," and it's become such a terrible cliché. Then again, there is a reason clichés have been around so long. "Exceeding customer expectations" is in the first line of our company's quality statement. We'll talk more about this vital point in Chapter 11 as it is key to customer retention.

Gift Giving

We are big on gift giving and put our logo on just about everything you can imagine — if you can put a logo on it, we have.

It goes back to my candy throwing days, but we enjoy giving our customers, suppliers, employees and other stakeholders fun, useful and memorable gifts.

Some people may view gift-giving as old school and in some ways it is. But done properly, it can go a long way toward branding and relationship building. More important than the gift is the personalized card that goes along. People appreciate personal attention and thoughtfulness. When done right, gifts can create a great code-shifting opportunity. Who doesn't like to get a gift at Christmas time?

Our company still sends out Christmas presents to our best commercial customers, and I write more than 500 personalized cards each holiday season to them. They are sent out primarily to OEM customers and dealers with whom we have close personal relationships. Sending gifts is a point of differentiation. Gifts should be practical, and they're most memorable when they are unique. If they can be used by the customer's family, that's even better. It's also important that the gifts be lightweight, so they are not too expensive to mail.

Our company, and most of our larger commercial and government customers, have gift policies that allow us to give/accept gifts from vendors up to $25, so we are very careful with gifts to them. We keep our promotional equipment supplier, Joe Hughes from K7 Promotions, very busy with everything from Darley boxer underwear and reading glasses to blankets. Who needs another ball cap, pen, coffee mug or calendar?

Whenever I receive a gift from a supplier, I'm always quick to send a hand-written thank you note or at least an email. It's worthy to note that our female customers acknowledge gifts at a significantly higher rate than our male customers. I suspect it is related to their EQ level.

At trade shows, we give away small, Darley-branded notepads that fit into a shirt pocket. They are useful and inexpensive gifts that people can use to write notes while on the show floor. In addition to being a friendly gesture, when someone writes a note, the chances it will be remembered go up, and, hopefully, the potential client will act after the show. We also give out Darley chewing gum; we have people who stop by our booth just looking for our gum! Maybe someday they'll become Darley Demanders.

Whenever we have a major customer or supplier who builds a new plant or moves, we buy a tree for him. We have it planted in a prominent place, ideally outside the CEO's office window, so he thinks of us as the tree and our relationship grows. It's another thing I learned from my father. I just received a note from a long-time customer, Kimball Johnson, founder of OEM customer Kimtek Research in Vermont. He wrote, "It has been about a year since Paul presented the 'Darley Tree' to us, and despite a very dry summer and fall it has flourished just like our relationship! As you can see the fall colors are already starting. We want to thank you all at Darley for your continued support." Kimball has purchased almost 2,000 pumps over the past 10 years, pays his bills on time and is a pleasure to deal with … talk about the lifetime value of a customer!

Gift-giving among businesses in the U.S. is not common any more, but in most Asian communities it's considered an important part of the selling process, particularly during the courting phase. It's not bribery; it's simply a token of appreciation for their time. If you are going to give gifts to Asian visitors, the gifts should always be in red wrapping paper as a sign of luck. On the other hand, blue wrapping paper signifies mourning or death … and it might be the end of your relationship.

18) *Pleasure/Passion/Purpose*

While in college, my father gently pressured me to become an attorney before coming to work at Darley. I wanted to follow his wishes because I knew it was important to him. I quickly discovered through undergraduate business law classes that I did not have the mind for it, nor did I enjoy it.

My mother died of cancer one month after I arrived at Marquette University for college, and I turned to Father Naus for guidance over the next few years. As we discussed my career path, he gave me a card that said, "You will rarely succeed at anything, unless you truly enjoy doing it." Thirty years later, I still have that card and think about the impact this small bit of advice has had on my life over the years. I pass this sentiment on to many people who are looking for career advice.

Today, I still migrate to those areas of the business that I truly enjoy and where I do well. I don't enjoy certain aspects of our business, such as legal, IT and HR issues. But I've surrounded myself with people who do and who are extremely good at them

It's one thing to enjoy what you are doing and quite another to be passionate about it. It's easy to see those who enjoy their vocation and those who hate their jobs. After retiring from the railroad, Heidi's uncle, Fred Bon, became a chauffeur to stay active. He came in contact with a lot of business people and can quickly size them up – there is usually no hiding it.

The importance of passion cannot be understated. If two companies are competing in the same market and are viewed as being similar, the one with passion or "fire" always wins! It can be an incredibly powerful differentiator. It can't be faked.

I pop out of bed like a piece of toast in the morning — I simply can't wait to get to work, even on weekends. It's my calling, my life's work, my legacy.

Everyone in the industry knows that my family and I share this passion, and we've even used it in the marketing campaigns that won us a CEBA advertising award. If you're not passionate about what you do, then your customers and coworkers will see it, and, most importantly, you will be unfulfilled. Find something else that you truly love to do, and you'll never work another day in your life.

If you're fortunate to find a job that aligns with your own core desires or passions, you're going to be successful at it and everyone involved is going to benefit. Passion is contagious. If you're excited about your products, company, industry and your customers, the more likely it is that prospects will feed off your passion.

Being in a business that serves warfighters and firefighters, it is very easy for Team Darley employees to feel an innate sense of purpose and passion. Nearly any business can find altruistic meaning; we're fortunate that ours comes so easily and naturally. In some companies, the purpose can simply be about creating good paying jobs for its employees.

If you buy into your company's purpose, it usually shows through very quickly and genuinely in small ways. It leads to enthusiasm and can be seen when sales reps talk of their company.

I'm always amazed by sales reps who talk about the company they work for in the third person. It's easily caught in meetings when they say things like "they" rather than "we" when referring to their own company! I can understand it in the first month of an employee being hired, but after that, it's usually a good indication that this person is not onboard with the purpose and team environment that need to exist. Personally, I find this type of behavior and apathy appalling, and I address it immediately with employees if I hear it. I also politely bring it to the attention of vendors or business associates if I hear them say it.

At Darley, all the employees refer to Darley as "our" company, partially because of this sense of purpose. We are one team. Being a part of Team Darley is a significant part of our own individual identity.

A strong sense of purpose is particularly important if you're looking to attract Millennials who place this high on their list.

I've seen many successful executives sell their businesses or have other large liquidity events. The newly free executive has an initial sense of euphoria. But soon, most are less happy and unfulfilled after their big payout than they were when they were out hunting down sales and growing their business. In a sense, they've lost their identity, their drive and their sense of purpose.

Bill Graham, a forum mate of mine, is perfect example. Bill had this experience when he sold his company, USA Blue Book, to Home Depot in 2008. He went out and bought a ton of toys, including cars, a ranch, and even a plane. None of these things brought him happiness. He found happiness when he got back in the game by buying and running a 100-year-old family wine store ... something for which he is very passionate.

My dear friend, John DeBlasio, is another example. After selling his defense company, Sallyport, in 2012, he went through a similar phase. He tempered it by getting involved in many charitable and political organizations. He immediately donated roughly 50 percent of his fortune. Most of it went to charity, but some went to his alma mater, West Point Military Academy, without any recognition. John is on many of my "lists," including being No. 1 on the list of guys who can marry Heidi if anything ever happens to me. That's a short list, so that says a great deal about John.

Another friend, Father John Balluff, the pastor at St. Mary's Church in West Chicago, always felt he had a predisposition to become a priest. It was his calling from an early age. He is building a new church for his parish. Believe me, he is one heck of a salesman when it comes to raising funds and selling the benefits of living a virtuous life. He has changed the lives of many and clearly has purpose.

People with purpose live happier, longer and more productive lives. The statistics relative to the number of years that people live after retirement are staggering. My sense is that they feel a lack of purpose in life.

19) *Positivity (Happiness)*

Most successful salespeople are positive. They see the glass as half full. Having a positive approach to life and their business is contagious, and by the very nature of being optimistic, good things happen to them and those around them.

Some might call it "karma" or the "Law of Attraction."

Dave Flando (No. 8), CEO of Corporate Suites Network, likes to say, "Change your attitude, and you'll change your luck." He has very high EI and is one of the most positive and fun-loving people I know.

130

He spreads his love of life everywhere. If you're having a difficult day, hanging with Dave will quickly bring your life scale up at least a few points.

Much can be said for karma: if you do good things, good things generally happen to you. Call it the Golden Rule, if you wish. Good begets good. Just like measuring your EQ, several websites exist where you can quickly and easily measure your positivity quotient on a scale of 1 to 10. Here is one such site:

Positive Intelligence: Measuring your Positivity Quotient

Similar studies are conducted each year with respect to which countries are the happiest. The top five are Scandinavian countries. Canada ranks 9th and the U.S. ranks 13th. The other superpowers — China, Russia and India — don't make the top 50 list.

Science Alert: World's Happiest Index: 2016

Even when encountering challenges in life, look at them from a positive point of view and learn from each experience. My forum mate, Cary Chessick, who co-founded multiple companies, including Positivityu.com, Rewards21.com, Butterflysaves.com and Restaurant.com, has increased success in each business with the use of positive practices.

Cary puts it this way, "There is a distinction between being 'happy' and the field of Positive Psychology. 'Happy' is defined as feeling or showing pleasure or contentment. 'Positive Psychology' is defined as the scientific study of human flourishing and an applied approach to optimal functioning. We all know that if we train our bodies we will get in better physical shape. If we train our brain we can increase the likelihood of saying, thinking and doing the right thing at the right time. You can train your brain with simple exercises, repetitive practice, and a desire to succeed. Walk up to someone at work and smile. If you smile, they will smile. You can change someone else's thoughts and feelings with a simple physical action like a smile. Give it a try and watch it work!"

Harvard lecturer Shawn Achor recently wrote the book, *Happiness Advantage: The Seven Principles That Fuel Success and Performance at Work.* He writes, "Most people want to be successful in life. And of course, everyone wants to be happy. When it comes to the pursuit of success and happiness, most assume the same formula: if you work hard, you will become successful, and once you become successful, then you'll be happy. The only problem is that a decade of cutting-edge research in the field of positive psychology has proven that this formula is backwards. Success does not beget happiness." Based on the largest study ever conducted on happiness and human potential,

Achor shares seven core principles of positive psychology that each one of us can use to improve our performance, grow our careers, and gain a competitive edge at work and be happier. Here is a quick video if you're interested in learning more:

You Tube: Happiness Advantage: The Seven Principles

Achor also writes about creating a daily habit by doing the following tasks for 21 days in a row: State three gratuities (while brushing your teeth, say three things that you are grateful about), journaling, physical exercise, meditation, and conducting random acts of kindness.

In business and spiritual books, the positive aspects of journaling daily are repeated often. Most suggest that you start off your day with whatever is on your mind, but with a focus on what you're grateful for, your dreams, or goals. One person who lives by this habit is Travis Ownby, who is one of the most successful salesmen in our industry. One thing I admire most about him is his faith-based principals. He journals daily and credits many of his personal, family and business successes and overall happiness to this seemingly inconsequential habit.

My brother, Jimmy, likes to tell the story of the Cherokee Indian chief talking with his grandson about the two wolves:

"A fight is going on inside me and inside of all of us. It's a terrible fight, and it is between two wolves. One is evil — he is anger, envy, sorrow, regret, greed, arrogance, self-pity, guilt, resentment, inferiority, lies, false pride, superiority and ego. The other is good — he is joy, peace, love, hope, serenity, humility, kindness, benevolence, empathy, generosity, truth, compassion and faith."

The grandson thought about it for a minute and then asked, "Which wolf will win?"

The old Cherokee simply replied, "The one you feed."

20) *Pragmatism/Practicality*

With salespeople, sometimes positivity needs to be tempered with being pragmatic and practical. Because so many successful sales reps are — by their very nature — positive, they can tend to be over-confident and too optimistic.

Being pragmatic means dealing with things in a realistic way that is based on practical matters and not only theory or feeling-based.

For example, when it comes to sales forecasting, positivity must be tempered with pragmatism. Many companies like Darley rely on sales forecasts to set annual financial budgets, conduct capacity planning, and determine capital expenditures. Our sales reps get buy-in from each significant customer on anticipated orders for the coming year. We use this information to ensure proper staffing and to drive our Enterprise Resource Planning (ERP) system. When sales reps are overly optimistic, it is critical that management temper these forecasts when setting production requirements.

We also use a Major Order Report (MOR) that shows sales in the pipeline and what our confidence level is on each significant potential order. In using this approach, we quickly and easily see the overall landscape of potential orders in the pipeline, and we know who is being too optimistic. It's a system that works, as our actual sales at the end of the year are generally within 1-2 percent of our forecast.

Too often a sales rep will say, "I've got an order!" when, in fact, he doesn't have a formal written purchase order yet. This practice can be dangerous, as many sales are lost during this time when the rep moves on. It's not an order until you have a physical order in your hand! Moreover, it's not a "sale" until the product or service is delivered, paid for and the customer is happy.

Chapter 8
Getting to Yes!

"I'm convinced that about half of what separates successful entrepreneurs from non-successful ones is pure perseverance."

Steve Jobs, co-founder and former CEO of Apple.

21. Proposition (Value Proposition)

22. Product/Palpable/Permeable/Payback Period

23. Probe

24. Problem Solver

25. Perceptible/Perspective

26. Proposal

27. Power of Persuasion/Prevail

28. Perseverance/Persistence

29. Proactive/Preemptive

30. Poise

21) *Proposition — Value Proposition*

For a salesperson, knowing your company's overall value proposition, as well as your product's features, benefits, and specifications, is the bare minimum. So much information is available on the internet that customers have a difficult time sifting through it to find the exact information they need, much less knowing what your company stands for and how they might benefit from it.

In all that clutter, your value proposition must be up front and center. You need to have a strong elevator pitch that takes less than two minutes. It must explain your company, what you stand for, your products, and how they might benefit a prospective client. You should also have a 10-second and 30-second pitch for the shorter "elevator rides." It must grab their attention and explain the promise that you will deliver.

Your value proposition won't be the same for every customer. You may have diverse types of customers in multiple channels. For example, what's important to your dealer may be totally different from your end-user. There is no sense in talking about things that simply don't matter.

It is critical to determine what product attributes are most important to your customer. You need find out who is buying your products and why! Then, tailor your message to focus on those specific reasons.

If you can get your customers to list the attributes they care most about and rank them, you can focus on what's most important—their true pain. However, getting them to make the effort is sometimes easier said than done. Compare your company's services and your product's performance, features, and benefits based on what is most important to your customer. Also, very importantly, remember: It's fine to make comparisons, but never slam your competition.

If you're unclear of your value proposition or unsure how to develop one, I would strongly encourage you to read this article on creating value propositions. You'll also learn more about creating a favorable point of difference and unique selling position.

HBR: Creating Value Propositions in Business Markets, 2006

22) *ProductPermeable/Payback Period/Palpability (Story Telling)*

Today's customers are much savvier than 15 or 20 years ago. They can Google information and have as much detail on your products as your best sales rep can provide. In a matter of minutes, they can research what blogs, rating services and other reviews have written about your products. (You should have someone monitor these sites regularly.)

Because of this, product training is essential for any salesman, while it is not as critical today as it once was. There is nothing wrong with not knowing the answer to a customer's question about your products. Never B.S. on the answers; go to engineering or the experts in your company, find out the answer, and get back to the customer quickly.

Whenever you discuss a product feature, you should explain the benefit of that feature. An easy way to remember how to clarify the advantages for each customer is to follow up each benefit with, "What that means to you is … ." The feature will most often resonate with the customer when he can see how it applies to his situation.

Often, customers need help with the justification to purchase your product or service, especially when you're not low bid. Be sure to give your customers rationale information such, as a payback period, so they can justify the purchase in their mind or to their supervisor. How will your solution save them money? How will it benefit them? What advantages will your product provide that can help them justify the purchase?

On sales calls and at trade shows, use props or cutaways of your products to show the features and benefits. 3-D printing and animation tools can produce some great "touchables" at a low price. Place the product in the customer's hand, so she can touch and feel and get a better understanding of the product.

Our defense sales representatives go to most meetings with a large duffle bag filled with the latest innovative tactical products. While every product might not necessarily be of interest to customers, we can focus in on what is important to them. Our military customers like to be aware of the latest products and due to travel restrictions imposed over the last five years, these meetings are one of the few opportunities for them to keep current.

Since these customers can't travel, we now hold our own trade shows on military bases, called "Darley Defense Days." We bring in our vendors and speakers, and even have had our friend, Clint Romesha, a Medal of Honor recipient, attend many of them. He is an amazing American, and his book, *Red Platoon*, is a page turner.

Link to review of Red Platoon by Clinton Romesha

Story Telling

Palpability can also be attained through a story. We were all raised hearing and reading stories that still subliminally impact us today. Stories can be incredibly powerful and allow the customer to get a better perspective on you, your company and your products. Stories will help them remember. It's important to understand that your customer and others have stories, too. Tell your story only after hearing their story.

Some of the best salespeople are exceptional storytellers. My father was a great storyteller, and his stories were always fun, engaging and had a purpose, a moral, or a lesson that resonated with his listeners.

Your story must be something that the prospect wants to hear and hasn't heard too many times in the past. Of course, I am proud of our company's history—but maybe a bit too much. Twenty years ago, I was addressing the dealers at the annual sales meeting for Central States Fire Apparatus, our largest OEM customer at the time. I began my presentation by telling our company history, which I had done in previous years. Their sales manager, Donley Frederickson, jokingly yelled from the back of the room, "No one wants to hear about company history. We've all heard it before!" He was right, and we still laugh about it today.

Central States Fire Apparatus was founded by Harold and Helen Boer in 1982, and most of it was later sold to Rosenbauer of Austria. Harold is stepping back a bit now, but his contributions to our industry and the hard-working people of South Dakota are virtually unmatched. The people who work there are trustworthy and hardworking people who make up the heartland of America. They were our first significant OEM pump customer, and they have

138

always been just a delight to work with—a lot of mutual respect here. Rosenbauer has pretty much left this company alone, but integrated high tech European innovation and processes that positively impacted the brand.

23) *Probe*

Asking high impact, probing questions can create great code-shifting opportunities. You should continually ask your customers questions: How is our company doing in meeting your needs? Is there anything we can do to improve? What issues are you trying to solve?

When questioning prospects, first ask about any objections they might have working with you. What concerns do they have relative to dealing with your company? As they share these with you, write them down and don't interrupt. Second, once they are finished, address the concerns one by one. Ask if you've fully addressed each specific concern before moving on to the next. At the end, be sure to ask if there are any other objections, roadblocks or concerns with purchasing your product. If not, ask for the order.

These are two critical sales steps, but every salesperson worth his salt who is calling on them is asking these same things.

When the time seems right, you need to prod them, delve deeper into their issues, and get to know them better. Find their true pain. What makes them tick? What is really on their mind?

Some high EI or critical questions that you might ask the prospective customer are:

- Why are you *really* buying from our competitors versus us?

- What is the one thing that you dislike about your relationship with them?

- If we could change one thing to help make you more successful, what would it be?

- Is there anything our competitor is doing that our company should be doing?

- What keeps you awake at night?

- One a scale of 1–10, how are things in your personal life?

- How is your family?

- What plans do you have for this weekend?

- Where do you see your company in five years?

139

You can't force these EI questions or you'll sound rehearsed and insincere. They must come naturally.

Getting to Yes — Find Out the Real Objection!

Most people refrain from telling you the real reason why they don't buy your product or service. How many times have you been in a restaurant where the food or service was just OK, or even not good, but when the waiter asks, "How is everything?" you reply, "Oh, it was fine." We don't want to deal with the hassles and hurt feelings that accompany the truth. This is just as evident in relationship sales, perhaps more so.

Per the below Help Scout website, only 4 percent of your customers who have a bad experience will share it with you, but they are twice as likely to tell others about your bad service. A whopping 78 percent of consumers have bailed on a transaction or not made an intended purchase because of a poor service experience. The Help Scout website has great customer service tips and is worth a quick read and sharing with your customer service team.

Help Scout: 75 Customers Service Facts, Quotes and Statistics

If you don't know the real reason why people select a competitor over you, work to get to the truth. Prod them and push them to provide the real reason.

At the end of the meeting, ask your customer if you have addressed all his questions and see if he might have any other concerns that would prevent him from giving you an order. If he doesn't, be sure to ask for the order again.

24) *Problem Solver*

To problem solve, you need to make sure that you're asking the right questions. Albert Einstein once said, "If I had an hour to solve a problem and my life depended on the solution, I would spend the first 55 minutes determining the proper question to ask, for once I know the proper question, I could solve the problem in less than five minutes."

With relationship sales, you are not selling a physical product; you are selling a solution to a problem—a value proposition. Customers want benefits, not product attributes per se. Focusing on attributes leads to price parity. Focusing on benefits leads to differentiation and potentially higher prices with better margins. Differentiation and providing value comes from rethinking what your value proposition is. Looking at competition is a start, but is not the complete answer.

Part of being a problem solver means helping your customer justify your product to others in his organization. Be prepared with facts such as payback periods, cost-benefit ratios and other justifications that he can use to make himself look good.

You need to make it easy for your customer to place an order. As a potential order is being developed, it's good to end all communications with a simple affirmation statement, such as asking if is there any additional information you can provide or restating your desire to work with him.

25) *Perceptible/Perspective*

The only perspective that matters is that of your customer. In relationship sales, you must be customer-centric and be the customer's advocate. Be perceptive and look at things from his perspective. If you can grasp what's important to him through observations, you will increase your chances of building a relationship and increasing your sales. These actions can be strong code-shifting opportunities. Become the customer's advocate within your company.

My uncle, Reg Darley, who just retired at age 85, ran our equipment catalog business for years and did an excellent job of it. He was always an advocate for the customer. As our company became more sophisticated with our sales analytics, we would argue to remove items from the catalog that didn't sell well.

Reg would tell the story about the local pharmacy in our hometown. The son took over the business and decided to remove all the magazines from the store because he felt the profit margins were not high enough, and they took up too much prime real estate in the front of the store. What the son failed to realize is that when people came in for a newspaper or magazine, they almost always bought something else. That family pharmacy has been out of business for a while, as it simply couldn't compete with the likes of Walgreens and CVS, but I always remember the story. As a youngster, I stopped going there when the same son cut the candy selection in half.

Another example of perspective comes from my dealings in China. In China and in the U.S., a $100 bill and a Yuan 100 are the largest denominations made in both countries. The Chinese Yuan 100 is worth about 15 U.S. dollars, but up until 10 years ago, we would think about U.S. $100 the same way most Chinese think about 100 yuan.

26) *Proposals*

For typical business transactions, proposals are easier to prepare than they used to be. Most of our quotes and proposals are generated through our ERP system, which kicks out professional looking quotes that we can quickly turn into orders.

Certain customized product quotes are prepared in Excel because it's quicker and we don't need to populate our ERP system with temporary part numbers. In these cases, the Excel files are always sent as PDF files. We do the same with proposals prepared in Word. Be sure to spellcheck the document. If you use a template from a previous quote, double check to make sure that another company's name is not reference from a previous document.

Always send proposals as PDF files. They are easier to read, un-editable and give a sense of permanency. People also feel more comfortable with PDF files because they are more likely to be virus free when opening them on their computers.

It is important that even quick proposals include all pertinent data, including payment terms, delivery time and FOB point. (Freight on Board determines who pays for and insures the freight — generally it's FOB Shipping Point, which means the customer pays for the freight. If it's FOB Destination, then the supplier pays for the freight and is responsible for any shipping damage). Watch for typos and other grammatical errors, and make sure hyperlinks are accurate. If at all possible, never ask for an extension on the proposal due date.

With larger quotes, prepare the proposal and then review it with a fresh set of eyes the next day, or have a coworker proofread it for you. They say you shouldn't judge a book by its cover, but when it comes to reviewing proposals, prospective buyers tend to do just that. The more professional the proposal, the better chance you have of winning the sale.

In our business, we submit many sophisticated government proposals, and believe me when I tell you the quality of the proposal is imperative and can mean the difference between getting an order or not. Further, don't make the customer search for answers about your compliance with customer specifications. Set up a "Red Team" to review the proposal with a very critical eye, as if it is the customer. Challenge what is written as a devil's advocate.

Before writing your next major proposal, read the article below for simple rules. Below is a summary of the tips.

CBS Money Watch: 10 Rules for Writing a Winning Proposal, 2009

- *RULE #1.* Write the proposal as a sales document

- *RULE #2.* Make sure the customer knows you

- *RULE #3.* Focus the executive summary on reasons to buy

- *RULE #4.* Keep the executive summary short

- *RULE #5.* Hit everyone's hot buttons

- *RULE #6.* Focus on the customer, not your product

- *RULE #7.* Thoroughly edit the boilerplate

- *RULE #8.* Follow the customer's outline

- *RULE #9.* Don't discuss costs in the executive summary

- *RULE #10.* Edit out the meaningless jargon

These days, many companies are doing away with printed materials. At a trade show, less than 10 percent of the literature picked up at the show goes home with someone. And of that, less than 10 percent gets acted upon. (Think about what happened to the literature you picked up at the last trade shows you attended.) That said, printed literature still does go a long way with formal written proposals and for high ticket items such as automobiles or fire trucks.

We still print and mail over 100,000 catalogs each year. We obviously blend this with user-friendly e-commerce websites, edarley. com and darleydefense.com, with roughly 100,000 SKUs. Few other companies in our industry still print paper catalogs, and it's become a point of differentiation for us.

27) *Power of Persuasion/Prevail*

No one likes to be "sold." When you think of salespeople, you probably think of the high-pressure, fast-talking salesmen who are trying to *persuade* you to buy something that you don't want or need. Plenty of those types of salesmen lurk out there and are an embarrassment to our profession.

With that understanding, many sales and self-improvement programs focus heavily on the power of persuasion, and you can learn some vital lessons from them. Zig Ziglar wrote, "Your most important persuasion tool you have in your entire arsenal is integrity." I couldn't agree more.

If you try to use persuasion *tactics,* like what's used at timeshare programs and other high-pressure sales organizations, you might be more ideally suited for transactional sales than relationship selling. In these cases, customers usually end up on the losing side of the equation, and once they realize it, they'll almost never make a second similar purchase. This is not relationship selling!

With that understanding, the below link from Toast Masters has some clever ideas, but be careful if you choose to implement all of them. Note that this link has 15 chapters.

Westside Toast Masters – The Rules of Persuasion

One example of high pressure sales happened to us recently when our company was shopping for a new CRM program. The sales rep was very professional, but continued to use time pressure as a sales tactic, telling us if we didn't act within 10 days, he could no longer offer this "special price." We had other options that were priced considerably less. His "scarcity" play was such a turnoff that we went elsewhere. Don't put undue time pressures on your customers in relationship sales. It will almost always backfire.

Persuasion needs to be low key; it can't be in-your-face. Most see right through these tricky sales tactics. It's about getting "yes" when the quick response is "no," because people are naturally afraid to say "yes." Be respectful and calm.

While I have an excellent driving record with no accidents and only a couple of speeding tickets over the past 25 years, I admit I tend to speed too often. In social settings with police officers, I ask "What's the best line you ever heard in letting someone off a ticket?" The best two responses were, first, from a Chicago police officer, who pulled over a vehicle with two Hispanic men inside. The officer asked if there was anything illegal in the car and the driver responded, "Just the two of us." They got a free pass.

The second best came from a small-town cop in Virginia, who pulled over a "city slicker" in a BMW going 60 MPH in "his" 25 MPH zone. The cop approached the car and said, "Boy, I've been waiting for you all day." The driver responded, "Well, I got here as fast as I could." He knocked the ticket down by 15 mph.

Both are true stories, illustrating the importance of being cool under fire, respectful, cordial and funny at times to improve your persuasion. As an aside, I believe there to be a strong correlation between someone's EI and his driving ability. I've never read any data on this, but accident-free drivers usually know their limits (self-awareness), know where to watch their speed around exit and on ramps (self-management), drive defensively and constantly observe their surroundings (social awareness), and adapt their driving to changing environmental conditions (relationship management). When hiring sales reps, it's a good idea to go on sales call with them and let them drive. Try it.

28) *Persistence/Perseverance*

In 2011, I was a finalist for the Ernst & Young Entrepreneur of the Year Award in Chicago. At the time, my Elmhurst Business Organization (EBO) forum attended the black-tie ceremony with me at the Hyatt Regency Chicago. I went through a series of interviews, and I was anxious to see my write-up by *Smart Business* magazine. I was initially embarrassed when I read it. It began, "There's almost nothing that could happen to Paul Darley in the business world that would present more of a challenge than what he faced in his late teenage years. At 16, his oldest brother committed suicide. Two years later, his mother died of cancer during his first month of college. And a few years after that, his best friend and cousin died (of cancer). While these would be unimaginably difficult for any person to endure, Darley chose to learn from the experiences and seize every day and every opportunity that presented itself. And if the opportunity was not there, he simply created it himself."

I'm still a bit embarrassed as I read it again. But like anything in life, it's the difficult times that define who you are and help to form you as a person. These times also pushed me to seize the day (carpe diem) and live life to the fullest.

About 25 years ago, I called on one of the more high-profile executives in our industry. Jim Hebe, CEO of Freightliner at the time, had just purchased the iconic fire truck brand, American LaFrance. We were bidding to build a private label pump for him. Jim took a liking to me, perhaps partially because he wanted to buy our company, but mostly because we both shared a passion for the fire service and hunting. I was nervous at our first meeting, but completely focused. I was enamored with his success at such a young age, and asked about his secrets to business success. Jim told me he focused on two things—cash flow and customer service at all costs. That stuck with me.

For six months, we worked hard to custom design a pump for him that met all his objectives. At the close of the eighth meeting, we received the order. I later learned that Jim had called my father, telling him, "Your son must have asked for the order 10 times while he was here. I finally just had to give it to him." Jim gave me one of our first shots at breaking into the pump OEM business, and I'll never forget it.

It might seem like a small thing, but it's critical and worth mentioning again. Far too many salespeople don't bother to make an "ask" from the customer during or at the close of the meeting. They are either afraid or think it's somehow inappropriate to ask a customer to place an order or ask for a second meeting. They couldn't be more wrong. To put it simply, if you want something, you need to ask for it.

On the flip side, be careful not to oversell. When the customer is ready to move forward with an order, sincerely thank them and shut up! Then, make it easy for the customer to place the order and stay on him until you get the firm order in hand.

Persistence does not mean being pushy; it must be respectful persistence. You don't want to be a pest. No one likes a forceful salesperson, and being one can result in a lost sale. Orders come because of educating the customer and making him feel comfortable with the decision to purchase from you. Pushy sales representatives give us all a bad rap. Give customers space to make their decision, but not too much space that they think you don't care. It's kind of like fishing: you need to keep the line tight, but don't pull so hard you break the line. And don't give them too much slack or they'll shake the hook.

Another forum mate, Tor Solberg, president of his 70-year-old family business, Solberg Manufacturing, has a motto of "Pleasant Persistence." He explains, "It's about 'touch' and being wanted around at a customer's place instead of being labeled as too 'aggressive.' We do this by keeping in contact in various forms — phone, email, in person, and marketing — always trying to have success stories that relate to the customer's business, so that they actually want to hear the latest news from us."

One person who knows persistence is Angela Duckworth, who wrote an instant *New York Times* bestseller in April of 2016 titled *Grit: The Power of Passion and Perseverance*. She shows that for anyone striving to succeed—be it parents, students, educators, athletes or business people—the secret to outstanding achievement is not talent, but a special blend of passion and persistence she calls "grit." Here is a great TED Talk video:

Grit: The Power of Passion and Perseverance

Grit and hard work can't be understated. My fishing buddy, Brett Christenson, is a highly successful money manager for Marquette Associates, who advises pension funds on where to invest their money. Like many of my friends who are successful executives, he started off with a paper route as a kid and worked his way through grade school, high school and college. They all have a strong work ethic that was instilled in them at an early age.

29) *Proactive/Preemptive*

Here is a riddle for you that my father loved to tell. "There are three frogs on a log and one of them decides to jump in. How many are left?" Think about it for a moment.

Ready?

Most people answer two, but the correct answer is three. The key word here is "decides." Just because he decides to do something, doesn't mean he does it. I see this point in some salespeople. Some are simply procrastinators. They will say, "I will put it on my to-do list." Don't put it on your list; just do it!

Too many sales reps sit back and wait for the phone to ring or respond to an email request for information or pricing. Waiting for the phone to ring is not selling! Follow-up is where selling begins. Set calendar follow-ups on each quote, generally one week out and then as often as necessary. After your first email follow-up, pick up the phone and reach out to the person to gauge his level of interest and qualify the prospect. Blind copy yourself on each email quote, filing it in a follow-up folder, and set calendar follow-ups using Outlook.

My phone doesn't ring like it used to ... and that's despite a long-standing ad campaign publicizing my home, cell and office telephone numbers, encouraging customers to call me. Email, however, is pretty much out of control. I typically receive between 300-400 emails per day, and I touch them once. I respond, delete them, file them, set a follow-up, or delegate them. Touch emails once and you'll find you have a great deal more time to be proactive. As a rule, I never leave the office without being able to see the bottom of my email inbox. Many of your competitors fail to make taking care of emails a priority and get caught up the email rat race or "email jail."

When reviewing your emails, it's quickest if you review them in the "Normal Folder Pane" setting with "compact" view. That way you can quickly review the contents of the email without opening it. If you use Microsoft Outlook, be sure to have "Clutter" installed. It will send many emails to this file folder that aren't junk, but that you might only review in your window pane and not open. It learns what emails you don't open and puts them there in the future.

Being preemptive like this leaves time for sales reps to be proactive with customers not just reactionary. Sometimes being proactive also means being preemptive. Rob Hallberg is the vice president of MB Financial Bank, one of the largest commercial banks in Chicago. He is an incredible salesman who has earned the respect of his customers and peers. One reason for this is that he has a rule: If you must deliver bad news to a customer, always do it in person, never over the phone or in an email!

Here's one of the favorites stories that my father liked to tell our employees: Every morning in Africa, the gazelle wakes up and knows that he must outrun the fastest lion. Every morning, the lion wakes up and knows that he must outrun the slowest gazelle. It doesn't matter if you're a lion or a gazelle, you've got to get up running. If you're smaller than most of your competitors, speed should be one of your greatest competitive advantages.

Most CEOs and top sales reps start their days with exercise and then arrive at the office before the hustle and bustle starts. They will tell you that this stretch is the most productive time of their day. If you have important tasks to work on, tackle them at the beginning of the day when you are fresh and focused. You'll also find that you have fewer distractions from phone calls, emails and people coming to you looking for guidance during this time.

30) *Poise*

You're not going to garner every sale, so it's important to accept "no" graciously. Use it as an opportunity to improve. Like most salespeople, it is an area that I need to work on. I don't take losing well. Whether it's a round of golf, my fantasy football league, or business (especially business!) — I am in it to win! In one instance (which I described earlier), I took losing a government contract so poorly that we went out and bought the company that won the contract. Today that company, Ohler Pump, is a critical component of our company's success and it typically maintains the highest profit margin of all our divisions.

Accept Rejection Gracefully

Sales reps tend to take losses personally and generally don't take rejection well. Usually it's not a personal issue, but if it is, try having another sales rep call on the company, or put it on the back burner for a while. If you handle rejection gracefully, a prospective customer will be more receptive to you the next time an opportunity arises.

Learn from Your Mistakes

The loss of an order doesn't have to be a complete failure. Use it to improve on the next one, and always learn from the mistakes. "Those who cannot remember the past are condemned to repeat it," wrote philosopher, essayist, poet and novelist George Santayana in *Reason in Common Sense* in 1906.

When it comes to the sales process, and business in general, every mistake that can be made already has been. When no lessons are learned from mistakes, a salesperson is "condemned" to repeat them, which likely translates into a very short career.

At Darley, we take time to have fun and celebrate special efforts when we win a contract. When we lose, we get together as a team for a post-award review. We analyze why we didn't get that award so

148

that the next time we face a similar situation, we improve our chances of success. We've found this self-examination is critically important to explore why we didn't get a contract. That debriefing provides us with critical information about our sales approach.

Don't be afraid to ask why you didn't get the contract. You can't always get input from customers, but probe to find the real reason. Sometimes it has nothing to do with your products or sales process. Explore your strengths and weaknesses, learn what you can improve, then do it. And always learn from the mistakes.

Because sales is a process, you can apply the same principles of continuous improvement that are used in manufacturing processes such as Lean, Six Sigma and Total Quality Management (TQM). Implement Corrective Action Reports (CARS) to prevent you from doing it again.

While there's something to be said for the school of hard knocks (where you learn from your mistakes), it's best if your salespeople can benefit from the experiences of others. Why reinvent the wheel? Something Mark Twain is quoted as saying rings true here: "When I was a boy of fourteen, my father was so ignorant I could hardly stand to have the old man around. But when I got to be twenty-one, I was astonished at how much the old man had learned in seven years."

Chapter 9

Profitable Sales & Pricing. Making a Buck for you and the Company

"The chief executive officer is also the chief sales officer. He or she is responsible for the success of the company and making a profit. The closer the CEO is to the everyday selling process, bringing in business, the more successful the company will become."

Jeffrey Gitomer, sales author, professional speaker and business trainer.

1. Profitable Sales (Not just any sale)

2. Pricing

3. Product Differentiation (Avoid becoming a commodity)

4. Parity/Partnership

5. Pathos

6. Perambulate

7. Placate

8. Promotion (Branding)

9. Perception is Reality

10. Positioning/Push vs Pull Strategies

31) *Profitable Sales (Not Just Any Sale)*

At Darley, we like to tell the story about the brothers in Florida selling watermelons. The brothers purchased a truck load of watermelons at $1 each, which was too high of a price. Their competition down the road also sells watermelons, but at the price of a buck each. The brothers quickly realize they are in trouble. If they don't lower their price, the produce is going to go to waste. So they lower their selling price to .75 cents. Soon sales are great and the brothers run out of watermelons and ask themselves, "What should we do? Well, we have to go and get more watermelons." I know it's a bit silly, but you get my point. Too many focus only on sales, not *profitable* sales.

Many think they can make profit up in volume, but this strategy seldom works. You should look at the situation from a contribution margin standpoint and conduct a break-even analysis so you know exactly how much you need to sell at varying prices to make a profit. The below link shows you how to do this quickly in an Excel spreadsheet:

Accounting Tools: Contribution Margin

Investopedia: Break-Even Analysis

If you have a product line or division that is consistently

unprofitable, you should cut bait quickly. When losing money in a market, we will say, "We have to go get more watermelons." We all know it's time to get out of the business and move on. Too many hang on too long due to the sunk costs involved or other emotional reasons. You always need to look at sunk costs as exactly that—sunk. Over the years, our company has admittedly been slow to cut bait on unsuccessful projects, usually due to emotional reasons.

I'm surprised by the number of firms that place equal weight on both sales and profits. There might be some strategic reasons to place more emphasis on growing top-line sales over bottom-line profits, such as preparing a company for sale or an Initial Public Offering, or when trying to enter a new market. But that's not a healthy or sustainable long-term business model. This type of growth is referred to as "glamorous growth," and it's a dangerous route for any company.

Glamorous growth happens more often than most realize. Look at Uber, for example: the ride hailing company has transformed the way people get around, but it lost roughly $2 billion in 2015 and $3 billion in 2016. Yet somehow, the company is valued at more than $50 billion. Companies with glamorous growth often grow too fast and run out of cash flow to operate their business, even if they're making a small profit.

Grocery stores promote a loss leader to draw in customers. Think of the low prices grocery stores sell turkeys for at Thanksgiving. While customers pick up their turkey from the back of the store, they buy other food items for their Thanksgiving meal on their way to the cash register. Customers buy the discounted item and then a few other things, too. The loss leader item generates a profit by getting customers into the store, and while the customers are there, they purchase other things. However, be careful with this strategy; it can be a slippery slope.

Companies need to monitor their salespeople and focus on the bottom line to survive. A salesperson should have some flexibility in negotiating deals with customers, but in many industries they don't. If they do, it is important that those salespeople have clear guidelines. Those responsible for creating compensation packages must understand the net operating profit that a salesperson's deals bring in — not just the gross revenue (sales) or gross profit (the difference between the selling price and purchased price, including manufacturing overhead, but before selling, general and administrative costs). It's a straightforward way to grow top-line sales. As CEO, I look at not only sales, but, more importantly, the profitability of those sales.

Some still view "profit" as a four-letter word. Not all salespeople focus on the profitability of their sales; those who do, however, have a better chance of moving up the executive food chain. No matter where one sits on the organizational chart, every person in the company must remain focused on the company's profitability. To achieve this profit, everyone must understand the cost of doing business.

Understanding the True Costs of Doing Business

Many employees don't realize how many costs are associated with running a business. Most workers know the obvious — salaries, travel expenses, health insurance, and so on. However, plenty of additional expenses — i.e., payroll taxes, product liability insurance, financing costs, warranty expense, bad debts, legal costs, website, electricity, building lease and maintenance costs, trade shows and conferences that employees attend — sometimes fly under the radar of new employees, even new executives.

Every CEO and manager must know and understand the cost to turn the key in the door each day. They should also know customer acquisition costs. Unfortunately, few do.

For starters, many confuse *gross profit* with *net operating profit*. Gross profit is simply the company's total revenue (total sales) minus the cost of goods sold. Gross profit is what a company makes after deducting the costs associated with buying or manufacturing its products. It doesn't include sales, general, administrative (SG & A), or other related costs.

I have even met people who think a million dollars in sales translates into a million dollars in profit to their company. These are usually the same ones who walk into a convenience store, buy a candy bar for a dollar, and think the store just made a dollar on the sale.

Net profit, or operating profit, is the actual profit after SG & A expenses not included in the calculation of gross profit have been paid. At the end of the day, if you're left with a net profit between 2 and 3 percent (before Uncle Sam takes his share), you're doing fairly well, as long as you have positive cash flow.

Most companies focus on Earnings Before Interest Tax Depreciation and Amortization (EBITDA). EBITDA measures free cash flow and adds back non-cash expenses, and it's a way to evaluate a company's performance without having to factor in financing decisions. EBITDA is a measure of how much cash the

154

company generates. When companies are bought and sold, the price is generally set on a multiple of EBITDA. These multiples fluctuate by industry, company size, and market conditions, but most companies are valued between four and 10 times EBITDA. If a company sells for a six multiple, then the buyer expects to recoup his investment within six years, taking into consideration his cost of capital or internal rate of return (IRR).

Here is a good report from Pepperdine that gives some typical multiples for different industries.

Pepperdine Report: Capital Markets Report, Company Valuations, 2015

Too many business people look at the cost of the goods sold and not the cost of selling those goods. If you earn a gross profit of $10,000 annually on sales to a customer, but that customer requires an excessive amount of maintenance, the customer might be costing your company money in the long run.

Markup Vs Margin

Many well-seasoned business people and sales reps confuse the difference between mark-up and margin, which can be a huge mistake. Most think the terms mean the same, but they do not!

If you purchase a product for resell and mark it up 50 percent, this action does not mean your gross profit is 50 percent; it's only 33.3 percent. Do the math. For example, if you purchase a component for $100 from a vendor and sell it for $150, the *gross profit* is $50. $50/$150 = 33.3 percent. Few companies can mark up something 50 percent, so it becomes even more critical when you mark up something only 15 percent; this has a gross profit of only 13 percent.

Buy yourself a calculator that can automatically calculates these at the push of a button, or better yet, download a free app for your smart phone by searching "Gross Margin Calculator."

Most companies have a tough time operating at gross margins under 20 percent. A few places, such as car dealerships, gas stations, and grocery stores, do it by automation, making it up on other products or services. Here is a good report that shows typical company gross margins. Remember, these margins are before selling and administrative costs.

Butler Consultants: Typical gross margins by industry

I love the scene in *The Jerk* where Steve Martin's character is guessing people's weight and age working at a circus, and he feels he's not doing a good job. The circus manager tells him he's taken in $15 and given away .50 cents worth of crap, which is a net profit of $14.50. The Jerk proclaims, "It's a profit deal! That takes the pressure off." While the circus manager should have said "gross profit" since it doesn't take into consideration all the overhead costs, it's funny and worth a quick watch:

You Tube: Steve Martin - Jerk - It's a profit deal

32) *Pricing*

As a sales rep, the objection you'll hear the most is, "Your price is too high!" Price is only going to continue to increase in importance in this information age, where discriminating buyers have so much more information than ever before. This is where your salesmanship kicks in. There are some basic approaches you can take to address this, but selling against price alone is a difficult task.

Be careful of going after deals when you have a customer who is solely price- focused. Most likely, that customer isn't going to remain loyal to you in the long run and could end up costing you money and brand reputation, especially if you've cut corners to reduce your price. If a customer is entirely price-driven, you don't have a personal relationship and it becomes more of a transactional sale than a relationship sale.

Setting Pricing

Pricing is more of an art than a science. Most companies will price their products based on their manufacturing costs and what their competitors are charging for similar products. But companies with product differentiation will generally price their products based on what the market will bear.

Selling on Price – Be Careful

Some sales reps compete only on price, especially if they represent a company that has low cost operations such as manufacturing overseas. If your product is the lowest cost and lowest priced, you should leverage that position, but be careful as competing on price alone is not selling and it's a dangerous game. Eventually, someone will be willing to undercut your price.

Markets that are totally cost driven are generally going to offer very poor customer service and poor-quality products. "You get what you pay for," holds true for just about everything in life. When this happens, you need to find ways to differentiate yourself and focus on other factors.

A competitor may be willing to lose money on a deal to win other

156

business. If a product is consistently lower in price, the lower costs are associated with low quality. When product problems occur with the lower price product, this company usually does not back the product.

Selling Against Lower Priced Products

If your competitor is consistently offering a lower price, you might want to infer that its product is "cheaper," not lower priced. Cheap denotes lower quality. Therefore, be careful with this approach, so you're not perceived as negative selling.

At Darley, while we have ongoing Lean initiatives, we are not the low-cost producer in our industry. As a result, Darley pumps are generally more expensive than our competitors', just as a Lexus is generally more expensive than a Ford. Our customers know that they get more due to our quality, personalized service, longer warranty, delivery and total cost of ownership.

Because of these services, we have a higher cost structure than our competitors. Unlike our primary pump competitor, by choice we manufacture all our products in the U.S., as opposed to sourcing low-cost products overseas. By maintaining this domestic construction, we can control the quality of our products. We pay our skilled employees well, and since we reinvest most of our profits back into the company, we have a high cost of capital based on all our reinvestment. Because of this structure, we'll be around to take care of customers in the long run, which makes it easier to err on their side when things go wrong.

Discuss Pricing Last

When price comes up in a discussion with a customer, and it almost always eventually does, the following approach can be very effective.

Ask the customer to put pricing aside by saying, "OK, let's take price out of it for a minute. Let's say I am the lowest price. Now what are your concerns relative to our product?" Once he agrees, look for ways that you can reduce your product offering and show how your product can reduce other costs so that his total acquisition cost is lower than your competitors'. Sometimes easier said than done, but it works.

You might want to ask your customer if he has a target price. It he does, you can figure that he is currently paying 10-20 percent higher than this target price.

Unbundle your Product to match the competitors lower price

Many companies bundle products or services. Most customers see through this tactic as a bait-and-switch approach. Bundling can be perceived as playing games, and customers will quickly punt when they catch on.

At that point, make apples-to-apples comparisons on your products. Focus on whatever his pain is and unbundle any additional features that you may have in your product that your competitor might not. These features could be components, but also look closely at payment terms, warranty, acquisition costs, switching costs, installation costs and training costs.

Ultimately, you need to find other ways to reduce the customer's overall acquisition costs and create economic value for him.

At times, companies might buy a modest bit of business and sell at little or no margin to get their foot in the door. This strategy might be used to enter a new market or in the hopes of selling a customer other products that don't have the same price elasticity. Here is a good article on determining the price elasticity of your product.

HBR: A Refresher on Price Elasticity, August 2015

Ultimately, if your product is viewed as a commodity, it's going to be difficult—if not impossible—to make money, unless you become the low-cost producer, and even then, it's a bad idea. Ultimately, though, you don't want to get into a position where you compete strictly on price. It is a losing game, not only for you, but for your customer.

33) *Product Differentiation - Avoid Becoming a Commodity*

When you fail to innovate, your product can easily become a commodity. Once a product becomes or is viewed as a commodity, a company's options are limited—make it for less, sell it for less, offer a better-buying experience (everyone says they offer the best customer service), or innovate.

Product differentiation or innovation is the key to avoiding commoditization. Once a product is viewed as a commodity, it all comes down to price—a viscous trap—because, for the short term, competitors can always drop their price to match yours. Avoid commoditization of your product at all costs.

Another way to avoid commoditization is to customize products for specific customers to reduce their overall acquisition costs. With this approach, businesses must carefully target perspective clients. Not every customer is right for this type of customized approach, as it can be very expensive to undertake. It is imperative to look at a project and determine, on the front end, if the potential cost is justified for that type of investment of time, money and other resources.

158

Relationship vs. Price — Where is the Value?

Most salespeople learn to sell on value, but they fail to understand that their perception of value is completely at odds with each potential customer's. Remember, it's not about you!

So why do our customers buy from us? In our OEM customer surveys, "relationships" and "customer service" are cited most often as the reasons customers choose us over another supplier. What about quality and competitive pricing? In today's competitive business environment, these attributes are simply expected. In fact, I'd argue that no company today can stay in business if it doesn't provide a high-quality product at a competitive price. Low quality is weeded out, and high, non-competitive prices are either adjusted down or do not find a market.

This subject could take up an entire chapter, but if you want to learn more, check this link from *Harvard Business Review* in 2010.

HBR - How to Stop Customers from Fixating on Price

34) *Parity/Partnership*

During college, I was a chauffeur in Milwaukee. One of my co-workers, Jim O'Brien (OB), and I became fast friends. Today, OB is a highly successful salesman for Premier Blanket Service, selling offset printing blankets to printing companies … a true commodity. Jim says, "My approach to selling is to take the position of customer advocate. I have to offer a compelling reason for a printer to try my products. This tactic takes creativity because I sell a consumable commodity. With access to all major product lines, I can offer them a targeted solution, not just a limited choice. You have to quickly show the prospect you have something better for them, that will make *them* look good and operate just a little better than with their current supplier. If I help them demonstrate savings, they take that to their next meeting." It helps tremendously that Jim has high EI, and people love to be around him. He's one of the funniest guys I know and has a knack for building relationships, both in business and his private life.

There must be something in it for both parties. For you as a salesperson, relationship selling can never take an "I won" approach or it's not going to last long. The only one who should ever say "I won" is the customer. It must be "win-win" for both parties. If it's not, one party, feeling it's gotten a bad deal, will never come back.

I've learned from the banking industry, and it applies to all selling relationships, that too often there is a lack of parity in relationships. One of the parties is begging or asking for something and "wearing knee pads." In most business relationships, the person who is wearing the kneepads changes over time. When I am the customer, I'm either on my knees begging for help or my suppliers are on their knees begging for our business. It's critical that you always remain respectful in all relationships, especially when you are not the one wearing the knee pads.

In the end, people remember how they were treated by others in their times of need. In business and in life, when people you know have been exiled or isolated by a group or are down on their luck, reach out to them. They'll always remember it.

At Darley, creating partnerships is one of our core values. We view business partnerships as a marriage, in that no one is ever forced unwillingly into a relationship. If they feel they are, chances are it won't stand the test of time. Partnerships never last if they lack equality. It's not easy to get your customer to view you as a partner unless you have a close working—and personal—relationship.

Once in a partnership, it's critical that both parties be respectful and don't take advantage of each other. Steven Rogers, a Harvard Business School professor who serves on our board of directors, has said to me more than once, "Pigs get fat, and hogs get slaughtered." If you're in a partnership, don't get greedy!

Partnerships take a long time to build, but can be ruined in minutes if you don't respect the parameters of relationship.

Negotiating

At some point, you'll most likely engage in negotiations with your customer. I've taken courses on negotiations over the years, including classes at Kellogg and from professional negotiators who we've hired for our sales training programs at Darley. Despite that, I don't feel I'm a strong negotiator. I'm not alone as statistics show that most U.S. CEOs are not naturally good at negotiations, and 80 percent of them leave money on the table.

For our Asian customers, negotiations are a common practice. Bo Zhang, the general manager of Darley China, is the master. He and his team enjoy it. When in these sessions with our Chinese customers, we feel like we are playing checkers, while they are playing chess. They are always a few steps ahead of us.

If you've never had a chance to take a professional negotiating class, I strongly suggest you do so, or check out videos available on Kellogg's websites:

Video: Kellogg Northwestern Negotiation Tactics 101 – Leigh Thompson

160

Many negotiations will be with those whom you have long-term symbiotic relationships, such as customers, suppliers, employees and even family, so you can't go into every negotiation with guns a-blazing. Look for ways to compromise and enjoy the thrill of striking a win-win deal.

Before going into any negotiation, I review my Kellogg negotiation notes I keep in my wallet. I pull it out three or four times a year, and I've added to it. Some things I try to remember are:

- Be ready to listen more than you talk. Be respectful. Keep your cool

- Be prepared and do the homework in advance

- Know your Best Alternative to Negotiating an Agreement (BATNA). This is same as your "Walk-Away" price or terms

- Don't give anything without getting something in return. Trade things of lesser and unequal value. Quid pro quo. "If I do this, what will you do?"

- Make the first offer with precise numbers. Ideally, it should be near their reservation price or BATNA

In all negotiations, always try to find common ground. Then, appeal to their sense of what is fair and equitable, while connecting with the other party on an emotional level.

35) *Pathos*

Pathos is appealing to one's emotions to prompt action. Some might call it the "sympathy sale." I'm not proud of it, but I've used it. I literally got down on both knees in front of long-time customer, Scott Vincent of West-Mark, begging to be his pump supplier for a large government contract. It worked, and we've since delivered close to 500 pumps under this multi-million-dollar contract. Scott and I are old friends, and we both had fun with it.

Don't play the sympathy card too often. Candidly, I feel an obligation to buy from some suppliers because they are such hard workers and rely on our business to support their families. At the end of the day, people buy from people largely for emotional reasons.

Some customers appreciate the dedication and persistence exhibited by sales reps and feel an obligation to give them an order to reward them for their efforts. We worked on one large prospective customer 25 years without an order. In his Christmas card each year, I would simply write, "Throw me a bone." He finally did.

161

Part of relationship selling is honest homage to the customer. All relationships should be revered. Customers react well when you give them VIP or LMB service. They know you truly appreciate their business and pull out stops in servicing them.

36) *Perambulate (Walk in their shoes)*

I realize this "P" is kind of a stretch, but it's critically important to relationship selling. Perambulate means to travel on foot. All salespeople should take the proverbial walk in their customer's shoes, spending a day in the life of their customers to gain an understanding of what their customers are going through. If you don't understand your customer's situation or how your product is being used, get out of your office and spend time in the field with your customers and end-users. The information you gain can be truly insightful.

The Godfather movies are known for their quotes relative to dealing with people. One of my favorites is when Michael Corleone, played by Al Pacino, is talking to his consigliere, Tom Hagen, and says "All my people are businessmen; their loyalty is based on that. One thing I learned from my father is to try to think as the people around you think...and on that basis, anything is possible."

When you put yourself in others shoes, you can garner incredible insights. It's not about you.

We conduct ongoing market research, from surveys to focus groups. These are an invaluable way to hone your value proposition through a better understanding of what your customers are experiencing. You can generally count on your customers for information about the market and their true opinions on you and your products. Don't expect major insights each time; instead, each perspective adds to the bigger picture.

Market research is great, but spending a day in the life of your customer can tell you even more about how you are perceived. The process is important because it provides a clearer understanding of their issues, of their pain, so as a salesperson you can better serve their needs. We also encourage this practice with all our engineers, inside sales reps, and anyone with customer contact. For more information, this *Harvard Business Review* article is timeless and one of my favorites.

HBR - Spend a-Day in the Life of your Customers, 1994

At Abbott Labs, new sales reps who sell cardio vascular equipment go into the operating room with the doctors. They observe open-heart surgery to have a better understanding of how his company's product is used. Now that's on the job training!

162

37) *Placate*

At some point, you are going to encounter an angry customer. How you deal with that customer to calm the situation and regain his confidence is the difference between losing a customer or building one for life. You can tell most about a company and your relationship with others when things go wrong. How you and your customers react in these circumstances pinpoints strengths and weaknesses in your relationship. Some sales reps run for the hills or bury their heads in the sand when trouble comes up. However, the best players use these potentially destructive situations as an opportunity to create code-shifts and turn lemons into lemonade, making the relationship even stronger.

Customers can get angry or rude for a variety of reasons. Some causes are legitimate; others are not, and how you respond makes all the difference in the world. I'm part owner of a company called Vital Signs in Elmhurst, IL. Don Meyers, the company president, called me recently.

"We've got an issue," Don said. "Our best customer is raking us over the coals. It's unfair." He explained the situation, and it seemed his company was in the right. Unfortunately, moral ground doesn't always matter.

He told me, "Look, we've got to take this one in the chin. We can't afford to lose this customer over a fairly minor discrepancy, regardless of whether we're right or not."

So, Don did just that. He placated the customer in a respectful manner. A week later, the customer called back and realized that she had made the mistake. Don didn't throw it in her face. Instead, he said he could understand her error, and he was happy that he could help. He gained a customer for life.

Forbes Magazine wrote an article on placating a customer:

Forbes Magazine: 7 Steps for Dealing with Angry Customers. August 2013

Briefly, the article recommends the following:
1. Remain calm
2. Don't take it personally
3. Use your best listening skills
4. Actively sympathize
5. Apologize gracefully
6. Find a solution

7. Take a few minutes on your own

These tips are great. I would add wait a day or two, then follow-up with the person on the phone, and send a personal, hand-written apology note with a small gift.

38) *Promotion (Branding)/ Push & Pull Strategies*

If you've never gone through a branding exercise, use the template below and come up with one for your organization. It will not only help organize your value proposition, but develop your brand essence and create higher loyalty with your customers. It's available on our website:

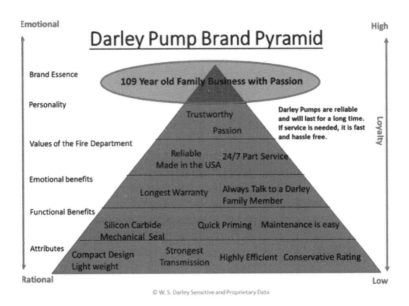

Branding Tree Template: Soldbypauldarley

Staying in front of your customers with consistent messages is an important way to build a brand, so we never stop spending time and money on branding. Our marketing director, Amanda Whitlaw, gets this and has been doing an awesome job on our marketing and branding for over 15 years. Her father worked for us for many years and she married Michael Whitlaw in our sales department. Our webmaster, Joe Catania, takes Amanda's lead. They are a strong team.

Besides advertising and other messaging, other soft costs go to branding—the type of building in which a company operates, for example. At Darley, we pride ourselves on our facilities. Operating from crummy, run down, or dilapidated-looking places reflects poorly on a company. When our customers visit our facilities, we want them to walk away with a very professional image. Over the last 25 years, we've invested heavily back in to our company, so we have the best plants and capital equipment in our industry.

Because we are a family business and none of our competitors are, we leverage much of our brand based on the passion we have as a family. This can't be replicated by our competitors. It is at the essence of what we are all about as a company and as a family.

Salespeople get branded, too. Remember, good, bad or indifferent, you have a brand, and you should be constantly working on improving your image. Ask people close to you to use three adjectives to describe you. Jeff Resch, a 40-year employee at Pierce/Oshkosh who just retired as Vice President and General Manager for Oshkosh Airport Products, says, "Over time, your reputation and your company's reputation become one in the same. If someone doesn't want to do business with you, they won't do business with your company."

When you ask for honest feedback, the answers can be very powerful. You might be surprised by what you learn.

The power of branding has been known for centuries. In the Art of War, Sun Tzu writes, "Appear weak when you are strong, and strong when you are weak." This line was written in China in the 5th century BC, but it applies today more than ever. The internet and social media can create overnight sensational brands and destroy brands equally as quickly.

39) *Perception is Reality*

My pal, Joe O'Neil, owned a restaurant and bar just off Michigan Ave., in the heart of downtown Chicago. Outside of "O'Neil's Bar and Grill," Joe posted a sign that read, "Voted #1 Cheeseburger in Chicago."

Tourists and locals flocked to his restaurant and sang the praises for the burgers. As it turns out, Joe's wife, Susan, was the only one who voted in his poll, but that fact was good enough for Joe. While there was nothing special about the frozen patty he quickly grilled up, customers thought it was incredible because of their perceptions. Joe can work a room better than anyone, and his patrons felt appreciated being greeted by the owner. Joe also gave customers an unexpected gift and little bit more than they expected by including a small bag of M&M candy with each burger.

How the market perceives you is reality for them and you. While you might think you represent one thing, how the markets perceive you is all that matters.

During the 1960s, our company introduced a new pump that did not have enough reserve pumping capacity. As a result, after about 10 years of use, some pumps had a problem achieving their rated performance. That occurred more than 50 years ago, and the effects of that poor marketing decision linger with some "Darley Despisers," who still refuse to work with us. To ameliorate the public's perception, when we manufacture a midship mounted pump for the USA market today, it won't pass our ISO Certification until it can exceed its rated performance by at least 15 percent. The market's perception of Darley has improved tremendously from 30 years ago.

40) *Positioning / Push & Pull Strategies*

How you position your company in the marketplace can significantly impact your brand. One of the most successful positioning stories is Avis, which in 1963 was second in the market to Hertz. Its ad agency, Leo Burnett, launched a successful "We try harder" campaign. Avis still uses it today, despite becoming part of the largest car rental company in the U.S.

To keep up-to-date and a step ahead, I talk to my competitors at least once a year. I ask them if we're doing anything they feel is inappropriate, or if there are any issues they would like to discuss or that they believe I should be aware of. It's all within the confines of FTC regulations. It might seem like an odd thing to do. We're certainly not going to reveal any big secrets to each other, but there can be advantages to competitors getting along. Studies have shown that industries where competitors are friendly and less rivalry exists are more profitable.

You can follow many different schools of thought when it comes to mentioning a competitor during sales calls or in advertisements. Most marketers agree with the premise: If you are the market leader, never mention the competition. If you're not the market leader or if you're not the primary supplier to a customer, it's fine to bring them up by name and make fair comparisons, while not talking negatively about them.

Relationship selling involves both push and pull strategies, each with tactics used to create demand for your product at the OEM, distributor or end-user level. The push begins with face-to-face contact with a distributor, where you build rapport, educate them on your product, and build a relationship so you can get the sale. As shown below, each of these groups in the sales channel has a different and unique need. We use different sales and marketing approaches when dealing with each segment.

TARGET CUSTOMER	WHAT THEY WANT		HOW TO PROVIDE IT
OEMs	Engineering Support Good Pricing Non-Competitor On-Time Delivery Good Payment Terms	←→	Personal Contact Focus On Where Less 5 Private Label - Stay Out Forecasted Flexible Credit
DEALERS	Field Support Relationships Equipment Partner What Makes Them Money	←→	Pump Schools Build Trust Special Pricing & Web Incentives
FIRE DEPARTMENTS	Hassle-Free Reliable Product Great Service & Warranty Feeling of Confidence/Ownership Proud About the Products	←→	Mechanical Seal Longest Warranty Accessible Direct Staff Team Darley

Pull strategies are where you create demand for your product by the end-user, and distributors are forced to sell your product, even if you're not the preferred choice.

We use a tagline called "Demand Darley" when we market towards our end-users, including our "Darley Demanders." When you consistently take care of our customers and build relationships, these end-user customers demand our products through the distribution channels they buy from. They are willing to sing your praises to others.

Chapter 10

Concentrate on what's most important.
80/20 is everywhere!

"I don't care how much power, brilliance, or energy you have, if you don't harness it and focus it on a specific target, and hold it there you're never going to accomplish as much as your ability warrants."

Zig Ziglar

1. Pareto Principal

2. Prioritize/Paramount

3. Prolific/Productive

4. Performance/Players/Producers

5. Paralysis/Pause

6. Patience

7. Pace

8. Pivoting

9. Panorama/Patterns

10. Paradigm shift

In life, everything can't be equally important; otherwise, nothing is. Time is a limited resource, and in sales it's critical that you properly manage your time and resources.

41) *Pareto Principle (80/20 Rule)*

I've mentioned the Pareto principle a couple of times before. Let's explore how to put the concept into practice. The Pareto Principle (80/20 rule) was named for Vilfredo Pareto, an Italian economist who discovered in 1896 that 80 percent of the land in Italy was owned by 20 percent of its citizens.

As he investigated further, he discovered that the same principle applied to almost everything in his life. Think for a moment: you probably wear 20 percent of your clothes most of the time, right? In business terms, for most companies, this rule means 20 percent of customers generate 80 percent of sales — and an even higher percentage of profits.

Many companies treat all customers the same. While admirable, it's bad business and isn't practical. If the largest portion of your business comes from a relatively select few customers, does it make sense to treat every customer the same? The secret is to treat everyone fairly, but not equally.

Yes, it's important to continually develop new customers and grow your business with the other 80 percent. But why would you spend the same amount of time servicing customers who have proven over time they're not making your company very much money, and, in many cases, losing you money? Especially at the risk of not being able to give "Concierge," "VIP," or "LMB" service to your best customers.

Publicly traded Illinois Tool Works (ITW) is a master at the Pareto Principle — the company applies 80/20 to everything. It's part of its culture. Its financial results are hard to dispute, with average stockholder returns close to 20 percent over each of the past 25 years.

Many companies successfully utilize this principle: The airlines with frequent flyer programs and Nordstrom hooked my wife, Heidi, years ago. We follow this theory with Darley Disciples and Darley Demanders. We treat all our customers well and with respect. At times, we might provide a special favor for a customer who is not in the top 20 percent, but not at the expense of Darley Disciples or Darley Demanders (who are in our top 20 percent).

The same principle applies to products. Look at your entire product line. I'll bet most of your sales come from roughly 20 percent of your SKUs. We have over 100,000 SKUs. Roughly 90 percent of our sales come from 10 percent of these SKUs. Most companies are similar. If you can sell your best-selling, most profitable products to your best customers, that's where you make your highest profit. Try to avoid selling low volume products, especially to smaller customers, which is a recipe for significant losses.

Below is a slide from Strategex, a Chicago consulting firm that works with many mid-to large B2B organizations, specializing in implementing 80/20 policies in their businesses, with dramatic business performance improvements.

What Does the Quad Chart Tell Us?

If you would like to learn more, check out this video from CEO Peter Philippi. It's a 25-minute video but well worth your time. Our management team watched it together at a recent meeting.

I know this is going to be hard to believe, but Peter Philippi proves that in virtually every company, 89 percent of business comes from that company's top 25 percent of customers, 7 percent from the next 25 percent, 3 percent from next 25 percent and 1 percent from the last quartile. This rule applies across nearly all industries, products and services. For most companies, the cost of servicing these customers is generally 25 percent from each quartile. Most companies will be making 150 percent (yes, 150 percent) of their profits on customers in their top 25 percent quartile, while losing money on the smaller customers.

Following the 80/20 rule helps understand the importance of segmenting your customers and products for maximum efficiency and profitability.

Certainly, small customers can be grown. You should target those rising stars and treat them with concierge service to see if you can turn them into a top 20 percent producing customer. In the meantime, make sure you spend most of your time with the customers who drive most of your business. It's all about prioritizing.

42) *Prioritize/Paramount*

Prioritization means staying focused on the most important things that need to be done. Things that are paramount and have the biggest impact on your business should be done first — and now.

I'm surprised at the amount of busywork people will do to avoid important tasks. The important things are generally more difficult and time consuming. Perhaps it's laziness on the employees' part, but more likely, they've simply never learned to prioritize. Managers need to work with their employees to set goals and establish priorities. Employees need to be taught to focus on the significant things at the beginning of the day. At Darley, that translates into starting the day with a bit of reflection and writing down the day's priorities on a fresh page in a notebook.

Use a prioritizing system to organize your day and focus on the day's top objectives. It can be something as simple as the page in your spiral notebook and task list or your calendar in Microsoft Outlook.

Having a schedule and knowing your priorities focuses you on the most important activities. Things will arise requiring your attention. Build that likelihood into your schedule as you create a daily, monthly and quarterly "catch up" task list, so things don't slip through the cracks. All employees should follow this method, not just salespeople. Whether you use a computer, fancy portfolio or a three-section notebook, it's the same simple process. You'll find you are more productive and enjoy peace of knowing you're on top of your commitments. Don't carry around the stress of a long to-do list. Just do it! You'll feel better and advance yourself.

As discussed above with the Pareto Principal, you need to prioritize your customers, too. Scott Edens is president of Fouts Brothers in Smyrna, GA, one of our most committed Darley Disciple OEM customers. It builds close to 100 fire trucks each year, and almost without exception, every one has a Darley pump. Scott talks about how the successful college football programs in the Southeastern Conference know they must draft the best players from their home state to stay competitive. Scott takes this same approach with respect to making sure he owns his core customer base. "These fire department customers become our best salesmen and most of our sales come from referrals from these happy customers."

He keeps his customers singing their praises with a great product at a fair price and by delivering LMB service. Scott is a producer. Fouts has grown tremendously under his leadership, and he is currently president of the Fire Apparatus Manufacturers' Association (FAMA).

43) *Prolific/Productive*

The performance of salespeople is easy to measure. Ultimately, once they're up and running and given the tools, it's simply a matter of tracking sales numbers, how profitable the orders are, and whether the salespeople are bringing in new business while growing their current customers.

Many companies set quotas for their sales reps and establish forecasts for their customers, so one can easily see variations from projections. If sales reps are compensated mostly on commission, they and the company are going to learn quickly if they are going to make it. Generally, you can tell if a sales rep is going to succeed within the first 12 months on the job, sometimes sooner based on the length of the sales cycle.

Customer satisfaction is measured by customer satisfaction ratings, profitability and reviewing the net promoter scores (NSP). Many analysts will argue to NPS being the overall best indicator of a company's health. NSP surveys ask customers if they would recommend this product or service to a friend. It sounds simple, but NPS are among the most accurate tools and can be very insightful. To learn more, check out this article:

Netpromoter.com: What is Net Promotor Score

44) *Performance/Players//Producers*

In any given industry, it's easy to find the players and producers.

By interacting with different sales groups, you can spot and differentiate the performers from non-performers — those who talk and those who act. The day of the schmoozer is pretty much gone because there is more accountability these days. As in baseball, you see the results quickly.

Sales reps who are prolific are highly productive producers. They become productive by setting priorities and working on what produces the best return for their time investment. Even their down time is productive—they send themselves emails and reminders on action items, keep a notepad next to their bed to record ideas at night and they prioritize just about everything in their lives.

In our fire industry markets over 1.2 million firefighters, and another 20,000 people who work for companies serving this market, are active in the marketplace. However, I would estimate that less than 5,000 are true players, who know how to read people, size up situations accurately, act and get things done. They are the players.

Players are found in both the companies and fire departments. They are the influencers, the early adopters, the change agents. They are the people heavily involved in industry associations, speakers at trade shows, and authors in industry publications. Usually, the larger the company or city, the higher the profile.

Karen Burnham, our FAMA executive assistant for over 20 years, commented to me once that the busiest people always raise their hand and contribute the most. That is true in many organizations. My father would tell me, "For everything that you say 'yes' to, there has to be something that you say 'no' to." At the time, he was trying to convince me not to serve on the Metra train board in Chicago after Dan Cronin, our DuPage County Chair, encouraged me to serve. I have a lot of respect for Dan and other public servants, but in my case, I should have listened to my dad. It was a clear case of, "No good deed goes unpunished," especially since I had no affinity for the cause and knew this was a "train wreck" waiting to happen.

The City of Charlotte, NC, is one of the highest profile fire departments in the U.S. Its former fire chief, Luther Fincher, is probably the most revered and respected chief in the country. Jon Hannan was his protégé and served as chief until August of 2017. We worked on them for over 20 years, trying to get them to purchase Darley pumps. Jason Darley, our national pump sales manager, was finally able to achieve this goal in the last few years by working closely with its head of fleet services, Captain Buddy Caldwell. The department's pain was personalized service, coupled with a reliable product, some proprietary features and training. Once the Charlotte Fire Department became a Darley customer, it quickly became a Darley Demander. We achieved similar results with Boston, Edmonton and other high-profile city departments.

Studies in our industry show that word of mouth is more influential than trade shows or advertising. Most industries have a publication which will share this type of research. When you can find the players in your market and influence them, they can be your key to opening opportunities and increasing the adoption rate for your products.

45) *Paralysis/Pause*

Often at some point in the sales process, a stall or pause occurs. The larger the purchase, the longer the pause.

Some customers simply don't want to decide, particularly when the switching costs are high. When you encounter this analysis paralysis, you need to stay in constant communication without being a pest, so it's good to alternate the methods of communication between phone calls and emails.

A customer might stall for a variety of reasons, so it's critical that you find out his true objection so you can address it head on. Sometimes the customer doesn't know why he won't act.

Your job as a salesperson is to learn what is creating his inability to act. When the pause happens, the best recourse is to start asking probing questions, but only when the time is right. Don't pressure a customer. It starts with a follow-up call to let him know how important his business is to your company, and restate your value proposition. Ask for a face-to-face meeting, if appropriate.

Some days you'll able to overcome his objections or inaction, and other times you won't. If he flat out tell yous he is not interested, know when to walk away and be graceful. Keep the customer on your follow-up list and remain cordial and helpful. Have patience. He will come around when the time is right.

46) *Patience*

Typically, salespeople don't have much patience. But if you are persistent and continue to knock on doors, you will find that customers at some point feel an obligation to work with you or throw you a bone.

In certain situations, it's good to slow it down. At times, the power of silence is stronger than saying anything. It's good to know when to simply shut up.

Salespeople need to know when to punt on a deal. You need

to decide when to put a potential customer on the backburner and not waste time. Is it worth the effort to convert this customer? Each situation is unique, but don't let it get personal. Always take the high road.

47) *Pace – Be the Pace Setter*

At its most basic level, business is about solving a problem and filling a customer's need — the better and more quickly a company can do that, the more likely it will grow.

At Darley, we cultivate a culture of speed. We view it as a huge competitive advantage over our larger or bureaucratictype competitors. The ability to make decisions and move quickly helps us win and keep customers. Many customers come to expect it. I love this article which talks to this concept:

Inc. Magazine: 4 Reasons Speed is Everything in Business, 2015

If you're a fast-moving company in an industry that is evolving quickly, maintaining your speed is even more important. If you want to learn more on this, read Jason Jennings book *It's Not the Big That Eat the Small, It's the Fast That Eat the Slow.*

When dealing with customers, it's important to keep the ball rolling or else projects seem to die. Whenever possible, be a pacesetter in your sales approach through prompt responses to emails, setting timelines, and gently pushing a prospective client. Many like to keep their email inboxes clean and will respond quickly just to act and not have to look it.

Be extremely careful if you plan to put time pressure on a customer, such as stating that this offer is only good until next week. This approach can be harmful when it comes to relationship selling. No one likes to be pressured. I've walked from deals where I felt this type of pressure simply because I was so angry with the approach. It's a bit like the game played at car dealerships, making you cool your heels while the sales rep goes to talk to the sales manager.

48) *Pivoting*

Successful companies pivot, and are quick to adapt and react to changing environments. Pivoting is the ability to change with the times and bounce back stronger. Some call it resilience.

Eastman Kodak, which thought digital cameras were a fad, put all its eggs in the film basket even years after the digital photography market had taken off. It refused to believe that the digital market would take off, or better said, it wanted to believe that print would always be the choice. Huge mistake.

176

In your business, challenge the status quo. Ask the tough questions about what is working and what is not. Every company and sales rep needs to reinvent themselves to change when old methods aren't working due to changing market conditions, such as new competition or technology.

General Peter Schoomaker would say, "No plan survives first contact." When that initial plan fails, you need to pivot. Ideally, one should anticipate charge far enough in advance, so you're not trying pivot when it's too late.

49) *Panorama/Patterns*

My grandfather was a big picture guy. I envision him telling the story of two salesmen from Chicago who sailed to Africa in the early 1900s. They were sent to see if there was an opportunity for selling shoes. They wrote a telegram back to their Chicago office: "Situation Hopeless. Stop. They don't wear shoes." The CEO responded: "Glorious opportunity. They don't have any shoes, yet."

Successful sales and business executives look at the big picture and the big opportunities that exist. It often takes little more time and effort to go after big opportunities than it does a small one.

Daniel Burnham, the famed architect who helped to rebuild Chicago after the Great Chicago Fire of 1871, was known for his famous quote, "Make no little plans; they have no magic to stir men's blood."

Moving too quickly on strategic issues can prevent you from seeing the big picture. Step back and look at megatrends taking place throughout the world, but also study the trends in your industry and company. Patterns can be very telling and provide a roadmap for where the market is headed.

Working your way up the sales promotion channel, your managers will be looking for people who can think outside their scope of work and see the big picture. What you've learned along the way in the trenches offers a perspective that most of your managers might not be aware of. When you can translate that experience into meaningful strategy to help the company, you will get noticed.

50) *Paradigm Shift*

Some pivoting can be so strong that it creates paradigm shifts within the market. Thinking outside the box can lead to changing the paradigm. However, it is far easier to talk about paradigm shifts than to create them. Major breakthroughs are generally going to be driven by data and addressing a customer's latent need that no one else has touched on. Unfortunately, it doesn't happen very often.

Everyone knows the story of Henry Ford, who supposedly once said, "If I were to ask my customers what they wanted, they would have said, 'a faster horse.'" He thought outside the box and gave them something they didn't know they needed. Ford did not invent the automobile; what he invented was a way to make them faster, cheaper and, thus, more accessible to everyone. Thirty years ago, nobody told Chrysler that its customers wanted a minivan, but it was a huge paradigm shift that had a great run.

Often customers do not understand a latent need they have. But if you collectively scour the environment and understand your customers' true needs, and combine that knowledge with your experience and the collective industry wisdom, you might come up with an innovation that can truly be industry changing. Darley was founded, in large part, on innovation and it's still embedded in our culture. My nephew, Matt Darley, is helping to ensure that we are focused on emerging trends and technologies that will transform our industry.

The U.S. Fire Service, it has been said, is 200 years of tradition unimpeded by change or progress. Paradigm shifts in most industries take some time to catch on. But if you can get to those early adopters or those willing to explore new innovations, people who aren't afraid to go out on a limb, you might be able to change the status quo, which will give you a strong competitive advantage.

I was fortunate to be part of one paradigm shift. In 2006, Darley began working with Pierce Manufacturing, a division of Oshkosh Corporation. We collaborated on a unique custom pump project called the PUC, which was initially an acronym for "Pump Under the Cab," and later "Pierce Ultimate Configuration." Traditionally, fire trucks had a pump compartment (or pump module, as we call them) behind the cab that was 60 to 80 inches long. Along with Pierce, we realized that the fire service was changing.

Fewer fires happen today than 40 years ago due to better electrical codes, building materials, fire sprinkler systems and fewer smokers. In 1975, fire trucks rolling out of the station were responding to a fire about 40 percent of the time. In 2016, it was less than 4 percent of the time. Fire departments are busier today than ever, but most of calls are for Emergency Medical Services (EMS) and other non-fire related calls. While the number of fire calls are fewer, the fires being fought are larger and costlier than ever.

Just as the role of firefighters has changed, departments needed a truck to respond to their new reality. For a variety of reasons, full-time, professional fire departments still send a fire truck on each EMS call. As a result, they need these trucks to be maneuverable and have more compartment space to handle the equipment to meet their new responsibilities. Fire departments also need trucks that can fight large scale fires when called upon.

Keeping the changing dynamics in mind, we worked closely with a Pierce team. It included industry change leaders such as Mike Moore, Chad Trinkner, Clarence Grady, John Schultz, Brian Piller and others. We gathered data, talked with our customers, and, collaborating with them, we developed a patented pump design that mounted underneath the cab of the fire truck, thus eliminating the large module behind the cab. This allows for a shorter wheelbase, which gave PUC vehicles better maneuverability. It also offers unique features that a traditional fire truck doesn't have, such as allowing firefighters to put the pump into operation more easily, easier maintenance of the pump and engine, easier access to the discharge hose storage, and significantly increasing the amount of compartment space. It became the first true multipurpose firefighting vehicle.

When Pierce first introduced the new PUC model, some customers did not like the untraditional look. But it didn't take long for the concept to catch on. Those traditionalists who initially said, "No, that's not for me," have come around.

In less than 10 years, Pierce created a huge industry paradigm shift to multi-purpose vehicles. Because our team was involved in creating the new model, we were both able to register some patents, and it has ended up revolutionizing the fire service. Today, it is the single most popular fire truck sold in the U.S., with more than 2,000 trucks in service since its introduction — this is in a market that builds about 3,000 pumpers a year.

Reflecting on this paradigm shift, Mike Moore at Pierce comments, "We really listened to the voice of the customer. They knew what the problems were, but they just didn't have the product to solve that issue." Using its engineering and new product development strengths, teamed with Darley, Pierce radically change the market.

Pierce recently came to us to develop another new pump product. We are proud to have partnered with it on the largest pump ever produced for the fire service. This new pump produces over 10,000 gallons per minute (GPM) from a pressurized source and over 5,750 GPM when pumping from draft. Pierce assembled a similar team as it had when developing the PUC, but this one also included Allen Huelsebusch, an Industrial Products Specialist from Pierce dealer Siddons-Martin, and Dave Fieber of Pierce. We believe this pump has achieved a new world record for the highest flow from a truck mounted firefighting pump.

Our chief engineer, Wayne Hable, and G4 family member, Kyle Darley, did an incredible job developing this new record setting pump. Wayne recently earned his Master's in Engineering from the University of Wisconsin at Madison with straight A's. Kyle is currently enrolled in the same program.

Pierce introduced this new industrial pumper at the FRI show in Charlotte in July 2017 and produced the below video that was released on Facebook the morning the show opened. It went viral and within 24 hours had over 100,000 views (over 200,000 within a week). The power of social media is amazing.

Facebook: Pierce High Flow Industrial Truck Video

Matt McLeish, the Pierce Vice President of Sales and Marketing, preaches about the importance of Aptitude, Attitude and Activity. According to Matt, "Meaningful, productive differences are achieved by those who possess the capacity, invest the will and put forth the effort." This new industrial truck was certainly an example of this and could potentially be another paradigm shift.

SECTION III

YOU'VE MADE IT TO THE C-SUITE! NOW WHAT?

Chapter 11

Transitioning from a Salesperson to a Leader

"Ideas are a commodity; execution of them is not."

Michael Dell

The essence of this book is about relationships and how a salesperson can increase sales and make the transition to business leader by using emotional intelligence and authentic leadership as a catalyst.

Great salespeople don't always become good managers or C-Level employees, just as not every great ballplayer is a great manager or even a great coach. It's been said Ted Williams, perhaps the greatest hitter baseball has ever seen, wasn't a good hitting coach because he couldn't translate what he did with the bat to others. His skills and knowledge as a superior hitter remained locked away, unavailable to the players he was trying to help.

It is true that leaders come in all forms. Some subscribe to the theory that an organization can only grow as much as the leader is capable. Others believe the company is limited to or only capable of what the team supporting him can provide. My thoughts lie somewhere in the middle.

No one book or class is ever going to provide an exact blueprint to make someone a successful CEO. But this article from McKinsey in August 2016 talks to the summary of interviews with 600 CEOs and claims to have bottled the process:

McKinsey: CEO Transitions. The Science of Success

There is certainly no substitute for experience — it takes time, patience, education and much self-examination. In 2004, HBR printed this excellent article, written by Harvard's Michael Porter, Jay Lorsh, and Nitin Nohria, which has some great tips for new CEOs:

HBR: 7 Surprises for New CEOs 2004

Of course, the ideas of what makes CEOs successful are constantly changing. This excellent study released in the June 2017 issue of HBR in an article titled, *What makes CEOs different,* is one of the best that I've read! It's hard to argue with anything here:

HBR: What sets successful CEOs Apart, June 2017

This study followed 17,000 executives over a 10-year period and found that the top performers demonstrate four specific business behaviors:

1. They're decisive, realizing they can't wait for perfect information and that a wrong decision is better than no decision

2. They engage for impact, working to understand the priorities of stakeholders and then aligning them around a goal of value creation

3. They adapt proactively, keeping an eye on the long term and treating mistakes as learning opportunities

4. They deliver results in a reliable fashion, steadily following through on commitments

This section of *Sold!* focuses on lessons I've learned running a business over the years. Some lessons came from mistakes I've made; some I've avoided by watching others make them. Hopefully, this can help you as you make the leap from sales to the C-suite, and give you guidance once you get there. If you're not there yet, you can use the material to get noticed by making suggestions to make your company more customer focused and profitable.

Get Noticed in Your Organization by Offering Solutions to Problems

The first step is to get noticed. An individual gets positively noticed by management with the same skills he or she uses to make sales. Sell yourself so you get noticed. Exceed expectations, follow up, deliver results and don't complain unless you have a suggestion that is fair to all parties. Do those things consistently and you'll already be far ahead of the vast majority of your peers who also have their sights set on moving up the organization.

One of the best ways a salesperson can impress executive level leaders is to solve the problems he comes across. As it's said, "Don't bring me problems; bring me solutions." A salesman recognized as someone who solves issues, moves the ball forward, and is a team player will move up the corporate food chain quickly.

No manager wants a subordinate who is constantly complaining about co-workers or policies without a solution. Many "rock star" sales reps become "falling stars" if they don't play well in the sandbox. Being a team player and getting along well with others is critical if you want to advance your career.

As I look through our organization, I'm constantly assessing who should take the next step with more leadership roles. In some respects, we look for people who are the squeaky wheels, but only when they offer specific ideas for improvements. We want individuals who take their marching orders, provide feedback and then buy in and charge the hill. The average age of a new CEO for a *Fortune 500* company is 52 years old, so if you're in a large organization, you need to get recognized early.

Too many employees need regular reminders, which doesn't necessarily mean that they're bad employees; it just doesn't bode well when it comes to leadership. Twenty years ago, Dan Peters, who is a close friend and president of Emergency One, the second largest fire apparatus OEM in the U.S., put it this way, "I'll never hire anybody who I have to follow up with. If I delegate a task I'm going to consider it done. If I later find out the action hasn't been accomplished, that person is generally not going to be on our team very long." We were talking about salespeople at the time, but it's a concept that applies to many areas. If you can't complete a task on time, at least let people know in advance and advise when they can expect to receive it.

Some salespeople get promoted simply because they've managed to stay around. Maybe they were good once and have become lazy. They're not so bad that it's worth firing them, but they certainly don't inspire, either. The problem with that kind of team member is they will scare away your best talent. Worse yet is the poor salesman, someone who can't do the simple blocking and tackling — getting his expense reports on time, or completing follow-up calls. If they can't even do that, they probably can't handle additional responsibility. Too often sales reps prove to be this way, and it quickly disqualifies them from moving up the corporate ladder.

20 Lessons about Business that I've Learned the Hard Way

I've learned the basics of running a business are simple: come up with a product that people need, produce and sell it at a reasonable price, and treat people fairly — all people. You need to make a profit, but don't let money be your only driver.

For leaders brought into the C-suite, the first 100 days are most critical and can set the tone for what's to come. I became president of our company in 1998. I remember well that my first goals were simply, "Be humble. Try to earn respect. Learn from successful leaders. Don't screw it up!" Almost 25 years later, those still apply.

Jack Welch was the top business leader at the time, and I honed in on his actions. I still remember he wrote, "The three most important metrics to measure a business' health are: 1) employee engagement, 2) customer satisfaction, and 3) cash flow." I took that to heart and still do. I would expand with the following 20 lessons:

Lesson No. 1: Take care of your customers at all costs, be their advocate and treat people like you want to be treated.

186

Tony Pierotti (No. 2) and I have been friends since the first grade and we even went to college together. Today, we live across the street from each other. When I began soliciting selling ideas from friends and business associates for this book in 2011, he was the first to respond. Tony is the president of Fairborn Equipment Co., a business he co-founded in 2001. He is one hell of a salesman, too! It's become quite the success story by taking care of its customers at all costs. As with our company, it's imbued in his culture. "You can't nickel and dime your customers," he says. "They simply won't come back if they feel that you are." Tony delivers LMB service to his best customers, and his team does, too.

Tony has many highly-qualified service technicians who are in the field installing and servicing loading dock lifts and other accessories. These folks are the face of the company with customers. He empowers the technicians to make decisions that are right for the customer while the technicians are on the jobsite.

Err on the side of the customer

Long-term relationships are first built during customer contacts or "touch points." I constantly preach that, when dealing directly with a customer, we must always err on the side of the customer. I stress that employees will never be reprimanded for taking care of customer too much in terms of empowering them to correct a customer service situation on the spot

It's easy to put into practice. Tell all your employees that they may, without additional authorization, spend up to $200 to take care of an unhappy customer. As an executive, you'll be too busy running your company. You don't want to be dealing with a $200 problem, so empower your people to take care of an unhappy customer on the spot. Our middle and upper managers have higher dollar thresholds to ensure prompt action is taken.

Make sure that if a discrepancy occurs, your staff is empowered to say, "I apologize. Hey, we are going to take care of you right now, and I will personally credit your account. Have we resolved this matter to your complete satisfaction?" It's a good practice to then send the customer a hand-written note or small gift.

What happens when you're right and the customer is wrong? Even if they're wrong, take the customer's perspective if you want him for the long-term. We all know the saying, Rule No. 1 is, "The customer is always right." Rule No. 2 is, "When the customer is wrong, see Rule No. 1." If it happens consistently with the same customer, either you have a process problem or a customer problem. It may be best to quietly and discreetly "fire" that customer, as I can assure you, he is most likely not as profitable as you might think.

Ritz-Carlton, a leader in the luxury lodging field, empowers its employees to take care of its customers. Ritz-Carlton has become a leading brand by rigorously adhering to its own high standards. It is the only service company in America that has won the Malcolm Baldrige National Quality Award twice. Its unique culture starts with the motto, "We are ladies and gentlemen serving ladies and gentlemen." One of its extraordinary policies permits every employee to spend up to $2,000 on any guest to ensure he or she is satisfied.

Nordstrom department store is another shining example. This 130-year-old family business is known for accepting returns regardless of reason or time. It has even accepted snow tires from a customer, even though it has never sold tires in its history. This policy is profitable for Nordstrom because many people will buy things with the idea that they will return items when they do not, which in marketing speak is called the "endowment effect." It's kind of like taking a puppy or a car home for a day to see if you like it. Few get returned.

Nordstrom also takes great care of their best customers through an effective loyalty program—this includes my wife, Heidi. In fact, I've asked Heidi to sprinkle my ashes in front of the store by our home when I die. That way, she can visit me every day. ☺

Under-Promise and Over-Deliver

You've heard the expression, "a baker's dozen." Do you know where it came from? Bread used to be the primary source of food in many societies. In the Middle Ages, laws went into effect requiring bakers to sell bread at a certain weight. Selling underweight loaves carried a strict punishment, up to and including the loss of a limb. To avoid running afoul of the law, and to keep customers happy, bakers began giving customers 13 buns instead of 12. Even after the law ended, bakers noticed that their customers were happier because they got more than they paid for. "Gee," they said, "that baker is my friend. I got a really good deal." Bakers rewarded their best customers, which led to long-term relationship sales.

How does the baker's dozen apply to business today? Zig Ziglar, one of the most prominent sales gurus of the past 50 years, focuses on this concept in his books and speeches. Ziglar's premise relative to sales is that the value of goods and services immediately diminishes upon receipt.

For example, the moment you drive that new car out of the parking lot, you think, "I overpaid," or "I should have bought the other model." You get a new couch at home, and your wife says, "We should have gotten the black one." On any substantial purchase, it's a natural inclination. Typically, the more expensive the product, the greater the buyer's remorse. Closer to home, virtually every consumer is convinced their cable and wireless phone companies are out to screw them.

To counteract buyer's remorse, a salesperson should under-promise and over-deliver. This is particularly important after the moment of truth when the transaction is completed. Lexus will wash your car every time you bring it in for an oil change. United Airlines will add 500 free miles to your account if a flight is late due to mechanical problems. Our company sends a small box of Red Hots candies with each shipment. The box says, "If you are not completely satisfied, please call us so we can improve our service."

We preach this slogan everywhere — from the inside of our catalog covers to the back of our business cards.

Create Raving Customers and Fans

I learned about raving customers, or Darley Demanders, long before I worked at Darley.

When I was in high school, my father needed some dental work. Late one night, he was suffering from a massive tooth abscess. He called his dentist, Dr. John Lynch, saying, "I hate to bother you at this late hour. I need to make an appointment for tomorrow. I'm in awful pain." This dentist asked if my father could do it right away. He picked up my father at our home and drove him to the dentist office, where he relieved him of the pain immediately. My father became a "Dr. Lynch Dental Disciple" that evening. My father has sung his praises for years.

Today, Dr. Lynch's dental practice is incredibly successful; he has several offices around Chicago. He began delivering excellent customer service in an industry that was never known for its customer service — it became a huge point of difference. It's reflected in everything he does. My sister-in-law, Karen Darley, is a dentist in his office and she has the same approach to customer service.

The Mayo Clinic is similar. Not only does it attract the best doctors in the world, but when you are scheduled for an appointment at 1:20 p.m., the doctor sees you at that exact time. It is a model in operational efficiency, it treats its customers with respect, and doesn't make its patients wait.

If you execute on the above and still have a customer who is difficult to deal with or unhappy, it might be time to gently let that customer move on. You want to do business with customers that share your values.

Lesson No. 2: Watch your costs/Watch your cash/Understand your financials

This lesson covers everything from your manufacturing costs, to hiring, to staying in moderately priced hotel rooms. Small things add up. Grandma Darley would be proud that I still use coupons when I pick up our weekly Sunday night pizza for the family.

If you are a smaller company and you aren't already operating with a financial budget, it should be one of your first moves. Seemingly insignificant things add up and performing against a budget lets you concentrate on the positive and negative variances quickly.

Don't try to expand your business until you have a clear handle on costs. If you have significant budget variances or aren't making money when your business is small, the problems will only get larger when you grow.

Sales execution costs are among the highest budget item for any company, especially as it rolls out new products or enters new markets. For some reason, these costs don't undergo the same scrutiny and justification process as things like capital budgeting.

Negotiate with your suppliers, but be respectful when you do. Nearly everything is negotiable, and if you're going to negotiate with your vendors, make sure you have all the facts upfront to leverage your position. Remember to trade things that are of lesser value to the other party, remember your BATNA, and don't be a jerk. You will find that most suppliers will respect your business acumen if you negotiate with honor.

Many companies will delay payment to vendors to make better use of cash, and suppliers know which customers consistently do. While it might preserve some cash, it's bad practice to string out vendors. That said, it's generally a better long-term strategy to negotiate longer payment terms or prompt payment discounts from your vendors. If you can get "2 percent 10 NET 30" payment terms, and pay in 10 days, that 2 percent discount equals 43 percent interest annualized on your money. You are way better off paying promptly with the 2 percent discount and borrowing from your bank at substantially lower rates. If you go this route, don't play games, and pay in 20 or 30 days and still take the discount. That's weak and underhanded.

190

Today, we write a fraction of the checks that we used to, as most of our payments are made via ACH. Our vendors get the payment on the same day that it leaves our bank and we save at least $3 per check because we're not cutting, signing and mailing live checks. This change is just one of the improvements recently implemented by our new CFO, John Gruber. John lives in our hometown and went to Marquette and Kellogg. He was well-vetted and is an excellent addition to our team.

Another important point comes from John Sztykiel, the former CEO of our largest supplier Spartan Motors: "Companies don't go out of business because they lose money; they go out of business because they run out of cash." Constantly monitoring your cash is critical, especially if you're growing quickly. Everyone says cash is king. I say, cash is everything! It is the lifeblood of every organization, and without cash flow to keep your business open, nothing else matters.

As part of our overall value proposition, we are lenient with smaller customers who have cash flow problems. While not always the best use of my time, I personally pay a great deal of attention to our accounts receivable. And over the years, we've only been burned a handful of times by customers going out of business. If your net operating margin is 5 percent (which is higher than most companies), and you are forced to write off a $50,000 bad debt for a customer, you need to generate $1 million in other business at this same margin to make up for this loss. Our credit manager, Samika Thompson, is a 20-year employee who does a great job managing our customer credit. When Samika decided to pursue a college degree 10 years ago, our company helped pay for it. A wise investment in our people.

Continually focus on your financial statements. You should know and understand your income statement, balance sheet, and cash flow statement 100 percent. Focus on the areas where you have positive and negative variances to budget and compare to prior years. What are you doing to increase assets and create shareholder value on your balance sheet? Be sure that you benchmark your organization against other companies in your industry. Companies like Sageworks collect this data from banks and other sources. Your banker or accounting firm should be able to provide it to you at no cost. Due to the diversification of our business, we blend and weigh data from different industries using varying North American Industry Classification System (NAICS) codes.

Other than the obvious ones, some of the ratios that I watch closely are return on equity compared to the stock market, return on invested capital, and profits per employee. We seldom hire when profits per employee is on the decline. When looking at extending credit to customers, we use financier Bobby Sanfillipo's favorite metric, which is the quick ratio. This is a measure of how well a company can meet its short-term financial liabilities (aka the acid-test ratio) which can be calculated as follows: (Cash + Marketable Securities + Accounts Receivable) / Current Liabilities.

Lesson No. 3: Stay with your long-term vision and plan, but be adaptable and pivot quickly

One of the great things about running a privately-held business is that you don't need to report to Wall Street on a quarterly basis. As a result, you can focus on the long term.

While your shorter-term tactics and strategies can and should change to adapt to shifting market conditions, stick to your long-term vision. At Darley, we have a 100-year plan to make sure that we keep our long-term vision, but we're constantly modifying our shorter term one-year and five-year plans based on changing market conditions.

Concentrate your efforts on things that add the most value to the organization and ensure that your employees are informed, empowered and working on the most important things. If you're doing the same thing today that you were doing two years ago, you need to step back and make sure you are focused on what's most important now.

Leonard Greenhalgh, a professor at Tuck, said it best: "In this era of globalization, no organization can assume its current competitive advantage is sustainable."

As you move up the corporate ladder, the decisions that you make will generally have higher stakes. Being quantitively quirky, years ago I created a simple spreadsheet that helps me to analyze any key decision. Below is a sample that my daughter, Audrey, and I used in 2003 when looking at colleges for her. For any situation, identify criteria important to you and then put a weight on it that reflects how important it is. Quality and fit/feel/size were most important to her. She went to the University of Illinois based on the highest score of 8.35 and her sister, Maggie, followed in her footsteps two years later. A great fit for both.

Audrey Darley College Search						11/1/2003
Criteria	Quality	Distance	Fit/Feel/Size	Price/Value	Catholic	Total Weighted Score
Weight	30%	15%	25%	20%	10%	100%
Miami of Ohio	8	5	10	6	0	6.85
Marquette	8	10	8	7	10	8.2
Illinois	9	9	8	10	0	**8.35**
Wisconsin	9	9	5	7	0	6.7
Northwestern	10	10	8	8	0	8.1
Notre Dame	10	9	3	7	10	7.5
	Scale is 1 - 10					

I use a similar matrix with most high stakes decision-making from looking at company acquisitions to setting our strategy, and even to capital purchases. It's particularly helpful when looking at acquisitions. In these cases, we always look for acquisitions where 1 + 1 = 3. As a strategic buyer, we don't pay for these synergies.

You can quickly set up a decision-tree spreadsheet like this one on your own or download one from my website at:

Decision Tree Matrix: SoldbyPaulDarley

Not all decisions need to be "this or that" decisions. Sometime the best answer lies somewhere between what initially appears to be the only two options. Going through this decision-making process helps leaders choose the best next steps to execute on strategy.

Lesson No. 4: Execute and hold people accountable

Planning and adjusting your plan are the fun and easy parts. Execution of the plan is the difficult part. Execution can only happen with collaboration from your entire team, and it's critical that your management team and others are capable to help you with implementation. Execution happens when passion and ambition meet. If there is no movement toward a goal, then your people are not working on the right thing.

For a great read on execution, I highly recommend *Execution: The Disciple of Getting Things Done*, by Lawrence Bossidy and Ram Charan. I first read it in 2002 when it came out. My main take-away was when you meet with your team on executing, you should have written minutes stating who is going to do what and by when. These should be shared with the entire team, so people are held accountable.

You can quickly see who produces and who doesn't. In short, delegate with specific action items and timeframes. It creates accountability.

Here is a link to the best quotes from the book:

Larry Bossidy & Ram Charan: Best Quotes from *Execution*

At Darley, to ensure we execute on our plan, we have a detailed tactical spreadsheet that lists what we are going to do, who is going to do it, due dates, and a "red, yellow, green" box showing progress. We share this spreadsheet with all our employees. Below is a snapshot of this.

Employee and Business Development	Build partnerships with our customers, suppliers and employees that develop opportunities and continue to make us competitive. Foster an environment of teamwork while continuing to create a professional high-tech image.			
Initiative	Tactics	Owner	Status	Last Change
Acquisitions	Target companies for acquisition and focus on companies in growth areas of fire and defense and core markets. Ideally Midwest pump manufacturing. Look at companies where we can leverage our marketing, operations and engineering expertise	PCD	Yellow	7/15/2017
	Assess current divisions for profitability and strategic fit	PCD	Green	10/1/2017
	Be careful not to over extend our ourselves in terms of debt levels	PCD	Green	10/1/2017
	Establish formal strategic alliances with key vendors	PCD	Green	9/1/2017
Financial Management	Constantly watch our cash position.	JG	Green	10/1/217
	Better Dashboard Reporting	JG	Green	8/6/2017
	Analysis of proper debt levels for maximum return while keeping a conservative approach to debt	JG	Green	9/1/2017
	Strong banking relationships with two key banks	JG/PCD	Green	5/1/2017

To make it more manageable for most employees, we synthesize our plan into a one-page document each year. This strategy keeps everyone focused on where we are headed. I'm always proud to see how many of our employees prominently post these annual goals and core values in their cubicles or shop work stations.

As an aside, I once came upon an employee who had a calendar that had "X" on past dates. That might be okay if you're in prison, but not at Darley company. It was immediately removed.

Lesson No. 5: Build a strong team that collaborates

I learned this early in my career. I remember "typing" a follow-up letter to a customer after a meeting at his plant. I made a literal "carbon copy" of the letter and shared it with my father. I anxiously awaited his "atta-boy" for a job well done. Instead, the letter came back to me, and he had circled all the places where I used the word "I." His simple note at the bottom was, "We are a 'we' company, not an 'I' company. No one does it alone." At Darley, every one of our employees refers to our company as "our company," regardless of their role.

As future leaders move up the corporate ladder, positions become fewer and farther between. The rungs on the ladder are narrower and farther apart. The higher you climb, the more peers you're leaving behind, which means on the way up, you must be careful not to knock others off their path.

Those who can build teams and help others to succeed while they're moving up the ladder will be more successful once they reach the C-suite. It's paradoxical, but the only way to earn or keep power is to give it away and empower others … in any relationship. When team members support one another, they build trust and mutual respect. They support each other. Executives need buy-in from coworkers to succeed, and that cooperation is not likely to come from people who feel you haven't had their back over the years, especially during demanding times. You can tell a great deal about an employee by observing how he reacts to adversity or a stressful situation.

In 2000, Heidi and I had a chance to meet George H.W. Bush (President No. 41) along with his wife, Barbara, at a function in Chicago. Barbara told a story of her son George W. Bush (President No. 43) coming home from a lacrosse game in high school. Barbara asked how it went, and George responded, "I got three goals." Barbara snapped back, "How did the team do?" That's a good lesson in teamwork and collaboration that has stuck with me ever since.

Collaboration is more important today than ever before, and once in the C-suite, you can't get anything done without it.

Lesson No. 6: Empower your people, then delegate

At an early age, my father told me, "Paul, if there is anything that you are doing that someone else could be doing, especially if they are better at it or lower paid, then they should do it, not you. You should concentrate on those things that give us the bang for the buck on your time and salary."

That moment with my father was over 30 years ago, but I still remember his advice like it was yesterday and I practice it daily. Because I have empowered her with the ability to do so, my executive assistant, Dawn Hjelmgren, is excellent at taking over tasks she sees me doing which she is capable of handling. She understands that my time can be better spent doing the things I'm best at.

When you reach the C-suite, don't get caught up in the "operational weeds" of your business. This concept is easier said than done, and historically I've have been a terrible example. If your team is incapable of handling it to your satisfaction, that is another conversation. But it should not be the reason for failing to delegate.

You will still need to put out fires, but it's more important that you plant seeds after the fire. If you're in the office 50 percent of the time, it's too much. The CEO should be out visiting customers, vendors, employees at other locations, and taking time to learn from others. When in the office, take time to slowly walk through the office.

Empowerment is one of our company's core values. We make sure our people are empowered to take the actions necessary to get the job done. Leaders must motivate their people, make sure that they're on track, and continue to communicate with them. Conveying information is particularly key when implementing new strategies or initiatives.

We conduct about 50,000 customer transactions each year, and things are bound to go wrong even with the best practices in place. If it's a process issue, fix the issue. The longer challenges go on, the more upset customers naturally get. No one likes the runaround.

When you move into new markets, empowerment becomes even more critical. You need to rely on their tacit knowledge to help you understand the market.

If someone is always looking for direction, he is not properly managed or self-motivated. At our company, we implemented a permission-based system called the "Ladder of Leadership." When an employee is facing an issue that may be outside his Job Responsibility and Authority (JRA) and he feels he needs approval, he advises his boss, "I intend to" take the following action … and 95 percent of the time, the employee is on the right path, as he is closest to the situation. This concept was developed in the U.S. military.

U.S. Navy Submarine Captain David Marquee takes this one step further with his "intent based leadership" theories outlined in his book, *Turn Around the Ship*. As a nuclear submarine captain, rather than have every person in his crew ask for his permission, they instead advise the captain *what they intend to do*. He can reject their suggestion, but 99 percent of the time, he agrees. It's a good lesson in time management, delegation and empowerment. Check out his YouTube video if you get a chance:

You Tube: Captain David Marquee, 2013

This concept of pushing decision-making down in the

196

organization came about in the late 20th century. It sounds simple, but when approached by an employee looking for direction on an issue that he is grappling with, simply asking, "What do you think we should do?" can be extremely powerful and empowering. The employee knows that you value his opinion, and he usually has the best answer.

As you begin to remove yourself from day-to-day operations, you might not be aware of all the dynamics surrounding a situation, so be mindful of "Seagull Management." This is where you go into meetings and situations where you are not fully aware of what's going on, you issue directives, and then move on. Think of the seagull that flies in, takes a crap, and flies away.

Lesson No. 7: Take care of your employees—especially the great ones

Ask CEOs about their most important asset, and they are quick to respond, "My employees." I won't dispute that, but it's only the productive and happy employees who are the greatest asset. I'd argue that employees who are not productive and happy should not be on your team.

Once you get the right people on board, you must take care of them and develop them. Successful executives understand the people who work under them. They know how to motivate them, engage with them, and ensure they are collaborative team members. Great leaders don't create followers; they create other leaders.

Treat your people right and fair, and it will be reflected in everything from employee turnover to customer satisfaction. When an adversarial person and situation negatively influences your team, get all the facts and address it quickly. It may hurt you in the short-term, but problems are likely only going to get worse. I've seen it time and time again, there is a huge sense of relief among everyone once this person is gone. We generally look to our "no jerks" policy and find the answer there.

Lesson No. 8: Communicate, Communicate, Communicate

Communication is critical. This rule applies, of course, to all stakeholders—suppliers, customers, shareholders and employees. Successful leaders must communicate effectively up and down channels. They show the same level of respect to the CEO as they do to the janitor.

One reason successful salespeople make good leaders is because of their ability to "read" people and convey a message. They're able to communicate a story and win over customers.

When communicating with employees, make sure your message is consistent and uncomplicated. It's good to be natural and engaging, but stick to the big message. For the past 20 years, we have an annual company theme that employees can understand and relate to, which is generally focused on the one thing that is most important to the company. I learned this from Jim Russell, who built a highly successful company that he sold to a private equity group. He has gone on to start several new companies since then, all in very fast-growing markets.

In the mid-1990s, we were growing fast and adding a lot of employees — mostly skilled laborers to run our machining centers and build fire trucks. We were hiring primarily from companies in very tough union environments which had shut down due, in part, to challenges with unions. We hired many of those people without doing proper vetting. In 1997, the employees at our main plant voted to join the Teamsters Union. We never thought that would happen, and we lost by one vote. Three years later, in 2000, several of the new pro-union employees managed to convince the rest of the team to strike. As a family business, we took it very personally. It got ugly. We ended up hiring replacement workers and looked very hard at moving operations out of Northern Wisconsin.

At the last negotiation meeting, the Teamsters flew in a lead negotiator, who said to the union representatives, "You have the best health insurance and the highest wages in the entire county. This company offers you a 15 percent increase over a three-year period, and you morons take them out on strike." That was at 9 o'clock in the morning; 15 hours later we had an agreement that did not include most of the rabble rousers.

The strike marked a challenging time in our company. It reminded us how important it is to have regular communication with our employees. Today we are stronger than ever, and we have few, if any, barriers between our shop and management. If we see issues starting to develop, we address them immediately. We're careful to take the time to educate our employees on what's going on in the industry, who we are as a company, who we are as family, and what we stand for. In short, we make sure that we are taking time to educate them on our culture.

We communicate continually and haven't had a union grievance filed in years. Perhaps our biggest mistake with those new employees was not taking the time to listen closely enough, educate, and inculcate them on the culture of our business. It was our job to remind

198

them why working for our company was a wonderful thing. We were a new, young management team making too many mistakes. Years later, we are still learning.

Lesson No. 9: Lead from the front/Earn it!

Leading a company, fire department, a military platoon or any organization is both a privilege and a huge responsibility; a leader casts a long shadow that everyone is watching.

Growing up in a family business and becoming president at the young age of 35, I always knew that I had to earn it! I took a great deal of pride in being the first one at work and the last to leave for years.

While the first few years are critical, you need to continue to build mutual trust with the people around you and be able to inspire them. Let your team know that you put their interests and the organization's interests first.

Leadership does not come with a title. It is earned each day by the small actions you take while working with people around you. They watch you closely — some inherently want you to fail for one reason or another, but most look to take direction and support you.

It's been said in many different ways, but great bosses are good communicators who share information, hire right, celebrate wins, and are empathetic to the needs of others.

Be the pacesetter, the example setter; be consistent, let your people know where you stand and, most importantly, create other leaders.

At Darley, we're all about creating leaders through our core values including employee empowerment, teamwork and recognition. It's reflected in our 2017 employee engagement scores, which were the highest since we started conducting them over 20 years ago. We trust you also see it in our team's ability to promptly, fairly and respectfully work with you.

Dr. Travis Bradberry recently posted the link below on LinkedIn and the Talent Smart website. Great stuff, but here are the 10 tips if you don't have the time to check out the link:

Talent Smart: 10 Things Great Bosses Do Every Day

- A great boss shares information

- A great boss puts a lot of thought into hiring

- A great boss looks for and celebrates wins

- A great boss is empathetic

- A great boss is accountable

- A great boss says thank you

- A great boss doesn't forget that people have lives outside of work

- A great boss is a great communicator

- A great boss creates leaders

Over the past 10 years, I've had an opportunity to watch and study many military leaders, and the common theme is that they always go first. By doing so, they quickly instill confidence in the troops they lead while earning their respect. If you have a chance, watch the TED Talk video below by Simon Sinek on military leaders. It has more than five million views and could change your entire approach to leadership:

Ted Talk: Simon Sinek, Why Good Leaders Eat Last and Make You Safe

Sinek concludes it all goes back to trust and cooperation. Show your employees and your customers that you care by "having their backs." Never ask others to do something that you wouldn't do yourself.

This same principle applies for all important people in your life. Ken Banaszek, my next-door neighbor, has had my back for over 30 years.

Military heroes naturally respond when asked, "Why would you do such a heroic thing for others without regard for your own safety?" by saying, "Because they would have done it for me."

Lesson No. 10: Hire slowly/Address employees quickly if they're off track/Fire quickly

I ask interview questions that no one can ever prep for in advance. Some questions are quirky — like me — but they can reveal a great deal about a person. By the time they get to me, they are generally well-vetted, so I don't waste time on the trite questions for which they have rehearsed answers.

In addition to asking a potential employee to sell me on the corner of the room (as described earlier), I also ask other questions that can give me a sense of his EQ:

- "What is the population of the U.S.? And the world?" You would be surprised how many people are so far off from the actual U.S. population of about 320 million, while the world's is roughly 7.4 billion

- "How many gas stations do you think there are in the U.S.?" I ask them to answer aloud because I'm more interested in their logic and how they approach it (Roughly 115,000)

- "What type of music do you listen to?" If they like a variety, it generally means that they get along with many different types of employees

- "All things being equal, what do you typically do when approaching a traffic signal that turns yellow? Do you stop or go for it?" For sales reps, I generally want someone who goes for it, but for HR, accounting, or engineering, I prefer someone who stops

I have about 25 different questions. While I generally don't socialize with our employees much, if I am hiring for a sales rep position, I always ask myself, "Is this someone who I would like to have a beer with?" This one question is a show stopper for many potential employees.

If I don't receive a follow-up email from a candidate within 24 hours of the interview, that also tells me about this person's drive, passion and persistence. Almost without exception, I will not hire them if I don't get a follow-up email.

Twenty-five years ago, I had a non-productive employee leave, and my response was one of relief. I remember informing my father of the good news that this employee was moving on. His response was, "Shame on you. If the employee wasn't good for the team, you should have done something earlier." He was right.

If we have a non-performer, we always try to get the employee back on track before parting ways. We put him on a formal Performance Improvement Plan (PIP), and if he can't improve to our standards, it's time for the person to move on, and everyone is better off.

I always say to our employees that there are no bars on our windows. No one should ever stay here if he feels he can do better elsewhere for himself or his family. I have one request; let's be sure to discuss it before you start to look at options outside of Darley. If it's in our mutual best interests, we should first look at improving the current situation that is concerning them.

Ask any CEO or manager and he will tell you that firing someone is the worst part of the job. Firing a person is difficult, and most leaders fail to fire soon enough. I am certainly one of them. For larger scale work reductions or layoffs, most CEOs will say, "You should cut deep with a sharp knife." I've never been comfortable with that logic, partially because of the loyalty and longevity of our employees.

In either case, part of it is the family culture and job-for-a-lifetime mentality that permeates our business, which is not all bad if the people are producing. Most business people will tell you that this approach is unhealthy and I tend to agree, But I err on the side of the employee if he has been a long-standing, loyal, hard-working employee. We try to get him on a PIP first.

When we have an employee who is a habitual problem, putting him on a PIP clearly lays out the specific changes that need to be made by specific dates, and the consequences if he don't attain an improved level of performance. Too often, poor performing employees change for a while and then slip back into their same old habits. It's best to have it laid out clearly, communicate on their progress, and have them sign the PIP.

Properly reprimanding an employee takes understanding and finesse. Far too often bosses forget the employees on the other end of their words have feelings. Below is the Liautaud Institute's *Eight Steps for the Emotionally Intelligent Reprimand* for providing a proper reprimand or "Inspirational Feedback."

1. MAKE IT PRIVATE: When your anger subsides (and only then), arrange for a personal meeting in a quiet location away from others, and arrange for no interruptions, with phone and computer off

2. MAKE THEM COMFORTABLE: Begin the meeting with the one thing you admire or respect most about them. Tell them you need their input because of the respect you have for them

3. DEFINE THE ISSUE: State exactly what you understand happened, and then ask them for their recollection. (Don't proceed until you both completely agree as to what happened, giving them the edge to minimize the impact)

4. AGREE TO THE CONSEQUENCE: Ask that person how that action negatively affected the company or you personally. (Don't proceed until you have a consensus)

5. AGREE TO THE CORRECTION: Ask what that person might do to correct this situation from happening again. (Let this come from the other party, and then suggest options only if needed. Don't proceed without a consensus)

6. AGREE ON A DATE: Set a date to discuss this topic again, so the other party can report how well he has done

7. CONFIRM YOUR BELIEF IN THE OTHER PARTY: Leave the other party with this, or a similar statement, "The meeting went well, and I'm convinced you'll make this change happen." (People tend to rise to the expectations of those they respect)

8. CONGRATULATE THE OTHER PERSON'S SUCCESS: Let him know that you look forward to your follow-up meeting, and congratulate him on his successes. If he is still a bit short, repeat the process at least once

This process enables the offender to acknowledge his own issue, and be keenly aware of how it affects others. Don't be afraid to print this process out and have the steps in front of you.

We take a less formal approach with some employees. If we have a hard-working employee who may be having personal challenges at home that are affecting his work, we are sympathetic and try to work with him. I'm reminded of my daughter, Audrey, 15 years ago, when she did not make the A volleyball team in 8th grade. She worked hard and the fact that she was cut from the team became a huge driver for her. Her high school was 10 times larger than her grade school, and by her sophomore year, she was named captain of the varsity team. She played with determination and grit. If she made a bad play, her coach would say, "Audrey, I'm not going to beat you up on this, because you're already hard enough on yourself." I try to take that same approach with our hard-working employees who might get off track and just need some guidance.

However, anyone can become a cancer in an organization if his behavior turns sour. It's best for everyone if you can find a way for the person to move on in a respectful manner, if possible. The performance evaluation process, the formal reprimand, and PIP are a few of the ways you can accomplish this task. It's best to have someone one else present during the difficult discussions and document what was discussed during the meetings.

Almost without exception, whenever we let a problem employee go, everyone in the organization feels a sense of relief that this person is gone. We are generally much stronger, even if we felt at the time that this person was indispensable.

Lesson No. 11: Praise others, and take time to celebrate the victories

It's strange. Over the years I've noticed many bosses don't offer praise very often. It's so easy to give and it is free. Sincerely patting employees on the back and thanking them for their efforts goes a long way. Catch your employees doing something right, and they'll repeat that action. Simply put, people who feel truly appreciated will go the extra mile for you.

There is an adage: praise in public and criticize in private. I agree, but why not praise in private, too? Sometimes when praise is one on one, it can be even more powerful.

This may sound difficult to believe, but study after study has shown employees value recognition for their accomplishments, upward mobility, and the ability to make a difference as more important than compensation. This is particularly true with Millennials, but their outlook may change as they begin to raise families and have to meet monthly mortgage payments.

At the beginning of our management meetings, we start with opening comments from each manager and guest on their meeting expectations. After they speak, I always take time to praise each one. I speak from the heart and say whatever comes to the top of my mind. It may be about a recent accomplishment of theirs or a special relationship they've developed. It's never rehearsed. The impact of this public recognition is amazing. I can literally see managers sit up in their chairs as we go around the room. I also encourage others to do the same, and sometimes I will receive praise and sit up, too. It's a simple and effective exercise that helps build stronger business and personal relationships.

This habit works with employees, customers and, well, any relationship. Compliments should be natural. They can't be forced or untrue, nor patronizing. It must be something you truly admire, notice or respect about the person. Sharing those thoughts with that person has an incredibly strong effect on your relationship. Recognizing employees for special efforts or a job well done is a privilege and duty for CEOs and other company leaders.

204

Be careful, though, as your praise must be sincere. Because so few people are willing to offer praise, doing so forges a stronger relationship with the other person when it does happen. It can become a code-shift moment.

It's important to hand out "atta-boys" at every level of the organization, but be careful praising large groups of employees on a project, as this can sometime backfire if those who contributed more feel slighted.

If you praise people regularly, it makes it easier to manage them when they're off track. They're more receptive to criticism when that's not all they hear. It's said that you can learn more from failure than you can from success.

Celebration is another one of our core values, and we're big on celebrating milestones that our employees reach and praising employees for a job well done. In additional to verbal and written acknowledgement of a well-completed task, we have a formal "Board of Praise" that is distributed quarterly. Any employee can nominate a co-worker, but we also include positive feedback from our customers about things that we did right. Too often, employees only hear the negative comments.

When we have a company victory — a large sale, a new safety record, or completing a large order — we always make a point to celebrate and give out heartfelt thanks. The salesman might have been the one to get the customer to sign the contract, but countless support people back at the office helped land that order.

Celebrating wins is the fun and easy part of business, but surprisingly few companies do it. Take time to celebrate employment anniversaries, retirements and extraordinary service to the organization. Recognize employee contributions big and small. It can be little things. I cook a BBQ lunch for all our employees during the summer. They come to the grill and pick up the food and I take a moment to thank each for a job well done and try to extol the servant leadership that my father did so well. Make celebrating a part of your culture.

It's good to celebrate failures too, if you learn from them. This habit is true at work, but also in life's successes and failures. As my forum mate Ozzie Giglio like to say, "If you're not living on the edge, you're taking up too much room." Push the envelope when the time is right.

A leader should limit praise of himself. He gets enough praise from other sources. When things are going well, the CEO must remain humble and deflect praise toward his team. When things go poorly, he should accept the blame.

Lesson No. 12: Get everyone rowing in the same direction. Make sure their goals and actions are aligned with the company's goals

I'm a huge advocate of setting goals. I've seen the power of it time and time again in authentic leaders and the organizations they lead.

Each year, I personally review more than 100 employee evaluations and I always focus on the employees' goals. First, I look to see if they are SMART goals. I don't get hung up on this, but the more Specific, Measurable Actionable, Realistic, and Time-based they are, the better.

Second, I look to see how the employee performed in achieving his goals from the previous year.

Third, and most importantly, are the employee's goals aligned with our company goals? Is this employee working on the right thing? If not, how can his manager and I help him to be more productive?

If you're going to cascade corporate goals through the organization, you must have everyone in your organization aligned. Executives need to be able to explain to their direct reports, in very simple terms, where the company is going and how that employee fits in and can help.

The employee's goals must reflect that direction and be aligned and focused so that everyone is rowing in the same direction. Lastly, the manager must make sure that the employee has the capabilities, training and tools to achieve this. Strategy execution in business is generally not a single major event; instead it is a serious of smaller events. These events are almost always the result of focused, meaningful goals.

I share the below slide with our employees during our annual state of the company address that covers our approach for cascading the company's goals throughout the organization.

To help ensure accountability and help from others, our employees share their goals not only with their bosses, but with their co-workers as well. I'm always proud when I see our corporate goals and the employees' own goals prominently displayed in their cubicles and stapled to the inside of their notebook.

BHAGS – Big Hairy Audacious Goals

Much has been written on Big Hairy Audacious Goals (BHAGs)[17] and most companies tried some version of it. We tried it at our company with mixed results.

About 10 years ago, our company adopted a five-year strategic plan to grow our company from $100 million to $500 million. It was a true BHAG. The first two years we were right on our sales targets, with great incremental growth, but growing at the same compounded percentage rate became insurmountable.

It became a major board topic for us. We asked, "Are these goals too aggressive?" We had some opposing views on our board. One board member said, "You can't set these unrealistic goals, because it's not healthy for the organization. People feel they aren't achieving, even though they're doing a fantastic job." Another asked, "Will your lofty sales goals overtax your production capacity? What about other departments? How can they be engaged in the effort? Will you lose credibility with employees if goals are too lofty? How are employees to align their own goals with unrealistic company goals?"

---

17   BHAG is a term coined by Jim Collins in his best-selling book, "Good to Great"

After two and a half years, we realized we were not going to hit our sales goals for years three through five, so we adjusted our sales forecasts downward. While we failed in achieving our five-year goal, we learned from it and managed to more than double our business during this time.

BHAGS forced us to look at the big picture. As one board members commented when we started our next five-year plan, "We've achieved incredible growth over the past five years. Sometimes when you shoot for the stars, you may just hit the moon."

Personal Goal Setting

Most employees also include their own personal goals. I like to see this as I want them to have balanced lives. During prospective employee interviews, I always ask prospective employees. "Do you set personal goals?" Most everyone quickly responds, "Yes!" But few people can tell me specifically what they are. I've had a few applicants pull them out and show them to me … we offered them a job.

Seven years ago, when my forum mate, Chris Krause, CEO and founder of National Collegiate Scouting Association, was 43 years old, he shared with me his personal life plan that included retiring by the time he was 50 years old, with a $50 million net worth. In my mind, it was a BHAG—a pipedream. Chris ended up exceeding all those goals before he was 50, and now spends time raising his kids, surfing in front of his California home, writing books, and performing part-time consulting for the company he still partially owns with a private equity group. This goal-setting stuff helps you stay focused, and it works. Just ask Chris.

Lesson No. 13: Get organized/Time management/Work on what matters the most/ Stick to your knitting—Work on those things that you enjoy and are good at doing

Those who deliver results are usually the ones who are organized, focused and following processes. We talked a lot about this in Chapter 10, but make sure that you're focused on those things that give you the best return on your time and resource investment.

If you've come up through the sales channel, continue to work your best customers—don't abandon them. Focus on the big opportunities, as they often don't take too much more effort to work than the small ones. Big deals are more likely to happen when a C-Suite employee is active in the sales process. Continue to plant those seeds and work on major opportunities.

To become a leader, a salesperson must understand the overall business environment and not just the environment or silo in which he travels. That understanding includes the various pains, not only of his customers, but the needs of his company's employees. Focus on the biggest issues facing your operations, be it in finance or engineering, and guide them by asking the right questions. You need an understanding of the microeconomic and macroeconomic environments in which your people work.

Leaders also learn about time management. Make the best use of your downtime while on an airplane or in your hotel room at night. When you get home, make sure you focus on your family before diving into work at night. Once your family obligations are met, look at how you spend the time from 7-10 p.m. Are you using it in a productive manner?

Lesson No. 14: Regularly take the pulse of your team— Employee evaluations and employee engagement surveys

You need to know how things are really going in your company. It's good to have people in the organization who tell you like it is. As CEO, you'll be the last one to hear about issues that are brewing in the shop or office. Maintain an open-door policy and don't shoot the messenger when you hear bad news.

Employee Evaluations

We conduct annual employee evaluations. No one likes employee reviews—neither you nor the employee you're evaluating. But at the end of the day, they are necessary for many reasons. Everyone should regularly get formal feedback about how they are doing, so they can be aware of areas where improvement can be made and be praised when they are doing well. It gives you an opportunity to formally let people know how they are doing so that they can continue to do the things that they do well and change the things that need changing. Smart managers focus in on those areas.

The key to an employee evaluation is to focus solely on the process and not bring personalities into it. Limit personal criticism. That said, people do sometimes need to be privately reprimanded for their actions. You never want to embarrass employees in front of their peers. Realistically, employee evaluations are equally important documentation if you need to fire an employee.

Until a decade ago, we used a 10-page annual employee evaluation form that was just brutal. In 2007, after reading an HBR article by business guru Larry Bossidy titled, "What your Boss Expects from you and what you should expect in return," we changed our entire process. Our forms are now two pages and more productive and straightforward for both parties. If employee surveys in your company need improvement, this article can help:

<u>HBR: What your Boss Expects from You and What You Should Expect in Return</u>

You'll note that these employee evaluation forms include a 360-degree evaluation where the employee also evaluates his boss. In addition to these, we also conduct online confidential surveys, where managers get honest and direct feedback to make improvements. Authentic leaders seek honest feedback and it helps in the self-awareness portion of EI.

Whenever an employee leaves our company for any reason, including retirement or being fired, I always conduct an exit interview regardless of his role in the company. I ask him to fill out an exit survey in advance; then we discuss the result in person. Asking for honest and direct feedback on changes that we can be making — and criticism in any area of the company — can be humbling, and incredibly helpful and self-improving. Those leaving usually don't have anything to lose and will give you straight talk. You need to swallow your pride and have big shoulders when you get this feedback.

Employee Engagement

Each year we conduct an employee engagement survey that we use to evaluate and improve ourselves and the company. This past year we received our highest ratings ever — breaking last year's record. We share the results with all employees during our August quarterly company addresses. We then break into smaller groups and discuss the results openly. We listen and act. If we can't act, we let employees know why. We also take time to reinforce the importance of what we do and how we take pride in providing life-saving equipment and supporting our firefighters and soldiers.

Once you become a manager or a leader, you realize that more and more people, inside and outside your company, will come to you looking for direction and comfort. Most of your life, you've had a boss to turn to in hard times; suddenly everyone's turning to you and it can be a lot to handle. It's important that you take time to be that person whom others can lean on — be a good sounding board. Think to yourself: how did your boss make you feel when you sought consolation? I'll bet you distinctly remember how he reacted to you in your time of need. These are most often code-shift moments.

When managing a sales team, be very conscious of how team members approach you after they've been on the road with much "windshield time." Speaking from personal experience and from managing sales reps, I've seen many times where a sales rep comes storming into the office after a long road trip. He was out on the road, working long days and nights, and had a great deal of time to think while driving between calls. He begins to feel unappreciated, overworked and underpaid. As you encounter these type of employees, let them vent, but it's even better to get out in front of it and acknowledge their hard work before they bring it to your attention. If these become frequent "bitch sessions," try to address it with a PIP. Generally, this person is not a team player and the sooner he leaves, the better.

Lesson No. 15: Don't put all your eggs in one basket.

Many small businesses have a few customers who represent 50 percent or more of their business. They have no other choice, as part of it comes from being a startup business and concentrating on taking care of those current, growing customers. Since Darley has been around for more than 100 years, and we have thousands of products and customers around the world, no one customer or product represents more than five percent of our business. We've done this through a diversification strategy to mitigate our risk and exposure to one market.

From personal experience, as you diversify, don't stray too far from your core businesses. Selling new products into new markets is extremely difficult. It's much easier to find new customers for your current products or new products for your current customer base. This website is pretty good if you want to study this topic in more depth.

STRATEGIC OPPORTUNITY MATRIX

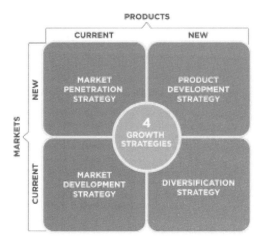

Lesson No. 16: Stay Humble. Protect and support the culture. Prepare for Succession

The most important thing about being a CEO is realizing that it's not about you; it's about the responsibility you have to make sure that things go well for your employees, stockholders and other partners. It can be an awesome responsibility, and worst thing you can do is get full of yourself. Remember, you are simply a servant.

A company's culture starts at the top. The CEO and other leaders of the business are stewards of the culture. It is their responsibility to support a culture that fosters the good things and change the culture when it needs to change with the times or when it's getting off course. Every culture is different, and new employees need to learn and embrace a set of attitudes and principles that define a workplace. No one would argue Google and IBM have the same corporate cultures. IBM exemplifies the starched white collar, while Google's "laid back" culture is at the other end of the spectrum. Most companies' cultures are somewhere in between.

I became a huge believer in setting and following core values at an early age. In the fall of 1982, while I was still in college, Johnson & Johnson (J&J) faced a crisis in the span of a few days when seven died in the Chicago area after taking cyanide-laced capsules of Extra-Strength Tylenol. The painkiller was the drug maker's best-selling product.

J&J looked at its core values, which placed consumer safety above a return on equity for its stockholders, and quickly recalled the product not only in Chicago, but in all markets. Back then, self-imposed recalls were unheard of in business, especially since it is rumored to have been made by a middle manager, while upper management was at offsite meetings.

The moves were costly. J&J spent more than $100 million for the 1982 recall and relaunch of Tylenol. Investors have had little to complain about since. If you had invested $1,000 in Johnson & Johnson shares on Sept. 28, 1982, just before the first Tylenol episode, it would be worth over $40,000 as of Oct. 1, 2017.

When I first joined our company after college, I started a company bowling league and softball team. I felt it created a strong bond in the company. After the softball games on Friday night, we would go out to a local bar. One Monday morning, my father called me into his office. He was angry.

"You have to stop this and now," he said.

I was shocked. I thought I was doing a great thing and impoving employee morale.

"In our family business," he explained, "if you're going to be a leader in this company, it's too difficult to go out with employees on weekends and then on Monday mornings command their respect."

In many regards, he was right, at least based on our company's culture at the time and my potential role in the business. For most, there is a fine line with respect to how personal a "boss/subordinate" relationships should be. "Relationships based on Respect" is one of our core values. While I'm respectful and courteous with all our employees, I don't have many personal employee friendships outside of normal business hours, by design. At Darley, it makes things too complicated when we do. We still have fun, including sports pools, picnics and holiday parties, but I'm careful not to cross the personal line.

I understand company cultures evolve and each is different. I've observed many company cultures where there are no boundaries. I admire the social interaction and friendships that take place with co-workers. This doesn't mean members of the Darley family and our management team can't be friendly with employees, but at Darley we carefully choose when, where and how it's done. That might change in years to come. I already see it changing in the next generation.

Amy Gallo, a professor at Harvard University, has studied and researched this subject of relationships within the workplace. If you're interested in learning more, search her name on Google or check out this video:

Facebook: Amy Gallo—Should you be friends with your boss or direct reports?

Teams are strengthened after enduring difficult times. One of the best ways to build a team is by being there for employees during their times of need. Try to find ways to assist them. Being there for someone during times of despair can be powerful code-shifting moments that endure for a career. In Rudy Giuliani's inspiring book, Leadership, he discusses this quite a bit in a chapter titled, "Weddings Discretionary. Funerals Mandatory."

I personally subscribe to this approach and have witnessed many times the power of unexpectedly attending a wake and supporting the grieving family. As a business leader, the impact of your presence can be profound. These small acts of kindness can have a profound effect on your employee relationships. At Darley, we don't do these things for self-serving business purposes; we do because it's the right thing to do. When you do the right thing, it's usually good for everyone involved.

With our remote locations, I can't make every funeral. But I always at least send a personalized card expressing my condolences in a private and personal tone. No one is ever entirely comfortable at a wake, but if you want to improve your emotional intelligence during these times, you might find this article of interest:

Funeral Etiquette Guide: Funeralwise.com

I still write a personalize birthday card to every employee. It's amazing the amount of feedback I receive from taking a few moments to write and mail these cards. I've seen CEOs with as many as 7,000 employees conduct this small act, and its benefits are incalculable.

Business Insider: CEO writes 7400 employee birthday cards each year; June 2017

These points lead to succession planning. Like execution, succession planning is not an event; it's a series of small, consistent acts that allow the company to have potential successors in line for key positions.

As a fourth-generation family business, we know the survival statistics and realize the importance of protecting our legacy, so we're constantly focused on succession planning through open sharing of information to the family and our key teams. This includes the

214

establishment of a G4 family forum and including G4 members in board meetings and management meetings. We constantly share information that will help them know how to run this business in the future. We also pay close attention to non-family member succession as we have in past generations.

I've watched a lot of family businesses go through this process and have learned a lot—mostly what not to do. If you're interested in learning more on our approach, you might want to watch this Northern Trust Bank video or these recent blogs from the Leaders with Courage Academy.

Northern Trust: Insights for Business Owners, Succession Planning – Paul Darley

Value Drivers: Leading with Courage Academy, How He's Building His Family's 109-Year-Old Business Paul Darley - Part I, June, 2017

Value Drivers: Leading with Courage Academy: How to fight fires: Family Friction, Generation Gaps, and Communicating Bad News – Part II of our conversation with Paul Darley; June 2017

In July 2017, I shared Part I above on my LinkedIn page after getting tagged in it. Within a week, it had been reviewed almost 10,000 times. It was the first time I ever posted or shared anything on LinkedIn and it was really cool to see.

Lesson No. 17: Don't panic

At some point, something will go wrong. Learn to deal with it in a mature and appropriate manner. If anybody in an organization sees the leader panicking and losing control, the ripple effects are detrimental to the organization and will likely last well beyond the current crisis. When those in the organization see the leader as decisive and calm, they, too, take on a similar demeanor.

While you can have your sleepless nights, stick to your long-term plan and make sure you're exuding confidence—never let them see you sweat. When employees see the manager stressed out, they, in turn, become stressed out, too. Tell employees the facts and don't sugar coat or embellish the situation. Most importantly, let them know what you plan to do about it and ask for their feedback when appropriate.

In the 1989 Super Bowl, the San Francisco 49ers were down by three points to the Cincinnati Bengals with 3:20 left in the game. The 49ers were nervously in the huddle when their quarterback Joe Montana entered and said to his teammates, "Check it out! Isn't that

John Candy sitting in the first row?" Cool Joe didn't panic and instead instilled confidence in his teammates. They knew they were going to win under his calm leadership. They went 92 yards downfield, with him throwing the winning touchdown with 34 seconds on the clock.

YouTube Video: The Drive - Joe Montana talks about John Candy in the Huddle

In 2012, we installed a new Oracle Enterprise Resource Planning (ERP) software system called JD Edwards. Like most large-scale computer implementation projects, it didn't go well. We went over our budget by more than $2 million and were 12 months behind schedule implementing it. We had a very difficult time getting accurate financial and production scheduling data. We went live on January 1st and had no financials for the year through November! We had to manage by cash flow. It's a very difficult way to run a business. That's adversity. So, how did we deal with it? We didn't panic. We managed to take care of our top customers and didn't lose any.

Our IT manager is my cousin, John Long, and he did a great job leading us out of the crisis, where tremendous pressure laid heavily on everyone. Today our ERP systems runs great — our assistant controller, Kim Cummuta, now has financials prepared within a few days of closing each period and our inventory and routings are accurate. We ship over 98 percent of our pumps and parts within 24 hours of the quoted delivery.

Lesson No. 18: Be a pacesetter, yet maintain balance and take care of yourself

Leaders face a dichotomy in trying to be a hard-working example-setter and, at the same time, maintaining a balance in their lives. Everyone who works hard knows what I mean — whether you're a fire chief, running a small business, a parent, a soldier, a sales rep, or anyone dedicated to their job. It's a balancing act. To have healthy business relationships, you need to have a sound mind and strong relationships at home. For this reason, the YPO symbol is a triangle, symbolizing the balance you should have with your work, yourself and your family.

Over the years, much has been written about the need for executives to find balance in their lives. The reasons range from being careful about not burning out, to being able to relate to your team better, to making sure that your family relationships are strong and intact. As of late, some schools of thought say that balance is overrated. I'm somewhere in the middle, but I am convinced that the

216

CEO must be the pacesetter for the organization. Communication and time management skills are critical to be successful at being the guide for the company without burning out or ruining his family life.

Twenty years ago, I attended a presentation by Jack Welch, a legendary business leader if there ever was one. He was in Chicago addressing a small group of YPO members at a luncheon. I figured Jack was speaking to pitch his new best-selling book, *Winning*. Later I learned he spoke at no cost, and all the proceeds from his book went to charity.

I found myself captivated, not only because he challenged so many generally accepted business best practices, but because he seemed to have all the answers. I especially loved the candor with which he spoke about leadership. Some concepts you've heard before:

- Surround yourself with a great team and help them grow

- Communicate expectations and let them know how they're doing

- Take time to celebrate the victories

- The important of balance

I was particularly interested in the discussion on balance, because at that point, I had none in my life. As Welch explained, leaders become ineffective when they don't occasionally step back. If they've done a good job of building a strong team and communicating the message clearly, managers should be able to trust their teams to perform when they're gone. He stressed that it is in these "down times" that leaders allow others to grow.

It also allows the CEO to focus on the most important strategic issues, which is his primary job. I used to laugh at this concept, picturing the CEO out of the office on the beach "working on his strategy," but now I embrace it because I see it in the most successful CEOs I know.

At about the same time as this Welch lunch, I was travelling roughly 250 days a year and was obsessed with growing our business. I was fortunate to have an understanding and supportive wife who raised our kids. It was before cell phones, and my youngest daughter, Sophie's, preschool called and caught me in the office, saying, "Mr. Darley, we can't get a hold of your wife, and Sophie is sick. Can you come get her?" I responded, "Absolutely, I will be right there!" I then had to embarrassingly ask, "Where are you located?" She was my third daughter, it was one block from my house, and I didn't even know where she went to school! That was a wake-up call.

I certainly wish I had been there more for my kids, but for most people working their way up the top, this sacrifice is one that we are forced to make. I have a renewed appreciation for my father's commitment to work, especially considering his accomplishments after losing both his oldest son and wife before he was my age. My mom had also lost two other children at birth after I was born. I can't imagine what my father was going through.

My forum mate, Bill Ryan, says, "The statute of limitations on bitching about your dad never being there for you runs out at age 30." I remind my kids of this idea often, so they only have a few years to complain. Bill is the founder and CEO of William Ryan Homes, one of the largest homebuilders in the country. As a third-generation home builder, construction is in his blood. He knows what he's doing and he loves it.

I truly love what I do and, God willing, I plan to work until I am at least 80 years old. My father always said, "I've never worked a day in my life," and I feel the same. This idea is true for many in my family because of the passion we have for our business and industry. However, it doesn't mean I won't make room for the next generations. I watch our G4 family employees closely, and I am constantly thinking about succession in our company. The succession planning process is the CEO's second most important job. The CEO's third most important job is the allocation of resources — both financial and human capital.

Young business executives show their dedication by working long hours and weekends. It is one of the ways successful people work their way to the top. By most measures, it's expected and part of earning your stripes and the respect of your co-workers. While there is nothing wrong with hard work and the occasional late night or even turning a weekend into a worked-end, doing it on a regular basis with 80-hour work weeks *can* have a negative effect on an individual, his family and the company, *if* not managed properly.

My YPO Forum mate, Ed Zeman, CEO of Zeman Homes, owns mobile home communities across the U.S. He is a big picture operator, and one of the most successful friends that I have. Ed has balance within his social, business and family life, and he lives life to the fullest with extreme passion. Yet he still manages to grow his company beyond his wildest expectations by delegating to a strong team and focusing only on major issues and cultural issues within his business.

As you move up in your career and build a family, you'll face more and more time constraints. Go where the fire is the hottest and don't waste time on insignificant tasks, issues or with people who are not important in your life or to the success of your business. (Numbering in silos might help you with figuring out who is most important in your life.)

Sheila Muldoon and I grew up across the street from each other and she's at the center of a close inner circle of grade school friends. She is a beautiful woman, but is considered one of the boys based on her straight forward approach to situations and life—she doesn't mince words. She likes to say, "I only care about people, who I care about."

When it comes to family relationships, make sure that you carve out time with your spouse where you can have alone time. Heidi and I try to do it every four days. We make sure we're together, just she and I, without our children or friends.

While most of my vacations are working vacations, I find myself feeling guilty when taking a vacation. I'm working on that, but as I've come to learn, taking time to be with your family does not count unless you're there mentally as well as physically.

It's a bit of a balance situation, but I've found that some of my best work comes during these times when I'm recharging my batteries. This time is when I am working "on" our business and not "in" our business. Writing this book has been therapeutic and has helped in recharging me. I'm kind of worried what I'll do now that it's published—but I sense it will have more to do with giving back and helping others.

While I take after my father in many ways, my father seemed to work hard all the time. He was a marathon runner, while I considered myself a sprinter, where I go hard for weeks or months at a time and then need to recharge. Find out which you are and adjust your work schedule and downtime accordingly.

As any workaholic will tell you, long hours at the office are not conducive to strong family relationships. I was fortunate to be married to someone who understood my passion for work. She did an awesome job raising the kids and I managed not to screw it up. She was always supportive of my time away—something can be said for absence making the heart grow fonder. Today I don't travel as much as I did 20 years ago and she will jokingly encourage me to get back on the road. I get it.

Take care of your health

Executives should take care of themselves by eating properly, exercising and getting regular doctor visits. You are of no good to anyone in the organization if you have a heart attack, stroke or even die. Health is your greatest wealth. I feel a bit hypocritical writing about this topic, though, since "play hard" has been a big part of my mantra for 20 years. But I do get regular health exams every six months locally, and I even go to the executive heath programs at the Mayo Clinic or University of Chicago, alternating every two years for a completely thorough check. I have CEO friends who have had their lives saved through these types of exams. We encourage and pay for our management team to have these in-depth checkups at least bi-annually.

Here is a great link to an article I recently read while at Mayo Clinic in Rochester, MN, in January of 2017. Some of these tips might surprise you.

<u>Mayo Clinic: 12 habits of highly healthy people</u>

We have a wellness program at our company. We offer free flu shots, hold health related competitions and wellness checks, and even pay for health club memberships for employees. Health isn't something we toy around with.

It's also important to have hobbies outside of business — all work and no play makes Jack a dull boy. My brother, Jimmy, heads up our pump sales and does an awesome job. He is a rock star, both in our business and with his band, *The Velvet Jimis*, which regularly fills venues in Chicago, including the House of Blues, Fitzgerald's, and The Wire. Their video, linked below, has almost 50,000 views:

<u>The Velvet Jimis—Just a lil bit</u>

Lesson No. 19: Continue to learn

For me, reading books wasn't enough. I joined YPO and went back to school to get an MBA. Although I had a Bachelor's degree in business, I had graduated 18 years earlier and knew I lacked many tools in my toolbox. I wanted decision-making tools, but also wanted to make sure I fully understood every aspect of our financial statements, which meant being able to read income statements, balance sheets and cash-flow statements — forward and backward.

I had a good handle on the culture of our business. After all, I had been immersed in it nearly my entire life. Going through the program gave me a needed sense of confidence.

At Kellogg's Executive MBA Program, a student is required to have at least 15 years of business experience before it will accept you because much of the learning comes from other students. I must confess, I went into that program thinking, "I really look forward to sharing my wealth of knowledge with the other students." My No. 1 take-away from the program was I couldn't believe how little I knew. It was an eye-opening experience.

Remember, you don't need to go back to business school for a full MBA program to improve yourself. If you have an area where you lack the knowledge and tools, plenty of universities and programs offer webinars and shorter seminars on most subjects. I still travel a great deal for business, so I subscribe to Business Book Summaries and *Trends Magazine* on CD, which I listen to while in the car and on airplanes.

Smart leaders learn from others and surround themselves with good people who are smarter than they are and who complement them in areas where they are deficient. They put exceptional people on their board and management teams — and create networks of people who are not afraid to challenge them. The more diversity on the team, the better. Unless you continue to learn, "you don't know what you don't know."

Lesson No. 20: Get help from others

One of the worst things a leader can do once he reaches the C-suite is to become complacent and isolated. The executive who stops learning starts losing. Continuing education is vital. This learning can come from reading books and magazines, internet searches, webinars, seminars, industry conferences and peers.

While many salespeople understand the sales process, to become an effective leader they've got to make sure they have a solid understanding of finance, operations and accounting. If the company is involved in manufacturing, having engineering experience is helpful.

No one has all the answers and it's critical that you surround yourself with advisors and mentors who give you candid "NO BS" feedback and provide clarity on the issues you are facing. We'll discuss that more in the next chapter.

Chapter 12

Advisors are all around you. Get help, and give help!

"The delicate balance of mentoring someone is not creating them in your own image, but giving them the opportunity to create themselves."

Steven Spielberg

It's lonely at the top, and every businessperson needs a sounding board — someone to bounce things off for advice on difficult decisions. For most executives, that sounding board means a peer group and/or a board of advisors or directors. One of the keys to running a successful business is to have trusted advisors both inside and outside the company. You need people with experience who have your back and won't mince words.

Advisors help to clear the fog on complex issues. They can come from many areas, from consultants, coaches, business organizations, peers and friends. Most successful executives give a great deal of credit to their spouse, and I'm certainly no exception. Spouses can tell you things that others can't—or won't, but it's good to have others you can turn to in times of need.

Consultants

Many executives turn to consultants for advice. Consultants can be helpful in addressing specific problems in areas where you and team have little knowledge of a subject. I'm tainted, but my overall experience is that consultants have a way of staying much longer than promised, running over budget and not bringing closure to the projects. Because most consultants are paid by the hour, an inherent conflict of interest exists not to finish the job. While they may offer great advice, many consultants seem to fail on the execution.

There are good consultants out there and if you can find a good one, you're fortunate. Use them on a project-by-project basis, but don't set them up with a comfortable office or they may never leave. If they're that good, you should hire them or put them on your board.

Executive Team

Most companies have a small leadership team at the top. They are called a variety of things, but in our case, it's the Executive Team. Our team is comprised of my brother, Peter Darley; cousin, Jeff Darley; cousin, James Long; and me. We are all third-generation family owners and run our business by an "cousin consortium," or "cousin collaboration."

The Darley Executive Team in 2017. From left: Jeff Darley, Paul Darley, James Long and Peter Darley

This cousin collaboration is great for the decision-making progress because we're able to bounce things off each other and we each have a unique perspective on things. We all aim to be supportive and respectful of each person's perspective. We also find that we push and drive each other in a way that is healthy for the company.

For most family businesses, it is important that management of the company mirror the ownership of the company. This setup is easier said than done, but it works for our company because we were fortunate to have at least one qualified individual from each of the three family ownership branches.

Our Executive Team meetings are held about one week before board meetings. We cover many operational and strategic issues at these meetings. The meeting's minutes are shared with our board, management team, G4 and stockholders. While we may have disagreements at times, we air these issues during our executive team meetings rather than during the board meetings. We generally go to the board united on issues. Most importantly, we all put the company's interest first.

No one harbors bad feelings and we don't go to bed mad at each other. Once a decision has been made, we move forward in a united front. Collectively, we are so much stronger than any one leader could be. Ultimately, the decisions we make are better than the decisions

225

one person could make on his own. This collaboration enables us to see issues through multiple lenses, see potential outcomes one person alone might not have come up with, and choose the best option to pursue.

Board of Directors

Most small businesses don't have a formal board of directors, but if you're a mid-sized company or plan to be one someday, I strongly suggest you consider one. We've worked hard to find the best possible board.

Our first outside board member was Willy Boos, who joined in 1994. He served our company faithfully, running our plant in Chippewa Falls for over 40 years. In 1997, we added Paul Faherty who was an attorney, family friend and a deacon at St. Luke Church in River Forest, where my grandfather donated the alter in 1921. We added some high-profile board talent over the past 20 years and there is no question, our board is one of the key reasons for our success and growth.

They help to professionalize the company. During the board meetings, we very briefly go over company operational, corporate and finance issues, and then we cover anywhere from two to four strategic issues. These discussions could be relative to an acquisition, important markets we serve, or how we should be adjusting our strategy to meet changing market conditions.

We follow YPO protocol in addressing those issues, which is explained in more detail later in this chapter, but it allows us to present the issue with relevant facts, uninterrupted, for 20 minutes. Board members then ask questions and provide advice on how they think we should be handling it. We find that this method enables us to focus on the important things and get feedback in a very distinct and timely manner.

In April of 2017, we were voted "The Board of the Year" for mid-sized companies ($100-$350 million in revenues) by *Directors & Boards Magazine*. Our board includes:

Steven Rogers. He is our lead director and was one of my professors at Kellogg. Steve recently moved from Kellogg to Harvard Business School. While at Kellogg, Steve was rated the No. 1 professor for 13 of the 17 years he was there. He also serves on the boards for SC Johnson Wax and Oakmark Mutual Funds. I asked him to join our board after our second finance class and he politely suggested I raise the question after I completed the class. He joined us in 2004.

Sam Skinner. Sam has had a distinguished career in both the

governmental and private sectors. He is the retired Chairman, president and Chief Executive Officer of USF Corporation, one of the nation's leading transportation companies. He was also president of Commonwealth Edison Company and its holding company, Unicom Corporation. Sam served as Chief of Staff to President George H.W. Bush and for nearly three years as his Secretary of Transportation. We met at a funeral and stayed in touch. He joined our board in 2008.

The Darley Board of Directors after being named #1 Midsize Board in America in 2017. Standing from left: Admiral (Ret) Joe McGuire, Garry Briese, Steven Rogers, Mary Jo Long, Sam Skinner. Seated from left: Jeff Darley, Paul Darley, James Long & Peter Darley

Garry Briese. Garry served on our Defense Advisory Board for three years before being asked to join our corporate board. He is the Executive Director of the Colorado State Fire Chiefs. Previously, Garry was the Regional Administrator for DHS/FEMA Region 8 and as Vice President, Emergency Management & Homeland Security for ICF International, a NASDAQ-listed professional services corporation. Garry is best known for his 23 years as the CEO of the International Association of Fire Chiefs. He's been a family friend and confidant for more than 30 years.

Admiral (retired) Joe McGuire. Joe is an incredible American who has served as president and CEO of The Special Operations Warrior Foundation since 2013 and he joined us in 2015. Prior to leading the Foundation, Joe was a vice president with Booz Allen Hamilton. He was a career Naval Special Warfare Officer (SEAL) and retired from the U.S. Navy in 2010, having served 36 years in uniform. Joe commanded at every level, including the Naval Special Warfare Command, and the Navy Component of United States Special Operations Command. Our family met Joe when he attended funeral services for Ted Fitz-Henry, a family relative who died in action while serving as a SEAL in 2004.

We clearly have no "yes-men" on our board. We want them to challenge us, and they do. They get their point across in a very logical, non-threatening, respectful manner with a viewpoint that's not as myopic as those of us who are living in this situation every day. In between quarterly meetings, I try not to bother them with too much correspondence because I don't want them getting caught in the weeds.

They're all great at giving us their sincere feedback and views on where they think we should be headed, as well as letting us know if they think we're headed in the wrong direction. They enjoy the experience and find it gratifying because we listen and execute so quickly.

As a privately-held family business, our board is weighted in favor of family members. In fact, that provision is written into our bylaws, stating that the majority of our board must be family members. In our case, we also have a family member on the board who does not work at Darley. My cousin, Mary Jo Long, an attorney with the Department of Child and Family Services, serves on the board to make sure that we are properly representing the needs of outside shareholders who don't work in the business. If you would like to learn more about our board, please visit:

Darley.com: Board of Directors

If you don't currently have a board, but are considering one, I would suggest that you check out this article on the importance of having an outside board of directors. Google this subject and you will find thousands of articles like it and few that talk about any negatives:

Forbes Magazine: Outside Board Members Bring Needed Experience and Perspective

Corporate boards are generally fiduciary in nature, which means that they serve as trustees for the stockholders. As such, they agree to be informed, act in good faith, and put the stockholder's interests first. If a member of a board of directors is found to be in breach of his fiduciary duty, he can be held liable in a court of law by the company itself or its shareholders. Don't let that stop you from forming or joining a board. If you are asked to serve on a board, be sure that you ask for a copy of their directors and officers insurance policy before signing up.

Board members at large, publicly traded companies can easily earn hundreds of thousands of dollars for their efforts. At Darley, and most small and mid-sized firms, they are paid a nominal meeting fee, but in line with industry standards.

If you consider forming a fiduciary corporate board, the benchmark compensation for independent board members is equal to the hourly salary of the CEO. Simply take the hourly rate of the CEO and multiply it by the number of hours that you expect from your board members per year. Most mid-sized companies pay their board members about $20,000 to $30,000 annually, which covers four quarterly meetings, committee work, preparation time, and work in-between the meetings.

Most board members are not in it for the money. They're part of the organization because they want to give back. In our case, they're also mentors who have had a positive and powerful impact on our business and me personally.

Advisory Boards

Many companies first set up advisory boards to see how the approach works for them. In our case, we set up a Defense Advisory Board (DAB) when we started our Defense Division business 10 years ago. We had no idea what we were doing, and we needed help. Hiring people with industry knowledge was critical. We made some great hires and some we regret, but I knew we needed help.

We assembled a non-fiduciary DAB which consists of retired military leaders:

The Darley Defense Advisory Board shown with top inside and outside sales reps in 2016

- Gerry Klein, a former Army Command Sergeant Major (CSM) who was recently inducted into the Ranger Hall of Fame

- John DeBlasio, a YPO friend who served in Iraq after graduating from West Point. We also performed a large defense contract together before he retired and sold his defense contracting business, Sallyport, at the age of 44

- Tim Abbott, another West Point grad and Army Special Operations intelligence officer

- Jeff Mellinger, an Army CSM who worked alongside generals Petraeus and Casey

- Jack Zeigler, a member of Army Special Operations for 30 years and now president of a defense contractor. He employs 150 people

- Captain Ozzie Giglio, another YPO friend who is a Navy Intelligence Officer for Joint Special Operations Command. He undertook numerous tours in Iraq and Afghanistan while growing his Harley Davidson dealership into one of the largest in the country with nine franchises

- Lt. General Ray Palumbo of the U.S. Army, who was a Defense Intelligence Officer and served as Deputy Undersecretary of the DOD, with a $13 billion budget

- Admiral Ron Rabago, who recently retired from the U.S. Coast Guard as a Naval Civil engineer

I look at the caliber of our DAB members, and I am incredibly humbled to be mentored by this level of leaders. They're not on our board for monetary reasons. In fact, we offer to double their modest stipend and donate it to the charity of their choice. Every DAB member donates his stipend to charity! They are here to give back, not only to Darley, but to those we serve. As military leaders, it comes very naturally to them as they have been giving all their lives. They set a notable example of good mentorship, and it's truly moving and humbling to have their support.

Stockholders

We have 36 stockholders and I communicate a lot with them. They get copies of the video-recorded quarterly company address, significant meeting minutes and monthly financials. We recently conducted a stockholder survey and they gave us high marks across the board and 100 percent responded that the amount of information we share with them is "About Right."

When you are transparent with your stockholders (and people in general), they will be direct with you. Stockholders in a family business are not known for being a shy group. This can be good or bad. In our case, it's good because they are incredibly supportive and they're asking the right questions.

About half of our stockholders work in the company, which is a high percentage by any fourth-generation standards. Those who don't work at the company are incredibly supportive. My cousin, Patricia Long Janecek, communicates her suggestions quite often, always with the company's best interests in mind. Her mother, Pat, who is in her 90s and is the daughter of our founder, still attends board meetings.

We have formed a G4 Advisory Board, which currently consists of seven fourth-generation Darley family members: Jason, Ryan, Kyle, Matt, Will, Kevin and Audrey Darley. They report at our quarterly board meetings and help address business issues. They also take the lead on running our family meetings and retreats. It's great to watch them grow and work together. They have complementary skills and are involved in sales, engineering and supply chain in all divisions of the company. Most importantly, they have good chemistry and get along well while supporting each other. This book was written largely in part as a "playbook" for them and future generations. The fifth generation (G5) is growing fast and will be here before we know it!

Peer Groups

Peer groups offer an opportunity to bounce ideas off experienced professionals in a nonjudgmental, confidential format, which can make all the difference in your company's business and help guide your success and assist you in seeing the pieces that may be missing from your puzzle. Support groups come in all types and sizes, from YPO and Vistage, to CEO Connection and The President's Forum. My brother, Peter, is in Vistage and learns a great deal from it. In addition to meeting monthly with peers, he also has a business coach who assists him in meeting his goals.

YPO Forums

I've been a member of YPO for almost 20 years. The organization has changed my life—in business, personal relationships and with my family. I currently belong to two YPO forums: one is a group of CEOs and presidents from Chicago; the other a group of CEOs who run their multigenerational family businesses. Most of the companies in my forum have at least $1 billion in annual revenues, but the members are all regular guys who put their pants on the same as you and me. In YPO we're all equals, regardless of the size of our company or thickness of our wallet. We receive tremendous take-home value in each forum.

YPO's monthly forums are confidential and follow strict protocols, generally comprising of 8-10 business leaders. During each meeting, at least one member addresses the group on a significant issue they are facing in the below format. Members never tell each other *what they should do*, they just listen, ask questions, share a common experience and let the people know they're appreciated. It's all done in a process-driven, nonjudgmental and respectful way.

The reason for not making specific suggestions is proven. YPO members present an issue to their peers once or twice a year. The issue they explain, in 30 minutes or less, has been absorbing much of their life for the last year. There are a lot of details unknown to the listener. The objective to help the member clear the fog on the subject they're facing and to help come to their own conclusion on the best path forward.

Often, these topics are soul-searching, "defining moments," or "watershed events" that are great code-shifts. When you dive that deep in a quick way, the relationships deepen quickly.

All the Windy City YPO forums follow the Process-directed Emotional Intelligence (PdEI) process. Meeting start promptly at 3 p.m. and end no later than 9 p.m. The below eight steps were developed by Jim Liautaud and used to achieve the identical outcome for each meeting:

(1) **Host's biggest issue.** This is a 30-to-60-minute, uninterrupted monologue with the group's full attention—body and face—directed to the presenter. No notetaking or side conversations. The presenter will usually start off by saying what he wants from the presentation.

(2) **Clarifying questions.** Upon completion of the presentation, the moderator asks for questions based on what was presented. Members are allowed a second question only after everyone has asked one.

(3) **Shared Experiences.** After clarifying questions, members share common experiences — if they have one — that the presenter can relate to their situation. Because this issue is generally the biggest one facing the CEO, members can never tell the presenter what he "should do." We only use only "I" statements, at the exclusion of any "you" statements.

(4) **Homework Option**. This step is optional (and sometimes dangerous). The presenter can ask others what they would do if they were in his shoes. This suggestion is limited to your one best, single sentence.

(5) **Closing Appreciation for the Host.** Members share the one thing each admired most about the presentation or about the host personally.

Break

(6) **Updates.** Each member of the forum shares one best and one worst event that happened since last meeting. Members will often supplement this with where their life is on a scale of 1–10. This step is limited to between three and five minutes. This Best/Worst exercise allows each forum member to be a bit more introspective on the issues that most affect their lives and why. In doing so, this reflection gives the members a much clearer insight into the emotional impact each of their fellow members is experiencing. We learn more about the values and nature of each member and walk away with a better understanding of what is most important to them. This leads to dialogue at the dinner table and the universal comfort of knowing others have had similar experiences as you.

Break

(7) **Dinner.** The meal is held in a private room, at a round table, with open dialogue. Everyone knows the strict rule against any sports talk, or discussion of politics or religion. We have plenty to discuss around dinner given the day's intensity. Dinner also provides that needed pause, combined with the warmth of bonding.

(8) **Closing Appreciation**. At the completion of dinner, the Chair asks each member to summarize, in one sentence, what each appreciated most from that day's meeting.

YPO is going through a lot of changes and has recently established forums for the sons and daughters of YPO members. My two oldest daughters, Audrey and Maggie, are both in forums and each one is benefiting tremendously from them. I'm proud to share that my daughter, Audrey, was recently named president of the Chicago Chapter of Young Next Gen (YNG). The chapter already has over 300 members and is the largest YNG in the world! They are doing great work.

YPO considers a "Young President" someone under the age of 50, and at this age we go to YPO Gold. The inside joke is that the "G" in Gold is silent. Previously it was known as WPO (World President's Organization). We have incredible opportunities for networking and lifelong learning. If you know anyone running a reasonably sized company before the age of 45, strongly encourage them to consider YPO. It's life changing!

Start your own group of Advisors

Sometimes you can take a good idea and apply it to something else. In my case, I've taken some of the concepts from YPO and embraced it with another group, Elmhurst Business Organization (EBO). I started EBO nine years ago with 10 business executives from our town of Elmhurst, a suburb of Chicago. We meet once a month and follow the same protocol as YPO. We embrace EI. Our goal is to develop better executives through what we call the EBO Process. We have kicked off three additional EBO forums and already have about 40 business leaders helping each other. It took little effort, but it is having a positive impact on these members.

These types of forum experiences don't need to be conducted on a large scale. One of my closest friends and neighbors, John Kosich, has a hot tub in his back yard. The two of us, along with Dave Wold, the CEO of Health Information Services, a large health care company, meet weekly in his hot tub and discuss business issues and personal matters, in a relaxed and fun setting. Some of the best input I've received in my life has come from times like these — in a relaxed informal setting over a couple of beers. "What's said in the tub, stays in the tub."

Many successful business people also have deep spiritual beliefs. I recently participated in a spiritual revival weekend retreat that was very powerful and helped free my soul. There were 15 or so of us who stayed together for over year meeting monthly. It was a great experience.

Mentoring Young Adults

According to *Forbes Magazine*, 75 percent of *Fortune 500* CEOs agree that mentoring played a key role in their personal lives and career. Once they've made it, they look for opportunities to give back. Another study shows that roughly 70 percent of executives would welcome the opportunity to mentor at least one young person who truly wants to be mentored.

I've been blessed by having several great mentors in my life. These have generally been older, highly successful business executives or leaders in our country's military, and who, for one reason or another, said, "I'm going to take Paul Darley under my wing and help guide him." It's truly a humbling feeling.

Every up-and-coming salesperson should find a business leader who will mentor and help guide them. In turn, every successful executive should serve as a mentor to future executives. Pay it forward.

Over the years, I have mentored about 20 young adults, some with more success than others. I'm currently mentoring several young men between the ages of 20 and 30. Some of them are doing incredibly well; others are not.

Sometimes I'm asked to get involved by the parents of young people who have strayed from their parents and need an adult to talk with who will not "act" as their parents. They may be in a transition phase, such as dropping out of school, or maybe they're having trouble with the law, drugs, or are still flipping burgers at the age of 27.

When I'm working with a troubled youth, I always begin the same way. I hold up my hand, spreading two fingers to form a V, and say, "Look, there are two paths you can take in life. Many want to pull you down this short, abysmal path. Once you get past the knuckle, it's generally very hard to come back and start down the right path on the other, longer finger."

Young people who are approaching this knuckle in their lives see their friends, if they have any left, on the right path moving up in their careers, starting families, and becoming good citizens. By the time they yearn for that life, it's often too late. If they don't want to change, I won't waste my time mentoring them. Sometimes you need to wait for them to hit rock bottom before they are willing to give change a try.

In my late teens, I could have easily gone down that wrong path. I had minimal guidance during that time—after my mother died, and my father was busy running our company. I give much credit to my high school sweetheart Heidi—I knew if she was going to marry me some day, it was only going to happen if I was on the right path. I'm not proud of it, but I grew up real fast and sowed my oats. In the words of Frankie Ballard, "How am I supposed to be old and wise, if I was never young and crazy?"

You don't have to be "seasoned" to start mentoring others. Many troubled teenagers can't imagine being able relate to an "old" guy like me, and relate better to younger successful people.

I get more enjoyment out of mentoring young folks who are on the right path, but merely need some guidance. These people may be those who recently graduated college, are starting a business, or taking the reins in a family business. I learn as much from them as they learn from me.

Whenever I take on a new mentee, I always lay out a   few simple rules:

- My job as a mentor is to help you understand your own convictions, see the big picture, and clear the fog on issues you're facing. I don't have all the answers, only you have those. I'll help you find them

- I will never tell you what you should do, but I will offer guidance.

- You don't have to accept my business guidance, and I won't be upset if you don't

- I'm only going to meet with you if you want to meet with me. The mentor-mentee relationship only works when both people are committed

- Everything we discuss is confidential

- I will listen more than I speak

- I will ask you probing questions

- I will only talk from my own experience

- Meetings start promptly as planned. Don't ever blow off a meeting

- You must have a positive attitude

- There must be mutual respect

I schedule a lot of my mentor meetings while I'm driving to our plants. I don't have interruptions and can give them my full attention during this time.

One of my mentees is Ryan Puccinelli, who started an office supply company with a college friend at the age of 25. Today, nine years later, Ryan's company, IQ Total Source, is highly successful. Like Darley, IQ Total Source has been listed in the *Inc. 5000* list of fastest growing companies for the last six years in a row. Ryan gets it. He understands his customers' needs, his suppliers, and the market itself, better than anyone his age. He's a natural salesman, but like most young business owners his age, he needs some advice on the financial, strategy and operations sides of his business.

Another mentee, Brad Nardick, is a YNG member and the son of a YPO member, Rob. Brad is working closely with his father to grow their awesome family business, Bazaar, Inc.

I've been mentoring Greg Hart for years. He is a young man who took my daughter to high school prom. He is an incredible representative of the Millennials and has set his sights on one day being President of the United States. He's been working for a defense contractor in D.C., and recently landed a job with Deloitte. He's moving into local politics and was just appointed as a board member for the DuPage County Board of Commissioners. Nothing will stop him.

Gary Rabine (No. 1 YPO friend) is the chairman and CEO of The Rabine Group of Companies. He has grown his business tremendously over the years, landing himself on the top of the Fast 50 list of Chicago's fastest growing companies many for of the last 10 years. Gary views mentorship as the most important gift he received throughout his entrepreneurial career. Gary's formal education ended at high school, and he credits his success to the great mentors he had.

He has a great deal on his plate and is one of the busiest guys I know, yet to give back, he founded and funded a non-profit group called True Mentors. True mentors match great leaders with young, aspiring mentees. The organization is making an enormous difference, and there is a long line of people lining up to be both mentors and mentees.

Quinton James, the founding partner of True Mentors. Against all odds, this fine young man grew up on the Southside of Chicago, went to college and landed a banking job. He felt a calling to impact 1 billion people, and founding True Mentors with Gary set him on this path.

True Mentors Information and Videos

Young executives and those in need of mentoring have many great places to meet others. Most universities and civic organizations, from the Jaycees, to the Lions, Kiwanis, Knights of Columbus, the local volunteer Fire Department, Chamber of Commerce or others, are begging for young people to join their organizations. Young people are their lifeblood.

Gary is also a mentor to Charlie Kirk. Charlie is an amazing young man who founded Turning Point USA, which mobilizes Republican college students on campus through a motto of "Big Government Sucks." It's an incredible organization, and many in the Trump campaign credit this grassroots effort in helping Donald win the 2016 election. Charlie spoke at the 2016 Republican National Convention, and he is a regular contributor to Fox News. Gary and I have a $2 bet on whose mentee will become President first.

Charlie Kirk: Turning Point USA

A hot new trend in this area is "Reverse Mentoring," where younger people can help the older generations stay up to the times. The new word for this is "rotnem." It's an odd name, but hats off to the person who came up with it ... it's "mentor" spelled backwards. Let's see if it catches on.

You're never too old to learn something new, as this *Forbes* article explains:

Forbes Magazine: Reverse Mentoring - What it is and why it is important

The older I get, the more important it is for me to give back. I feel so passionate about mentoring that I recently agreed to take on the role of chairman for the YPO Mentorship Program in the Chicago YPO Gold Chapter, where we have a long list of mentees awaiting mentors. YPO has set up a cloud platform to help facilitate this process. If you take the time to mentor someone, I promise you'll find it a rewarding experience.

Chapter 13
Profit and Corporate Social Responsibility

"We make a living by what we get,
we make a life by what we give."

Winston Churchill

On the very first day of business school, students learn that the primary purpose of any business is ... to generate a profit. Is this wrong?

My freshman year in high school at St. Ignatius College Prep in Chicago, I took a radio class. On the first day, the teacher asked, "Why do you think radio stations exist?" Students raised their hands and answered: to deliver the news, to entertain us, to play music. I was the 10th guy to raise my hand. I remember saying, "To make a profit." I felt a little capitalistic about it, but the teacher applauded me.

As a kid, I was always very business-minded and always hustling for a buck. I'm embarrassed to say it, but I was driven by money. But I am proud to say that I was also driven by the thrill of the hunt. I still am.

Most successful entrepreneurs and salespeople are driven by money to some degree. It's OK when making money is one of your drivers, but it can't be the only one — especially after you reach the point where you take care of your hierarchy of needs: providing for yourself and your family.

I distinctly remember a management meeting about 25 years ago, when we all filled out surveys that included this question: "What is the purpose of our business?"

Every manager, except one, answered that our primary purpose was to make a profit. We looked around the room at each other, wondering who didn't get it; that person ended up being my father.

"We are about serving our customers, creating good jobs and giving back," he said. "If we do that, the profits will come."

The room was silent. He was right. Dr. Martin Luther King Jr. once said, "Life's most persistent and urgent question is: 'What are you doing for others?'" It's a profound question, but one that is easily answered by those we serve — and by Bill Darley.

As an angel investor with the Marquette Golden Angels, I've watched many entrepreneurs over the years fail and others succeed. Almost without exception, the ones who failed were the ones who were totally profit-centric. The customer-focused and goodwill-centric businesses were the ones who made it, provided they had high EI, passion and grit.

Are Companies Greedy?

In the 1987 movie *Wall Street*, Michael Douglas plays business tycoon Gordon Gekko. During the meeting, Gekko says, "Greed is

240

good." While I certainly don't believe that, I do believe companies need to be profitable.

Serving the community and making a profit are the two sides of the corporate coin, separate yet conjoined. Fail to do one and you won't do the other. Taking that thought a step further, if a company is not profitable, it can't continue to serve its customers, create jobs and make contributions to society.

Years ago, I used to be very uncomfortable standing in front of our employees and talking about profits. When I first became president in the mid-1990s, that discomfort was because the topic wasn't part of our culture. Now I share almost everything going on in the company. These topics include major issues we're facing, like strategy, sales performance and how we are performing against our profit budget. Rather than show dollars, we show profits in terms of percentages and compared to previous years.

If you lead a private company, the level of information you choose to share with employees can be a delicate issue that is determined by your company's culture. You always stand a chance that information you share will be used against you in some way, particularly if you're perceived as making too much and not sharing the wealth with your employees.

If you don't tell employees what's going on, they'll make something up that will be worse than the truth. Employees have a right to know the truth. By being transparent, employees have a better understanding of where we are headed, then they can see things from our management's perspective: good, bad or indifferent. Equally important, this transparency, honesty and no BS straight-talk are a huge part of being an authentic leader which leads to our overall success. Employees get it and know if the company does well, so do our employees.

At Darley — and most small to mid-size companies — we reinvest almost all our after-tax profits back into our businesses. In Darley's case, we do it to grow the company for the next generations of Darley's, as well as for the children of our current employees. Everyone knows that my generation of owners are simply caretakers or stewards of the company. They know that our family is there is serve the business; the business is not there to serve the Darley family.

Giving Back — Corporate Social Responsibility (CSR)

Every Darley employee feels blessed that we are in a business which contributes to society by making and distributing lifesaving equipment for firefighters and equipment that supports and protects our country's warfighters and firefighters. This feeling of giving back is particularly important to today's Millennials.

It's humbling and rewarding to know that our work and products help them do their work, and it's an honor and privilege to be in an industry where we can assist those who give so selflessly.

As we enter new markets, such as we've done with defense supplies, water purification, residential fire sprinkler systems, drones and homeland security equipment for homeowners, we always consider their alignment with our Corporate Social Responsibility (CSR) plan. Will we be serving humanity? We also ask if can we do it profitably?

Some refer to this outlook as a triple bottom line (TBL), which is an accounting framework with three parts: social, environment and financial. My YPO Family Business Forum mate, Chris Herschend, says TBL is about People, Planet and Profits. Chris should know, as his business is the largest family-owned entertainment company in the world, owning numerous amusement parks and even the Harlem Globetrotters. They focus keenly in this area. Chris is same guy who likes to say, "If you know how to sell, you'll never go hungry."

Bryan Schwartz is a close YPO friend and an attorney who, until recently, led a large law firm in Chicago. He recently left the law firm he helped found in 1999 to head up a mid-sized manufacturing company. In 2007, Bryan and I led an initiative to get our YPO member companies to adopt formal Corporate Social Responsibility (CSR) Plans. For some reason, it was met with limited success — CEOs were either too busy or simply didn't care. Both of our companies embraced it, and it's been rewarding for us and those customers we serve. In short, we declared that we would be good corporate citizens and developed a plan to do it.

As part of our CSR plan at Darley, we support more than 250 charities each year through our company and the Darley Family Foundation. Most of our giving is directed to the communities where we serve and live. Each year, we set aside about 10 percent of our after-tax profits for charitable donations. Kevin Sofen, our Business Development Manager, is leading our CSR efforts now and taking us to new heights with significant environmental and humanitarian support.

Some recent articles and books are very critical of CSR for publicly traded companies. I don't understand that point of view. While we support these causes for their benefit, not our own, it's interesting to see the good that comes back to us.

My mantra today is quite different than it was 30 years ago.

242

In my teens, it was, "Everything happens for a reason." When I hit my early 20s, it changed to, "Carpe Diem (Seize the day)." At age 30, it changed again, to "Work Hard, Play Hard." When I was 43, it changed again. I was at a YPO regional conference with my wife. We sat at a round a table with five couples and discussed our personal mantras.

I said, "Oh, mine's 'Work hard, play hard.'"

Someone else offered theirs and said, "Mine is like Paul's, but it's 'Work hard, play hard, and *give back.*'"

"*Give back.*"

I remember how that hit me like a dagger. How had I been missing this last key part of my mantra? I was embarrassed and immediately reshaped my mantra. Now, the older I get, the more important giving back becomes. My mantra will probably change again in my 60s and 70s as my career begins to wind down and I look to leave my own legacy. I know that giving back will only grow in importance. Heidi's mantra has always been very simple: "Be kind," which is very descriptive of her.

Paul and Heidi Darley at a charity auction in 2015

Random Acts of Kindness

Giving back isn't only about writing checks. It could mean helping your friends, family, charities, civic organizations or even strangers. Discreet random acts of kindness are stronger than any other type of giving.

Heidi and I were recently waiting in a lobby at the Mayo Clinic for our biennial executive health check. A young woman who was a cancer patient with a bandana on her head casually commented that she liked Heidi's hat. Without even thinking, Heidi immediately removed it and gave it to her. It is small acts of kindness like Heidi's which make the world such a special place. Pay it forward and sprinkle a little kindness wherever you go, and you will help make the world a better place.

These acts have the most impact on those who are at the bottom of the socioeconomic pyramid because they need it the most and don't expect it. For example, this person could be cleaning the bathrooms at the airport or hotel. Whomever it ends up being, do it discreetly and watch their gratitude.

All of us, of course, are heavily influenced by our upbringing — including me. My mother had an enormous impact on how I see the world. She was all about giving back. My mother also instilled strong values in each of us, such as hard work, integrity, treating others like you like to be treated, and putting your faith in God but being sure that you take responsibility for your actions. I try to live by the Golden Rule. Pretty straight-forward.

On a personal level, Heidi and I find ourselves migrating to giving back to organizations that offer the most for those in need. Ultimately, one of the greatest charges of a leader is to make the world a better place than it was when they started, to make a positive impact.

My cousin, Jeff Darley, and his wife, Patti, were recently named the "Philanthropists of the Year" for Chippewa County, Wisconsin. They and their family are extremely active in their community. A close friend, Ken Wegner, CEO of the Jel Sert Company (makers of Wyler's drink mixes, Mondo, Fla-Vor-Ice, etc.), and his wife, Julia, received a similar award for DuPage County, outside Chicago. In both cases, they wrote significant checks to charitable organizations in their communities. But more importantly, they rolled up their sleeves and contributed to charitable boards where they put their business acumen and fundraising skills to work. As Ken and Julia, say, "To whom much is given, much is expected" (Luke 12:48).

Keep in mind, not all giving needs to be local. One of the charities

Heidi and I support is A New Day Cambodia (ANDC), a housing center (aka orphanage) in the capital city of Phenom Penh, which I recently visited. ANDC was founded by a very close friend of mine, Joe O'Neil, who is the senior ticket manager for the Chicago Bulls. Joe first visited Cambodia and founded ANDC about 10 years ago with another Bulls' employee. According to Joe, "They are the poorest of the poor, and I was so moved by it that I just had to do something. To date, the ANDC has taken over 130 kids out of the garbage dumps and put them into the ANDC center. We give them housing, food, education, medicine, and love."

One of these children, Sreylin, was picking garbage in 2009 and in 2015, she was named one of the "100 Women Who Will Change the World" by *Newsweek* magazine. That same year, she also met with Michelle Obama in the White House. Amazing work. If you get a chance, check out the website:

A New Day Cambodia

Our board member Admiral Joe Maguire is the former commander of the Navy SEALs and currently the executive director for the Special Operations Warrior Foundation. This amazing charity provided a college scholarship to his daughter and to hundreds of other sons and daughters of those soldiers who died protecting our country. Here is its worthwhile website:

Special Operations Warrior Foundation

I came to know Joe when he attended the funeral services for Navy SEAL Ted Fitz-Henry, who was killed in 2004 while serving our country. Ted was an American hero who was married to my cousin, Michelle Fitz-Henry. Michelle came to our family as an abandoned distant relative at age 13 in 1976, and left as a sister at the age of 21. She went on to serve in the Air Force and then as a firefighter/ paramedic in Oak Park, IL.

My next-door neighbor of 20 years, Dave Kleinhans, sold his dot-com company in 2001, shortly before the bubble burst. He has since devoted his life to giving back and now teaches Honors Physics at Fenwick High School in Oak Park. In 2017, he was recognized as the Educator of the Year. Principal Peter Groom praised Dave by saying, "Three things that strike me most about Dave are his humility, genuine love for his students, and the ability to motivate his students to perform beyond their own expectations." Many members of my family attended Fenwick, including my father who was an all-American swimmer there, and was recently inducted into the Fenwick Hall of Fame.

As important as giving back is, it seems some executives look for philanthropic opportunities for the wrong reasons—a tax deduction, career advancement, or for corporate or personal recognition. But there should be only one reason to give back: it's the right thing to do!

Of course, it's so amazing to see the rewards that come to you from doing good. Call it karma, good will, God's work, the Law of Attraction or whatever else you'd like, but I truly believe that when you do good things, good things happen to you. Conversely, if you do bad things, in general, bad things will happen.

Not too long ago, we looked at our corporate giving over a 10-year period. We learned that we were giving disproportionately to our churches, hospitals, local communities and schools—all of which were worthy of our support. However, it dawned on us that we weren't giving significantly to the communities we directly serve—the fire service and military. From that moment forward, we made a concerted effort to give more to those groups.

One of my lifelong friends, Peter Harmon, and his wife, Joan, recently started a business that I invested in. They said, "We're going to pledge a percentage of our net income to the following charities." This type of business model is becoming very popular these days—especially with Millennials. You see these with Kickstart and other grassroots funding initiatives.

While this idea is admirable, and I've seen many companies make similar pledges on donating a percentage of revenue. It's best that companies should get on their feet first and donate a percentage of their profits later. Giving to charity is honorable and rewarding when you're making money, but if your business has yet to turn a profit, quit corporate giving to charity. When you're not making money, you're the charity.

Some don't care if you are helping charities, and others say, "Look, if you're going to raise the price of my product to give to your charities, you aren't addressing a pain point for me. Lower the price; I'll give to charities of my choice."

While support needy organizations, you cannot forget the people in your own organization and others close to you. We get requests daily from our employees, customers and political organizations to support one charity or another. We try support as many of these as possible, but we can't support them all. The bottom line is that you have many ways to give back. Money is certainly the most obvious, but money isn't always what's needed. In fact, one of the most important ways to give back is with your time and talents.

Learn from those who had it and lost it

Statistics show that 78 percent of NFL and 60 percent of NBA players file bankruptcy within five years of "retirement." One was former Chicago Bulls player Bob Love, who recently talked about the importance of relationships and friendships. Addressing YPO kids, his words apply to anyone.

Bob began, "You know, statistically, your net worth at the end of your life will be the average of your five closest friends." I don't know if this statement is true, but Bob wasn't talking only about financial worth. His message was: "If you hang around with losers, you're going to be a loser, and you're going to get yourself in trouble. If you hang around with winners, you're going to be a winner. The money might be there, too, but that's a byproduct."

Bob talked about his own experiences and admits he was hanging out with the wrong crowd when he was a professional basketball player. Six months after leaving the NBA and having his jersey retired by the Bulls, he was broke, couldn't find a job, and his entourage was gone. Bob had a stutter, making it was difficult to talk. He admitted he wasn't very employable.

He eventually found work as a busboy at the diner at Marshall Fields — an upscale department store. Marshall Field, the Chicago philanthropist owner of the empire bearing his name, offered to pay for speech therapy sessions. Bob took him up on the overture, and he eventually overcame his stutter and returned to the Chicago Bulls to become its director of community relations.

It's been said by more than just Bob: Network = Net worth, but don't let the money be the driver. As Warren Buffett puts it, "It's better to hang out with people better than you. Pick your associates whose behavior is better than yours, and you'll drift in that direction."

This thought resonates as I look back at my Marquette roommates Sean Curley, John Fortunato, Steve DeJohn, Tom Schott and John Thomas. They all are incredible fathers, husbands and community leaders who have excelled in their lives and are leaving their mark by contributing significantly to society.

Leave your mark

I was in the seventh grade at St. Luke's Grade School and still vividly remember our teacher, Sr. Eleanor, breaking down and crying in front of the classroom. She explained that a close nun friend of hers was dying. The woman had no family and felt she would soon be forgotten by the world. She never left her mark. In my mid-20s, my best friend, Jim "Vinnie" Kerr's, biggest fear was being forgotten as well, as we discussed this seventh-grade experience. Death experiences, including this one, impacted me significantly, and they became part of my drive for writing this book.

My father loved to say, "A legacy isn't something you leave behind. It is something that you build each day. Ultimately, you will be judged not on how successful the company is under your watch, but on how successfully the next generation takes the reins and works together on making the business a success." That stuck with me and I know it did with my siblings and cousins, too.

As you start to ponder your legacy, think to yourself: What is the best use of your talents? Of your life?

My parting advice is to find a way to leave your mark on this world and make it a better place. You'll find contentment as you do.

Thank you for reading *Sold!* Now, go out and change the world!

Chapter 14

Bill Darley Quotes

Below is a list of quotes from Bill Darley. Not all are originals, but he enjoyed sharing them with our employees over the years. His quotes would be posted in our lunchrooms, in the shop and even in our bathrooms.

- At Darley, our difference is not measured only by the goals we set, but in how well we go about achieving them

- I am Responsible and Accountable!

- At Darley, you must treat our customers as you would like to be treated

- One of the secrets of life is enjoying the curves it throws at you

- At Darley, instead of just planning for the next quarter, how about planning for the next quarter of a century?

- The final test of a leader is that he leaves behind him, in other men and women, the conviction, knowledge and will to carry on!

- It's not how many ideas you have. It's how many ideas you make happen

- Every morning in Africa, a gazelle wakes up and knows it must outrun the fastest lion. Every morning in Africa, a lion wakes up and knows it must run faster than the slowest gazelle. It doesn't matter whether you are a lion or a gazelle. When the sun comes up, you better be running

- Business at Darley will/continues to change before I finish this sent…. That's good

- We have met the competition, and it is us. We must stay ahead faster and better than our competitors without innovation

- Who's in charge of change? You are! OK, so just do it!

- Why Darley? For those of you who are blessed with the ability to tell the difference, "It's our Service and Results that are/will be evident!"

- I am an engineer. I believe all questions should start with "What if?"

- If it ain't broke, take it apart and reassemble it anyway

- At Darley, we're proud to help customers make everything possible

- So, if you need to turn your vision to innovation, partner with Darley

- Our difference is not measured only by the goals we set, but in how well we go about achieving them

- We should look at the current global situation as the Chinese do: "Wei-ji"… means "Dangerous opportunities"

- Incredible opportunities exist. We must continue to seek solutions to the existing complex challenges

- At Darley, and in your personal lives, continue to question everything, to take nothing for granted, and to seek the truth

- To all of you at Darley and in the Fire Service who work so hard to protect our Families, our Communities, and our Wildlands…Thank you!

- Our approach should continue to be: It's not our product; it's our customer's product

- If we need to change, we will continue to do it

- A lion ate an entire bull and felt so good about it he started to roar. He kept roaring until a hunter came along and shot him. Moral: When you're full of bull, keep your mouth shut

- Attention! Leaders at Darley cannot only maintain your integrity 90% of the time! "It's got to be 100%"!

- Follow the 3 Rs. Respect for self. Respect for others. Responsibility for actions

- "Yu-Shi-Ju-Jin" means Look out world, here we come! (Since 1982 in China)

- Don't just walk by those you work with, but get "nostril-to-nostril' with them and take time to "breathe in their world." (Not to be taken literally!)

- A legacy isn't just something you leave behind when you die. It's something you build every day you live!

- Some people/companies see problems. Others like us/our company see opportunities

- At Darley, we/you should continue to create change and be prepared for it

- Whatever you do, continue to lead with confidence or step out of the way!

- To: Executive Team & Board of Directors. Continue to take us where we've never been before

- At Darley, we will continue to live with Integrity, Accountability, Hard Work & Commitment

- Don't throw out the internet Baby with the Dot.com bathwater

- A Boss does not want you to think. A Leader wants you to think

- At Darley, we have "Trained Leaders"

- My expectations of Darley Team Members are Have a winning attitude, Practice the Golden Rule, Seek Excellence, Capitalize on Diversity, Stay Focused. Participate

- Do it right (the first time)

- Trust everybody, but cut the cards!

- Retirement! Half the money, twice the spouse

- Don't mistake my strong sense of ethics for a weak sense of economics or leadership

- To all at Darley! Don't just wish for something. Do something about it!

- At Darley, I've seen extraordinary insights come from uncommon perspectives! Continue to continue to make us the best of the best!

- To all who work with me at your Company — W. S. Darley: I've tried my entire career at Darley and in my personal life to listen to people first, then talk, suggest, decide or listen more. Listen first, talk later!

- "Small danger in certain cases of listening too closely to customers

- If I had asked my customers what they wanted, they would have said a faster horse." – Henry Ford

- All of you/us should communicate with your/our customers frequently. If you do "They are talking to you and can't be talking to a competitor!" Look ahead, be proactive—don't just wait for orders to come in! Some day they will/could stop!

- About half of the job of management is trying to figure out where Darley is going to be 5 to 10 years down the road, and the second half is execution

- It's what we do and decide every day that establishes our Code of Ethics

- You never saw a fish on the wall with its mouth shut

- A ship in a safe harbor is safe, but that is not what a ship is built for

- "Shall I go to heaven or a-fishing" – Henry Thoreau. "Heaven can wait." – Bill Darley

- Why Apparatus! At Darley, it appears that our business changes/ can change every six months! So perhaps we continue to look forward in all Divisions rather than dwell in the past

- Newton's Rule of Inertia: Objects at rest tend to stay at rest. So keep moving!

- Work is not a place; it's an activity!

- If the student surpasses the teacher, that is an honor to the teacher

- God made the world round, so you couldn't look too far down the road. That's good!

Index of Friends and Family

The 50 Ps of Relationship Sales

Chapter 6 — The Sales Foundation. Build Relationships. Solve a Pain. Follow a Process

1) People (Relationships)

2) Private Conversations/Principled

3) Pacify a Pain

4) Process

5) Prospecting

6) Penetrable/Potential (Qualify the prospect)

7) Preparation/Practice/Pitch/Pre-call Planning

8) Pertinent/Pithy/Precise

9) Primary Point of Contact

10) Presentation

Chapter 7 — Separate Yourself from the Pack; Be Professional and Enjoy the Ride

11) Phollow-Up (Follow-Up)

12) Point of Difference (Be different or die)

13) Presence/Personality/Persona (Likeability)

14) Professionalism/Polished/Politeness

15) Promptness/Punctuality

16) Personalize/Personal Service/Praise/Promises and Pledges

17) Pleasure/Passion/Purpose

18) Proclivity/Predispositions

19) Positivity (Happiness)

20) Pragmatism/Practicality

Chapter 8 — Getting to Yes! Overcoming Objections

21) Proposition (Value Proposition)

22) Product/Permeable/

23) Probe

24) Problem Solver

About the Author

Paul C. Darley is Chairman, CEO & President of W.S. Darley & Co., a fourth-generation family business and world leader in the firefighting and defense industries. Under Paul's leadership, the company's sales have increased more than 1,000 percent.

During his tenure as CEO, Paul has traveled to 80 countries and delivered more than 500 industry speaking engagements. He is a past president of the Fire Apparatus Manufacturers Association (FAMA) and served on the board of directors of Fire & Emergency Manufacturers & Services Association (FEMSA) for seven years. Paul currently serves on the board of the National Defense Industry Association (NDIA) for the Great Lakes Chapter.

Paul is also involved with numerous charitable and service organizations. He is a former chairman of the Chicago Windy City Chapter of Young Presidents' Organization (YPO) and currently serves as a trustee for Dominican University.

In 2010, W.S. Darley & Co was named the Loyola University Illinois Family Business of the Year. It was recognized by Marquette University in 2009 as Alumnus Family Business of Year. Paul has conducted numerous family business speaking engagements, including "Resolving Sibling Conflict in Family Business" at the annual Family Business Magazine Conference.

A graduate of St. Ignatius College Prep in Chicago, Paul earned his bachelor's degree in marketing and finance from Marquette University and an MBA from Northwestern University's Kellogg School of Management. He also earned a two-year post graduate degree in Emotional Intelligence from the University of Illinois.

Paul lives in Elmhurst, Illinois, with his wife of more than 30 years and their three daughters.